LECTIONARY PREACHING RESOURCES

Series A

Edited by
Francis Rossow and Gerhard Aho

Publishing House
St. Louis

Permission to use sermonic studies that have previously appeared in *Concordia Theological Quarterly* has been granted by *Concordia Theological Quarterly*, Concordia Theological Seminary, Fort Wayne, Indiana.

Sermonic studies that previously appeared in *Concordia Journal* have been reprinted by permission of *Concordia Journal*, Concordia Seminary, St. Louis, Missouri.

The original source of each study is indicated in the Scripture Index.

The Scripture version used in each study, if a specific version is quoted, is indicated after the reference heading. Quotations marked KJV are from the King James or Authorized Version of the Bible. Quotations marked RSV are from the Revised Standard Version of the Bible, copyrighted 1946, 1952 © 1971, 1973. Used by permission. Quotations marked ASV are from the American Standard Version (1901). Quotations marked NEB are from THE NEW ENGLISH BIBLE (NEB) © The Delegates of The Oxford University Press and the Syndics of the Cambridge University Press, 1961, 1970, and are used by permission. Quotations marked NASB are from the NEW AMERICAN STANDARD BIBLE © The Lockman Foundation 1960, 1962, 1963, 1968, 1971, 1972, 1973, 1975, and are used by permission. Quotations marked TEV are from the Good News Bible, the Bible in TODAY'S ENGLISH VERSION. Copyright © American Bible Society 1966, 1971, 1976. Used by permission. Quotations marked NKJV are from The Holy Bible, New King James Version. Copyright © 1979, 1980, 1982 by Thomas Nelson, Inc. Used by permission.

Copyright © 1986 by Concordia Publishing House
3558 South Jefferson Avenue, St. Louis, MO 63118-3968
Manufactured in the United States of America.

All rights reserved. No part of this publication may be reproduced, stored in a retrieval system, or transmitted, in any form or by any means, electronic, mechanical, photocopying, recording, or otherwise, without the prior written permission of Concordia Publishing House.

Library of Congress Cataloging-in-Publication Data

Main entry under title:

Lectionary preaching resources.

"Contains sermonic studies for the Gospel and Epistle readings from Series A of the three-year lectionary. The primary source for these studies is previous issues of the Concordia journal and the Concordia theological quarterly"—CIP galley.
   1. Bible. N.T.—Homiletical use. 2. Bible. N.T.—Liturgical lessons, English.
I. Rossow, Francis C., 1925-   II. Aho, Gerhard. III. Concordia journal. IV. Concordia theological quarterly.
BS2392.L43 1986   251   85-28000
ISBN 0-570-03991-6

---

1 2 3 4 5 6 7 8 9 10   MAL   95 94 93 92 91 90 89 88 87 86

CONTENTS

Preface   9

First Sunday in Advent
    Romans 13:11 – 14 — Henry J. Eggold   11
    Matthew 24:37 – 44 — Stephen J. Carter   12

Second Sunday in Advent
    Romans 15:4 – 13 — Martin H. Scharlemann   14
    Matthew 3:1 – 12 — Stephen J. Carter   16

Third Sunday in Advent
    James 5:7 – 10 — Edwin Dubberke   17
    Matthew 11:2 – 11 — Andrew H. Bartelt   19

Fourth Sunday in Advent
    Romans 1:1 – 7 — Richard Klann   21
    Matthew 1:18 – 25 — Gerhard Aho   24

The Nativity of Our Lord: The First Service
    Titus 2:11 – 14 — Francis C. Rossow   26
    Luke 2:8 – 20 — Gerhard Aho   28

First Sunday After Christmas
    Galatians 4:4 – 7 — Francis C. Rossow   30
    Matthew 2:13 – 15, 19 – 23 — Alfred Fremder   32

Second Sunday After Christmas
    Ephesians 1:3 – 6, 15 – 18 — Ronald Irsch   35
    John 1:1 – 18 — Alfred Fremder   37

The Baptism of Our Lord:
First Sunday After the Epiphany
    Acts 10:34 – 38 — Robert G. Hoerber   39
    Matthew 3:13 – 17 — Andrew H. Bartelt   40

Second Sunday After the Epiphany
    1 Corinthians 1:1 – 9 — Francis C. Rossow   42
    John 1:29 – 41 — Harold H. Zietlow   44

Third Sunday After the Epiphany
    1 Corinthians 1:10 – 17 — Andrew H. Bartelt   46
    Matthew 4:12 – 23 — Warren Messmann   47

Fourth Sunday After the Epiphany
    1 Corinthians 1:26 – 31 — Andrew H. Bartelt   49
    Matthew 5:1 – 12 — Quentin F. Wesselschmidt   51

Fifth Sunday After the Epiphany
    1 Corinthians 2:1–5 — David L. Bahn   53
    Matthew 5:13–20 — Quentin F. Wesselschmidt   55

Sixth Sunday After the Epiphany
    1 Corinthians 2:6–13 — David L. Bahn   57
    Matthew 5:27–37 — Roger J. Humann   59

Seventh Sunday After the Epiphany
    1 Corinthians 3:10–11, 16–23   62
        Harold H. Zietlow
    Matthew 5:38–48 — Roger J. Humann   63

Eighth Sunday After the Epiphany
    1 Corinthians 4:1–13 — Gerhard Aho   65
    Matthew 6:24–34 — Roger J. Humann   67

The Transfiguration of Our Lord:
Last Sunday After the Epiphany
    2 Peter 1:16–21 — William J. Schmelder   69
    Matthew 17:1–9 — Louis A. Brighton   71

First Sunday in Lent
    Romans 5:12–19 — William J. Schmelder   73
    Matthew 4:1–11 — Francis C. Rossow   75

Second Sunday in Lent
    Romans 4:1–5, 13–17
        Quentin F. Wesselschmidt   77
    John 4:5–26 — Gerhard Aho   79

Third Sunday in Lent
    Ephesians 5:8–14 — Quentin F. Wesselschmidt   81
    John 9:24–41 — Gerhard Aho   83

Fourth Sunday in Lent
    Romans 8:1–10 — Louis A. Brighton   86
    Matthew 20:17–28 — Louis A. Brighton   88

Fifth Sunday in Lent
    Romans 8:11–19 — Henry J. Eggold   89
    John 11:47–53 — Francis C. Rossow   91

Palm Sunday: Sunday of the Passion
    Philippians 2:5–11 — Henry J. Eggold   94
    Matthew 26:6–13 — Gerhard Aho   96

Maundy Thursday
    1 Corinthians 11:23–26 — Gerhard Aho   98
    John 13:1–17 — Gerhard Aho   100

Good Friday
    Hebrews 4:14–5:10 — Gerhard Aho   102
    John 19:30b — Gerhard Aho   105

CONTENTS

The Resurrection of Our Lord: Easter Day
    Colossians 3:1–4 — Gerhard Aho 106
    John 20:1–9 — Henry J. Eggold 109

Second Sunday of Easter
    1 Peter 1:3–9 — Lowell F. Thomas 110
    John 20:19–31 — William J. Schmelder 112

Third Sunday of Easter
    1 Peter 1:17–21 — Richard J. Schultz 114
    Luke 24:13–35 — Henry J. Eggold 116

Fourth Sunday of Easter
    1 Peter 2:19–25 — Richard J. Schultz 117
    John 10:1–10 — Henry J. Eggold 119

Fifth Sunday of Easter
    1 Peter 2:4–10 — Jerrold A. Eickmann 120
    John 14:1–12 — Henry J. Eggold 122

Sixth Sunday of Easter
    1 Peter 3:15–18 — Jerrold A. Eickmann 124
    John 14:15–21 — Richard G. Kapfer 126

The Ascension of Our Lord
    Ephesians 1:16–23 — Bruce J. Lieske 128
    Luke 24:44–53 — Richard G. Kapfer 130

Seventh Sunday of Easter
    1 Peter 4:13–19 — David E. Seybold 132
    John 17:1–11 — Andrew H. Bartelt 134

Pentecost: The Day of Pentecost
    Acts 2:1–21 — David E. Seybold 136
    John 16:5–11 — David E. Seybold 138

The Holy Trinity: First Sunday After Pentecost
    2 Corinthians 13:11–14 — Francis C. Rossow 140
    Matthew 28:16–20 — Richard Klann 143

Second Sunday After Pentecost
    Romans 3:21–28 — John F. Johnson 145
    Matthew 7:21–29 — Terence R. Groth 147

Third Sunday After Pentecost
    Romans 4:18–25 — Mark R. Oien 149
    Matthew 9:9–13 — Daniel H. Pokorny 151

Fourth Sunday After Pentecost
    Romans 5:6–11 — Mark R. Oien 153
    Matthew 9:35–10:8 — Steven C. Briel 156

Fifth Sunday After Pentecost
    Romans 5:12–15 — Francis C. Rossow 158
    Matthew 10:24–33 — Terence R. Groth 161

Sixth Sunday After Pentecost
    Romans 6:2b – 11 — Gerhard Aho   163
    Matthew 10:34 – 42 — G. Waldemar Degner   165

Seventh Sunday After Pentecost
    Romans 7:15 – 25a — George S. Robbert   166
    Matthew 11:25 – 30 — Arthur F. Graudin   168

Eighth Sunday After Pentecost
    Romans 8:18 – 23 — Harold H. Zietlow   170
    Matthew 13:1 – 9 (18 – 23) — Mark R. Oien   172

Ninth Sunday After Pentecost
    Romans 8:26 – 27 — Erich H. Kiehl   173
    Matthew 13:24 – 30 — L. Dean Hempelmann   175

Tenth Sunday After Pentecost
    Romans 8:28 – 30 — George S. Robbert   177
    Matthew 13:44 – 52 — George R. Kraus   179

Eleventh Sunday After Pentecost
    Romans 8:35 – 39 — Wayne A. Pohl   181
    Matthew 14:13 – 21 — Richard J. Schultz   182

Twelfth Sunday After Pentecost
    Romans 9:1 – 5 — John W. Klotz   184
    Matthew 14:22 – 33 — Ken Schurb   186

Thirteenth Sunday After Pentecost
    Romans 11:13 – 15, 29 – 32 — John W. Klotz   188
    Matthew 15:21 – 28 — John F. Johnson   190

Fourteenth Sunday After Pentecost
    Romans 11:33 – 36 — Gerhard Aho   192
    Matthew 16:13 – 20 — John F. Johnson   193

Fifteenth Sunday After Pentecost
    Romans 12:1 – 18 — Gerhard Aho   196
    Matthew 16:21 – 26 — Edwin Dubberke   198

Sixteenth Sunday After Pentecost
    Romans 13:1 – 10 — Wayne E. Schmidt   200
    Matthew 18:15 – 20 — Edwin Dubberke   202

Seventeenth Sunday After Pentecost
    Romans 14:7 – 9 — Wayne E. Schmidt   204
    Matthew 18:21 – 35 — Gerhard Aho   206

Eighteenth Sunday After Pentecost
    Philippians 1:3 – 5, 19 – 27 — Erwin J. Kolb   207
    Matthew 20:1 – 16 — Gerhard Aho   209

Nineteenth Sunday After Pentecost
    Philippians 2:1 – 11 — Erwin J. Kolb   210
    Matthew 21:28 – 32 — Jonathan F. Grothe   212

Twentieth Sunday After Pentecost
    Philippians 3:12 – 21 — Gerhard Aho 214
    Matthew 21:33 – 43 — Gerhard Aho 216

Twenty-First Sunday After Pentecost
    Philippians 4:10 – 13, 19 – 20 — Andrew H. Bartelt 218
    Matthew 22:1 – 14 — Gerhard Aho 220

Twenty-Second Sunday After Pentecost
    1 Thessalonians 1:1 – 5a — Roland A. Hopmann 222
    Matthew 22:15 – 21 — Jonathan F. Grothe 224

Twenty-Third Sunday After Pentecost
    1 Thessalonians 1:5b – 10 — Roland A. Hopmann 226
    Matthew 22:34 – 40 — Dale A. Meyer 228

Twenty-Fourth Sunday After Pentecost
    1 Thessalonians 4:13 – 18 — Rudolph H. Harm 230
    Matthew 23:37 – 39 — Francis C. Rossow 232

Twenty-Fifth Sunday After Pentecost
    1 Thessalonians 5:1 – 11 — Rudolph H. Harm 235
    Matthew 25:14 – 30 — Gerhard Aho 237

Third-Last Sunday in the Church Year
    1 Thessalonians 2:8 – 13 — Roy A. Suelflow 238
    Matthew 23:1 – 12 — Gerhard Aho 240

Second-Last Sunday in the Church Year
    1 Thessalonians 3:7 – 13 — Roy A. Suelflow 243
    Matthew 24:1 – 14 — Gerhard Aho 244

Sunday of the Fulfillment:
Last Sunday in the Church Year 246
    1 Corinthians 15:20 – 28 — Francis C. Rossow 248
    Matthew 25:1 – 13 — Gerhard Aho

Scripture Index 251

PREFACE

The sermon studies in *Lectionary Preaching Resources: Series A,* for the most part, originally appeared in the *Concordia Journal* (Concordia Seminary, St. Louis, Mo.) and the *Concordia Theological Quarterly* (Concordia Theological Seminary, Fort Wayne, Ind.). A few new sermon studies were prepared to provide a comprehensive resource.

In a joint meeting the editors selected those they regarded as most likely to help the pastor in his weekly sermon preparation. These studies were edited to conform to a uniform length and style for the present volume. The Three-Year Lectionary as presented in *Lutheran Worship* was used for text selection.

These sermon studies provide a practical resource to the pastor in his weekly sermon preparation. The "Sermon Notes/Introduction—Outline" format provides the pastor with helpful suggestions for both the content and the structure of his sermon. By working through the notes, one can quickly grasp the thrust of the text; the outline suggests one possible sermonic approach to the text. Studies have been included for every Sunday and major festival in the church year, thus making this an ongoing resource for every iteration of Series A.

It is our hope that, under God, these studies will prove to be a blessing not only to the pastor who consults them but ultimately to his hearers as well.

THE EDITORS

First Sunday in Advent

EPISTLE   Romans 13:11 – 14 (KJV)

Sermon Notes/Introduction

V. 11: "And that": and this, too. "The time": the period at which we have arrived, the "hour" (RSV). "Believed": came to believe (ingressive aorist). "Our salvation": our transfer to heaven. "Nearer": namely, to us. *V. 12:* "The night": the present world age. "The day": the heavenly age. We do not know the time (Acts 1:7; 2 Peter 3:4 – 14). Jesus points us to the flood and to Sodom and Gomorrah. "The works of darkness": the works of the devil. "Let us decisively put away from ourselves" (aorist middle), separate ourselves from all such works—the danger of yielding to them. "Let us once for all clothe ourselves" (aorist hortative subjunctive). "Weapons of light": cf. Eph. 6:13; light refers to God, whose attribute is light. *V. 13:* "Honestly": becomingly (ASV), with decency (NEB). "Rioting": carousing (Goodspeed); cf. 1 Cor. 10:12; Luke 2:34. "Chambering": prostitution, sexual promiscuity (NASB); cf. 1 Cor. 6:15 – 20. "Wantonness": indecency (Goodspeed), sensuality (NASB). "Envying": jealousy. All are samples of the works of darkness. *V. 14:* "But put ye on the Lord Jesus Christ": namely, as your armor. "Provision for the flesh": put a stop to gratifying the evil desires that lurk in your lower nature; the body is so responsive to sin; cf. Rom. 6:12; 7:23. "Putting on Christ": (1) appropriating His righteousness (Is. 61:10; Matt. 22:12); (2) as our armor of defense and offense (Eph. 6:13). Take Christ for your sanctification.

Sleep is a gift of God, a great restorer of energy. But there comes a time when we have to wake up. So also spiritually, we are to arouse ourselves from the insensibility of spiritual sleep.

Sermon Outline
WAKE UP

I. Your salvation is near (v. 11).
   A. It is in Christ: He is our salvation.
      1. He came into the world to be its Savior (Luke 2:11; Luke 19:10).
      2. He accomplished our salvation.

           a. He kept the Law (Gal. 4:4).
           b. He suffered our punishment (Is. 53:5–6).
        3. The goal of His work is our salvation (John 3:16).
           a. We have it now.
           b. We will have it perfectly in heaven (John 14:1–6).
     B. This salvation is nearer than when we came to believe (v. 11).
        1. We may die at any time.
        2. Christ may come at any time (Matt. 24:27). Therefore, wake up. Don't be insensitive to such a glorious prospect. Use the Word of God to be strengthened.
II. You must take time to prepare for His coming.
     A. Cast off the works of darkness (v. 12).
        1. Examples are listed (v. 13).
        2. All are inspired by the prince of darkness to lead us astray (1 Peter 5:8).
        3. Don't indulge the flesh (Rom. 6:12; 7:23).
        4. Drown the Old Adam by daily contrition and repentance.
     B. Put on the armor of light (v. 12).
        1. That means put on Christ (v. 14).
           a. Appropriate His righteousness (Is. 61:10; Matt. 22:12).
           b. It is our armor of defense and offense (Eph. 6:13).
        2. Walk decently (v. 13).

Daily drown the Old Adam; daily put on Christ by faith and bring forth the fruits of faith. That's staying awake.

HENRY J. EGGOLD

First Sunday in Advent

GOSPEL   Matthew 24:37–44

Sermon Notes/Introduction

A new church year begins unnoticed by a world bent on self-destruction and preparing feverishly for a materialistic Christmas celebration. The world's Christmas begins on the Thanksgiving weekend and culminates a month later with sentimental words about "peace on earth" and "happy holidays" serving as a narcotic against the harsh realities of modern life.

Jesus in Matthew's gospel predicts both the fall of Jerusalem (vv. 4–22) and the signs of the end when He will come again in judgment (vv. 23–31). He tells a number of parables that describe the disciple's attitude as he waits for the end. In our text Jesus compares the end-time to the days of Noah when unbelievers were totally unprepared as they continued with "business as usual." He also characterizes an unprepared householder who counts his loss only after the thief has robbed him unexpectedly. The need to watch and be ready is the key thought of the text. Jesus is coming again.

The season of Advent begins today, ushering in a new church year of God's grace. We look to Jesus Christ our King, who first came into our world in Bethlehem's manger, who comes daily into our hearts through Word and Sacrament, and who will come again in triumph on the Last Day. This morning we look at Jesus' announcement of His final coming. In a world and sometimes a church that is oblivious to the signs of the times, our text trumpets the Advent message that the Son of Man is coming.

Sermon Outline
THE SON OF MAN IS COMING

I. He comes in judgment on the unprepared.
   A. Two examples describe the consequences of being unprepared.
      1. People in the days of Noah lived openly in sin and conducted "business as usual," ignoring God's threat of judgment. Their destruction followed.
      2. An unprepared householder discovers too late that a thief has unexpectedly robbed him.
   B. People today often are unprepared because they fail to watch for the coming of the Son of Man.
      1. As in the days of Noah, people engage openly in sin and become preoccupied with pressing daily affairs, including hectic Christmas preparations. They ignore God's threat of judgment on the unprepared.
      2. Christians, too, like the unprepared householder, may fail to keep watch against the temptations of the Evil One and are caught unprepared to meet the Son of Man.
II. He comes in mercy toward His people.

A. A watchful and prepared Jesus came the first time to live and die for the sins of the world. As He speaks in our text, He is preparing for the cross. Advent reminds us of His first coming for us.
B. The Son of Man comes to us in the Word and the sacraments to prepare us for His final coming. He makes us watchful.
C. The Son of Man will receive us to Himself when He comes on the Last Day.

As we prepare again to celebrate Jesus' birthday, we heed the warning to watch and be prepared because we know not the hour when the Son of Man will come. He supplies us with His unfailing mercy to make us watchful and prepared.

STEPHEN J. CARTER

Second Sunday in Advent

EPISTLE   Romans 15:4 – 13 (KJV)

Sermon Notes/Introduction

Our Lord lives among us even now in and by His Word. That fact, too, belongs to our celebration of Advent.

From this Word we learn of His coming in Bethlehem and of His return in glory at the end of the age. From it we also discover that Jesus Christ dwells among His people in the expectation that we live at peace with one another and glorify God with one voice (vv. 5 – 6).

This means that we have been given God's Word as a way of undoing Babel.

Sermon Outline
UNDOING BABEL

I. Judgment at Babel (Gen. 11:1 – 9): Confusion and Dispersion.
   A. Division and tension remain as historic realities.
      1. Over 150 different nations are represented in the United Nations.
      2. In Africa alone various tribes are divided by no less than 700 languages and dialects.
      3. Mankind is fragmented by hundreds of different religions, each with its own claims on the individual.

SECOND SUNDAY IN ADVENT

- B. Factionalism threatened the life of the congregation at Rome in Paul's day.
  1. The strong in faith were arrayed against those who were still weak (chap. 14 and 15:1–3).
  2. Jewish Christians and Gentile converts were ranged against each other (vv. 7–9).
- C. Tensions and divisions still plague Christian congregations.
  1. The strong and the weak are against each other.
  2. Personality clashes like those that created party strife in Corinth (1 Cor. 1:11-12) still occur.
  3. Family cliques, special interest groups, and personal ambitions constitute threats to peace in the church.

II. God's Gift of Unity.
- A. God's unity is at work in the church.
  1. It works in the Scriptures as a teaching instrument.
     - a. The Old Testament already offered what the apostle calls *the* hope (v. 4), namely, the hope of a united people.
     - b. In the text before us we have the apostle's appeal for the kind of harmony that expresses itself in common worship (vv. 5–6).
  2. It works in the Incarnation (Christmas) as a rallying point for one people (v. 7).
     - a. It demonstrates God's truth (faithfulness) in keeping His promises to Israel (v. 8).
     - b. It manifests His mercy toward the Gentiles (v. 9).
  3. Christ's work and life serve as a model (v. 7).
     - a. We accept one another for what we are.
     - b. We are a people of joy and peace from God (v. 13).
     - c. We are the assembly of hope (v. 13).
- B. God's unity transcends all of mankind's divisions.
  1. The sharpest of all historic rifts is between Jew and Gentile.
     - a. It is aggravated by the gift of God's law.
     - b. It is healed by the coming of Christ. (Here see Eph. 2:11–18.)
  2. The church is the extension of Christ's work of reconciliation.
     - a. It is the assembly where Christ Himself exalts the name of God (v. 9b).

    b. It is the place where Gentiles join Jews in praising the Lord (vv. 10–11).
    c. It is the place where Gentiles put their hope in the "root of Jesse" (v. 12).
 3. The church exists to gather one people.
    a. The people thrive on the patience and comfort derived from the Scriptures (v. 4).
    b. They live with a single-minded commitment (v. 5).
    c. They glorify God with "one mouth" (v. 6).

Today's Epistle speaks of undoing Babel as *the* hope of mankind. This hope begins to be realized in the church. Its life is a foreshadowing of that time when countless thousands from every nation, kindred, and tongue shall be gathered before the throne of the Lamb to sing His praises forever and to serve Him through all eternity. (Here see Revelation 4.)

MARTIN H. SCHARLEMANN

Second Sunday in Advent

GOSPEL   Matthew 3:1–12

Sermon Notes/Introduction

Advent stresses preparation for the coming of Christ. It is appropriate that John the Baptist is described in the Gospel for the Second Sunday in Advent. Arriving on the scene with the credentials of an Old Testament prophet (his wilderness location, dress, diet, and message), John attracts crowds. His strong message of repentance and baptism also for Israelites alienates some but strikes home with many in preparation for the Messiah's ministry.

When a presidential visit is anticipated in a local town, the word spreads; people gather; everyone is straining to catch the first glimpse of a helicopter or motorcade. An advance speaker addresses the crowd as it waits. In our text John the Baptist appears at the Jordan River as the advance man with a timely message for Israel and for us. He is announcing the new reign of God.

Sermon Outline
ANNOUNCING THE NEW REIGN OF GOD

I. The new reign of God stirs up interest!
 A. Israel responds to John's appearance.

1. The people are dissatisfied with world conditions and Israel's plight. They feel hopeless and long for deliverance.
    2. John's person and message place him in the tradition of the Old Testament prophets and raise Messianic hopes of a new reign of God in the Davidic line.
  B. We also respond to John's message.
    1. We experience a general dissatisfaction with world conditions of war clouds and national economic difficulties.
    2. John's message about a new reign of God to solve our problems sounds exciting. A Walt Disney World church sounds pleasant and enjoyable.
II. The new reign of God calls for repentance.
  A. John the Baptizer shocks Israel from the Pharisees to King Herod with a radical exposure of sin and a call for the baptism of repentance.
  B. John exposes our sin and summons us to the same kind of radical repentance that exposes our desire to reign over our own lives.
III. The new reign of God changes hearts!
  A. John's message leads many to conversion as they are prepared to embrace the Messiah's reign in their hearts.
  B. John's message points to the Messiah who died and rose again for the world's sin, and our hearts are rekindled through Word and Sacrament in the Advent season to embrace Christ's new reign in our hearts and lives.

Conclusion: As John the Baptist announces the new reign of God, we respond with more than superficial interest. Led to repentance, we find ourselves transformed by the Spirit to announce God's new reign in Christ to others.

STEPHEN J. CARTER

Third Sunday in Advent

EPISTLE   James 5:7 – 10 (KJV)

Sermon Notes/Introduction

The "waiting" character of Advent seems to escape most Christians. The coming of the Lord, so long awaited by the Old

Testament believers, has happened. Repeated celebrations of the nativity seem to preclude any further waiting, and yet after the most joyous celebration of the Savior's birth, the believer must "come down to earth" in the everyday struggles with burdens, grief, injustice, persecution, etc., that make up life in our sin-alienated world. Thus it is important for the Advent preacher to focus people's attention on that time of fullness of salvation when the Lord comes again. Meanwhile we live in a time that demands patient waiting.

There was a poor woman in Atlanta, Georgia, who for years had been supported entirely by charity. During this time she suffered from a disease that brought her great suffering. Now she was at the point of death and every moment was thought to be her last. Knowing her great faith, her friends were almost hoping for the moment of release. One of them said to the woman, "Are you ready to go?" "Yes," she said.

Sermon Outline
READY TO GO BUT WILLING TO WAIT!

I. Our confidence is based on the promises of our Advent Lord.
   A. We know the promises fulfilled in His first coming.
      1. The promised Burden-bearer was described by the prophets. (See esp. Is. 53, etc.)
      2. In His ministry Jesus did bring relief to people suffering under sin and its consequences (today's Gospel).
      3. Jesus is still touching people with His healing, renewing power today (Matt. 11:28). (The preacher should give current illustrations of Jesus' activity among the members of the congregation.)

By faith and experience we know the Lord has kept His promises of salvation. But what we have seen is only the beginning.

   B. We confidently await the fullness of glory yet to come when Christ comes again (vv. 7–8, also the symbolic picture of His kingdom in the Old Testament Reading).
      1. We will see Jesus face to face and be like Him (1 John 3:1–2).
      2. We will have the fullness of His eternal presence (Eph. 1; Rev. 21:4; Ps. 16:11; Rom. 8:18).

Many Christians take God's promises in Christ rather lightly, and yet how beautiful, rich, and full they really are!

II. Knowing the promises works in us the patience needed for waiting through the "delays" before fulfillment (v. 7; Rom. 5:3 – 5).
   A. Believers are definitely not exempt from burdens.
      1. Persecution and injustice are common and to be expected (context, v. 10; Matt. 5:11).
      2. The Lord disciplines His people as He sees need (Heb. 12).
      3. Impatience under trials only adds to our problems (v. 9).
   B. We need to learn to "wait on the Lord" (Ps. 27:14).
      1. Christian patience is not Stoic resignation: "What will be will be."
      2. It is rather a confident going with the will of the Lord, knowing that He has His purposes at work (Rom. 8:28).

Patience is a Christian virtue much more sorely needed in our lives than most of us would admit. It is not easy to have or practice.

III. Whatever happens, we know the presence of the Lord's strength and help.
   A. This is the message of the Incarnation, which we are preparing to celebrate soon.
   B. It continues among us through our faithful use of the Word and sacraments.

Under the gracious instruction and comfort of the Holy Spirit we who know the Savior who has come and the Lord who is yet to come are able to face the "todays" of life with patience, confidence, and a sure hope.

EDWIN DUBBERKE

Third Sunday in Advent

GOSPEL   Matthew 11:2 – 11 (RSV)

Sermon Notes/Introduction

1. The weeks before Christmas are a time of "great expectations." Caught up in all the hustle and bustle, one wonders if the celebration of Christmas itself isn't a bit of an anticlimax. Is it all worth it? What will be left of our "expectations" *after* Christmas: new toys that never worked as they did on television? massive bills owed to our (real?) Master, Charge?

dried out trees and empty-looking living rooms? the hopes of "peace on earth" dashed again? The problem, of course, is that many expect the wrong things.

2. John the Baptist wanted to be sure he was waiting for the right things. We are not told *why* he sent his disciples to ask his question. Was he truly in doubt? Did he misunderstand and hope that Jesus would somehow cause his release from prison? Did he simply want his disciples to be properly confirmed in *their* expectations? We are informed only that John heard about the *erga* of Jesus, which certainly seem not to have been the apocalyptic acts of judgment predicted last Sunday in Matt. 3:7–12, but rather the gracious deeds of mercy, healing, and forgiveness. In any case, John was awaiting *ho erchomenos* (and note how Matthew neatly answers the question for his readers before it is even asked by referring to the works "of *the Christ*" in v. 2). At least John's great expectations were *Messianic*, which is more than can be said of most people's expectations today. But what kind of Messiah was this to be?

3. Whatever was on John's mind, Jesus answers first by speaking *to* John about Himself and then *about* John to the crowd. Jesus' miracles only attest to His primary mission: to bring Good News to the spiritually downtrodden, that is, those in need of God's grace and forgiveness, those to whom our Lord offers rest (Matt. 11:28–29).

4. Yet many are "scandalized" by this kind of Messiah. How many miss the whole point of this "Gospel" in our world as well: those who expect the spectacular—miracles by which they can claim God's power on their own terms or the apocalyptic fireworks of a countdown to "Armageddon"; those who see Jesus as a "liberator" not from spiritual poverty but primarily from socio-economic and political oppression (compare the Jewish hopes in Jesus' day); or those who want simply their own version of "good news," whatever makes them happy, be it anemic, atheological wishes for "peace on earth" on Christmas cards or just a good dose of holiday cheer. How easy for modern man to stumble on the simplicity of the Gospel: that the only hope for us "poor, miserable sinners" comes as a baby wrapped in rags and lying in a manger.

Sermon Outline

For what are we waiting? Advent is a time of preparation and expectation. But many will miss the greatest expectation and thus celebrate a hollow Christmas because they do not know what they are really waiting for.

"GREAT EXPECTATIONS"

I. Confusion over Jesus' Mission.
   A. Many in Jesus' day had the wrong ideas
      1. About Jesus' Messianic ministry;
      2. About John's prophetic ministry.
   B. Even John himself was not sure.
   C. Many today misunderstand the coming of Christ and thus the very essence of Christmas as well.
      1. They have their own ideas and misconceptions without ever hearing Jesus' own words.
      2. They hear Jesus' words but stumble on the call to humbly confess that we *all* are the "poor in spirit."
II. Clarification of Jesus' True Messianic Mission.
   A. His life and "works" bear witness to His grace and power over life and death.
   B. His mission is to "evangelize" the poor, to bring the Good News of forgiveness and life.
   C. His kingdom is the fulfillment of Old Testament prophecy; He is the prophetic Word made sure.
III. Confession That Jesus Is Also *Our* Coming One.
   A. We, too, misunderstand and perhaps expect the wrong things of our coming King.
   B. Thus, sinfully "poor in spirit," we, too, receive the Good News that Christ, a *Savior,* is born.
   C. The message of the kingdom of God continues to come to us whenever we confess our spiritual poverty and hear again and again the daily message of forgiveness and life in Christ.
   D. Thus, we live in "great expectation"—now in Advent, as we prepare for the true joy of Christmas; daily in confession and forgiveness; and finally, when our coming One comes again.

ANDREW H. BARTELT

Fourth Sunday in Advent

EPISTLE   Romans 1:1 – 7 (RSV)

Sermon Notes/Introduction

Before leaving Corinth to deliver the collection of the Greek-speaking congregations for the relief of (mainly) Jewish Christians in Jerusalem, the apostle Paul also made preparations for his next missionary objective: to preach the Gospel in the western provinces of the Roman Empire, particularly in Spain. When Paul and Barnabas were "set apart" and called to special mission work at the command of the Holy Spirit (Acts 13:2), the Christians at Antioch in Syria were the sending congregation for the work in Asia and Greece. Apparently, Paul thought that the Christians at Rome could similarly function as the anchor community for the conversion of the people of Rome's western provinces.

The lands bordering on the Atlantic Ocean were considered at that time to be the "uttermost ends of the earth." Paul's policy not to labor where others had offered the Gospel (Rom. 15:20) conformed to the eschatological objective of the apostles stated by the Lord Himself (Matt. 28:20) just before His ascension. At this time, Paul could very well approach the Roman Christians from the perspective of one who had been victorious through Christ in Macedonia, Achaia, and the eastern provinces of Rome. Regardless of obstacles, he believed the Gospel, as the power of God for salvation to everyone who has faith, could not fail.

Sermon Outline
MISSION GUARANTEED

I. It is guaranteed because of Paul's divine call.
   A. Paul had become the *doulos* (slave) of Christ his Master, who had bought him for a great price—His own blood.
   B. Paul had been designated and called directly to be an apostle (Acts 9:1–2; 22:1–2; 26:2–3).
   C. Paul had been "set apart" (vv. 5–6) "to bring about the obedience of faith for the sake of His name among all the nations, including yourselves who are called to belong to Jesus Christ." As a former Pharisee, Paul had been "set apart" for the Law (Acts 9:13–16). Now he had become a "chosen instrument" of God for the Gospel.

We are also equipped for mission by God's call to discipleship for the sake of Jesus Christ, having been given all the necessary equipment to succeed.

II. It is guaranteed because of the content of the Gospel.
   A. It is the good news concerning His Son (v. 3a). The Son in His own person is the "Spirit of Holiness" (John 4:24; 2 Cor. 3:17). He is "very God of very God" (John 1:14; Ps. 2:7).

    B. Christ was "descended from David according to the flesh" (v. 2b). The Son of God assumed the human nature as a descendant of David. He was one of us in weakness and human limitation (2 Cor. 8:9; Matt. 8:20; Is. 53:3), but without sin (John 8:46; 2 Cor. 5:21; Heb. 4:15; Heb. 2:14–15; Heb. 7:27).

    C. By His resurrection from the dead He was designated Son of God also according to His human nature (Matt. 28:19; Phil. 2:9–11; Eph. 1:20–23). The resurrection from the dead is the turning point of history for Jesus Christ and for us.

His sharing of our human nature is also a guarantee of His promise. This coming of the Son of God into the flesh is even more important to us than our creation.

III. It is guaranteed because of the power of the Gospel.

    A. The Gospel—*euaggelion*—is the "good news" that we have been recalled from exile. The greater exile is that of sinners from the household of God.

    B. The Gospel was "promised beforehand through His prophets in the Holy Scriptures" (v. 2b). Paul was always careful to make it plain that his preaching and teaching conformed to that of the prophets (Acts 13:32; 26:22).

    C. The record of God's promises in the Old Testament was a decisive witness pointing to its fulfillment in Jesus Christ. Hence Paul repeatedly uses the expression "in accordance with the Scriptures" (1 Cor. 15:3–4).

The promise that His Word cannot return "empty" but must accomplish that for which it was sent (Is. 55:11) is God's own guarantee for the success of our mission.

The meaning of the "mission guaranteed" is the "grace and peace from God our Father and the Lord Jesus Christ." (Compare John 14:27; Luke 10:5; Num. 6:25–26.) When Christians receive His grace and peace, they also receive His life and salvation. The objective of the mission is guaranteed by Him who is the author of grace, peace, truth, and the new life in the risen Savior. In view of the coming of the Lord, mission work in His name is the only unfulfilled task of the Christian church.

RICHARD KLANN

Fourth Sunday in Advent

GOSPEL Matthew 1:18 – 25 (RSV)

Sermon Notes/Introduction

"Of the Holy Spirit" (v. 18) asserts the divine origin of Jesus Christ—that He was conceived of God, not of man. The Third Person of the Trinity prepared Mary for the incarnation of the Second Person of the Trinity. Joseph, being a just man who tried to conform to the Jewish law, planned to use the most private form of legal divorce, handing the letter to Mary in the presence of only two witnesses to whom he need not give his reasons. Here we note delicate thoughtfulness for her whom he loved and to whom he was bound by the Jewish betrothal as if in marriage (v. 19). The angel reminded Joseph of the greatness of his ancestry (v. 20) to assure him that his resolution was right insofar as Joseph knew the circumstances, for the line was to be kept pure, but also to urge him to take Mary so that the promise would be carried out in his family and no other. Joseph would formally give the child the name Jesus. Jesus, in His own person by virtue of what He is, shall save (v. 21). "From their sins" emphasizes that salvation from sin through Christ had to precede the restoration of Israel, which Joseph and all true Jews desired. The angel stresses "virgin" on the basis of Is. 7:14; God's past utterance is seen as requiring the present action (v. 22). The child was to be called not only Jesus but also Emmanuel, the manifestation of God in our midst (v. 23). Joseph's faith is seen in his immediate obedience to the commands received (v. 24).

The central thought of the text is the immanence of the transcendent God. The goal of the sermon is that the hearers will live in the awareness of God's closeness to them in Jesus Christ. The problem is that they often live as if God were far removed from them and does not partake of their humanity. The Gospel-means is that God condescended to us in limitless love.

These words appeared on a church bulletin board: "If God is far away, who has left?" We often live our lives with little awareness of how close God really is to us. It may be the weekly worship service or a tragedy in our lives that sensitizes us to God's nearness or to the need for Him to be near. The text reiterates this reality of our Christian existence: God is with us.

Sermon Outline
GOD IS WITH US

I. He is with us as the God-Man.
   A. He who is with us is true God.
      1. He was conceived by the Holy Ghost in a virgin (vv. 18, 20b).
      2. He is without sin (Heb. 4:15).
      3. He is not merely godly but actually and fully God (v. 23b; Col. 2:9).
      4. He was, is, and remains God (Heb. 13:8).
   B. He who is with us is true man.
      1. He was born of a woman (v. 25).
      2. He assumed a human body, wants, and feelings.
      3. He lived in the real world, experiencing joy and sorrow, acceptance and rejection.
      4. Jesus, the God-Man, is with us still (Matt. 28:20). Since He assumed our human nature, He will never cease being a man.

II. He is with us with His salvation.
   A. He came to save from sin (v. 21).
      1. Sin is a terrible reality.
         a. It corrupts.
         b. It separates from God.
         c. It condemns.
      2. Only God and Mary's Son could save us (Acts 4:12).
         a. As man He kept the Law and died in our stead.
         b. As God He was able to bear the suffering and to rise from the dead.
   B. Let Him be your Savior.
      1. Do not make prayer, faith, or piety your Savior.
      2. Jesus alone saves from the guilt, punishment, and power of sin.
   C. His salvation is a daily reality (Ps 85:9; 27:1).

Concluding thought: The Advent message is that God has come to be with us as the God-Man with His salvation. How close God is to us!

GERHARD AHO

The Nativity of Our Lord: The First Service

EPISTLE   Titus 2:11 – 14 (KJV)

Sermon Notes/Introduction

1. The relationship of the Series A readings for Christmas Day to one another is delightfully transparent: the Old Testament Reading (Is. 9:2 – 7) foretells the nativity of Christ; the Gospel (Luke 2:1 – 20) records His nativity; the Epistle (our text) probes the meaning of His nativity.

2. In the verses before and after our text, Paul recommends a number of specific virtues. Hence it should not surprise us to find as strong a sanctification emphasis in our text as there is a justification emphasis. In fact, throughout the text Paul insists that Christ came to our world for two reasons: (1) to save us and (2) to make us good people. These two emphases, of course, are one; what we in these sermon notes put asunder, St. Paul and also God's holy Word elsewhere join together. Where God justifies, He also sanctifies. Where faith is, there are also good works.

3. Although the assignment of this pericope to Christmas Day will naturally cause the preacher to concentrate on the first coming of Jesus (described in v. 11), it is interesting to note that the reading also refers to the second coming of Jesus (mentioned in v. 13).

4. The King James translation "a peculiar people" in verse 14 may today be misunderstood in the sense of an "odd," "queer," or "eccentric" people. This rendering, however, if understood correctly, is entirely appropriate. One of the meanings of the word "peculiar" listed in the dictionary is this: "exclusive, unique ... belonging distinctively or especially to one person, group, or kind." For instance, we might say of a certain plant that it is "peculiar" to a certain geographical area, meaning that only that area has it or grows it. That is the meaning of the word "peculiar" in the King James translation. Christ gave Himself that we might be God's "peculiar people," that is, that we might belong exclusively to God, be His private property and no one else's. The King James rendering is particularly serviceable for the outline below.

Sermon Outline

In many ways Christmas is peculiar. The Son of God, who is a spirit to begin with, takes on flesh and blood. He is born, of all things, of a virgin and, of all places, in a stable! He chooses for His birthplace a small town instead of a more prominent city nearby. Lowly shepherds rather than important people are the first to know about what has come to pass in Bethlehem. Not only the event itself is peculiar, but also the whole idea behind it is strange. Why should God do all this? Why should He leave the heavenly mansions for a 33-year sojourn on that infinitesimal speck in the universe called Earth? Why should He show concern for that creature of clay called man?

Our text makes clear the purpose of these peculiar events: to make us "a peculiar people."

CHRIST CAME TO MAKE US GOD'S PECULIAR PEOPLE

I. This means literally that Christ came to make us God's private property (justification emphasis).
   A. Christ bought the property (redeemed "us from all iniquity," v. 14).
      1. The price Christ paid was death. "The blood of Jesus Christ ... cleanseth us from all sin."
      2. The price Christ paid was damnation. "My God, my God, why hast Thou forsaken me?"
   B. Christ also improves the property (purifies "unto Himself a peculiar people, zealous of good works," v. 14).
II. This means in a sense that Christ also came to make us people who are actually peculiar—in the familiar, colloquial sense of the word (sanctification emphasis).
   A. Not that Christians are—or should be—odd, queer, or eccentric,
   B. But that Christians have a pleasant twist about them. As a result of Christ's work on them, something delightfully novel and refreshingly strange happens to them.
      1. Definition.
         a. They are peculiar as an oasis would be in a desert.
         b. They are peculiar as light would be to a mole.
         c. They are peculiar as sugar would be in a bitter, brackish diet.
         d. They are peculiar as a living person would seem on a battlefield covered with corpses.
      2. Example.
         a. Someone giving sacrificially may seem odd to us.

b. Someone turning the other cheek, loving enemies, etc., may seem abnormal to us.
c. Someone living at peace with people of other races may seem peculiar to us.
d. Someone remaining loyal to an undesirable spouse may seem unusual to us.
e. Someone giving up fame or wealth for a career of service to God and people may strike us as strange.

The peculiar events of Christmas have this purpose: to make us God's peculiar people. That literally means, to be sure, to make us God's exclusive, private property. But in a sense it also means to make us people who are actually peculiar, pleasantly peculiar. If society should ever be completely Christianized, such conduct, of course, will be the norm; it will lose its peculiar character. And in heaven for sure it will. There we shall recognize that what we did on earth, peculiar as it seemed at the time, was all along the thing to do.

FRANCIS C. ROSSOW

The Nativity of Our Lord: The First Service

GOSPEL   Luke 2:8 – 20 (RSV)

Sermon Notes/Introduction

The shepherds were keeping watch to guard the flock against thieves and marauders (v. 8). Into the night of the world Jesus came as the true Light. A symbol of this truth was the heavenly light (v. 9). The shepherds were afraid in the face of divine glory and holiness. But they had no need to fear (v. 9), because the angel's message was not of judgment but of salvation, not only to the shepherds but to all people (v. 10b). The shepherds were representatives of all lost sinners to whom was born a Savior from spiritual enemies. The Savior was both the promised Messiah and the Lord without peer (v. 11). The "sign" (v. 12) was a reference to Is. 9:6. The song of the angelic host was a triumphant declaration that God is glorified in heaven where angels see the realization of His counsel of love. On earth peace is established between God and man, and God is reconciled with the world (v. 14). The shepherds believed without seeing, accepting the message as from the Lord (v. 15). They became witnesses of the truth without leaving their daily vocations (v. 20).

The central thought of the text is that doxological worship involves the whole person. The goal of the sermon is that the hearers worship God with their whole being. The problem is that Christians fail to grasp the essentials of worship and so do it mechanically. The means to achieve the goal is that God has met our need and renewed us to worship Him.

Christmas worship services are usually beautiful and uplifting. Not only this service but every Christian worship service can take its cue from the first Christmas service.

Sermon Outline
THE FIRST CHRISTMAS SERVICE— A MODEL FOR CHRISTIAN WORSHIP

I. It is a model in its message.
   A. The message was declared by a unique messenger (v. 9).
      1. Angels were often privileged to bring a message from the Lord (Matt. 1:20; Luke 1:26).
      2. Preachers of God's word are also unique—they are called angels (Rev. 1:20; Gal. 4:14).
   B. The message was directed to the hearers.
      1. It was not speculative, abstract, or unrelated to people but concrete and applicable ("to all the people," "to you," vv. 10–11).
      2. It met the hearers at their point of need.
         a. They needed a Savior from sin.
         b. They needed deliverance from fear (v. 10).

In Christian worship we hear the message of the everlasting Gospel delivered by messengers whom God has sent (Rev. 14:6).

II. It is a model in its praise.
   A. It praises God for what He is.
      1. He is the highest One (v. 14), in whom we live (Acts 7:28) and whom we cannot fully comprehend (Rom. 11:33–36).
      2. He is worthy to be adored by the hosts of heaven and also by men on earth.
   B. It praises God for what He has done.
      1. He made peace between Himself and men (v. 14; Rom. 5:1, 10; 2 Cor. 5:19).
      2. In Christ, He made us objects of His good will.

In Christian worship we praise God in hymns, prayers, and other responses. It is God-centered activity.

III. It is a model in its worshipers.
   A. They were attentive.
      1. They really listened.
      2. They regarded what they heard as God's Word ("the Lord has made known," v. 15).
   B. They believed.
      1. They would go to Bethlehem (v. 15).
      2. They went with haste (v. 16).
   C. They confessed.
      1. They shared with others what they had heard and seen while continuing in their occupation (v. 17).
      2. They honored God in what they said and did (v. 20).

Christian worship involves people who listen attentively, respond in faith, and confess that faith by word and deed.

Let this Christmas service and all our worship be modeled after the first Christmas service.

GERHARD AHO

First Sunday After Christmas

EPISTLE   Galatians 4:4 – 7 (KJV)

Sermon Notes/Introduction

1. The fourth verse of this pericope, especially the phrase "made of a woman," clearly connects this reading with the Christmas narrative. At the same time the phrase "made under the Law" connects it with the account of Jesus' circumcision in the Gospel for New Year's Day (Luke 2:21).

2. Our text is the climax of a discussion begun at the end of chapter 3 and continued at the beginning of chapter 4, a discussion tracing the Christian's radical change in status; that is, if the Christian is indeed through Christ a son and heir of God, then he should not be a slave to rituals, ceremonial laws, ascetic practices, work-righteousness, and a variety of other "beggarly elements" (v. 9) that Paul mentions.

3. There are a number of interesting parallels in this pericope. The most obvious one is that the Son of God becomes a man in order to make us men sons of God. More specifically, He shares our condition, becomes a human being like us ("made of a woman"), subjects Himself to the law of God to which we are subject ("made under the Law"), so that we might enjoy His condition ("that we might receive the

adoption of sons"). Or to put it differently, the Son of God enters the human family so that we might belong to the heavenly family. Another parallel is the fact that in both Jesus' case and ours, one process automatically initiates another. Jesus' being "made of a woman" prepares Him for His also being "made under the Law." And in our case, our receiving the adoption of sons by Baptism (v. 5) triggers the sending forth of God's Holy Spirit ("because ye are sons, God hath sent forth the Spirit of His Son into your hearts," v. 6). Further, our being sons of God logically makes us also heirs of God (v. 7). A final parallel, less evident perhaps, is that there are *two* sendings or commissionings in our text: (1) that of Jesus Christ ("God sent forth His Son," v. 4) and (2) that of the Holy Spirit ("God hath sent forth the Spirit of His Son," v. 6).

4. Paradoxically, the Holy Spirit is both a cause and a result of our sonship with God. Frequently, the Scriptures point out that it is the Holy Spirit who through the message of Christ crucified and risen makes us believers in God, sons of God. But verse 6 of our text emphasizes another glorious truth about the Holy Spirit—that He is the pledge or proof or evidence of our status with God, a "bonus" or "extra" that God sends to reassure us of our sonship, a substantial "earnest" or "down-payment" of the full inheritance we will someday enjoy when we join God in heaven. (See 2 Cor. 1:22 and Eph. 1:13–14.) The Holy Spirit is both the *means to* and the *evidence of* our relationship with God through Jesus.

5. Note that in verse 5 our salvation is described both negatively and positively. Thanks to Jesus we get rid of one relationship (redeemed from being under the Law) and we enter another relationship (receive the adoption of sons).

6. Incidentally, note that all three persons of the Triune God are mentioned in this brief pericope. Here, as so often elsewhere in the Bible, the doctrine of the Trinity is quietly assumed rather than overtly proclaimed.

Sermon Outline

All the pericopes for this season (Christmas and the New Year) overwhelm us with the bountiful grace of God. There are no limits to His kindness. He gives "full measure and running over." He goes the extra mile. He gives *two* coats where none is deserved at all and where at most only one is hoped for. Our text is one more example of God's doing more than we can ever expect or wish for: He not only sends us His Son but He sends us His Holy Spirit as well.

GRACE ON GRACE FROM THE GOD OF GRACE

I. The God of grace sends us His Son.
   A. The Son of God becomes like us.
      1. He is "made of a woman" (v. 4).
      2. He is "made under the Law" (v. 4).
   B. As a result, we become sons of God in the eyes of God.
      1. Through Christ we are, first of all, freed from our slavery to the Law (v. 5).
      2. Through Christ we are then received into the family of God (v. 5). But there is more.
II. The God of grace sends us His Holy Spirit.
   A. The Holy Spirit enters our hearts.
      1. He effects our sonship; through the Gospel He enables us to acknowledge God as our Father ("crying, Abba, Father," v. 6).
      2. He evidences our sonship ("because ye are sons," etc., v. 6).
   B. As a result, we are not only the sons of God but also the heirs of God (v. 7).
      1. The presence of the Holy Spirit in our hearts is the "downpayment" on our future inheritance designed for present enjoyment.
      2. The presence of the Holy Spirit is a guarantee of the even fuller inheritance we shall someday enjoy in heaven.

What shall we then say to these things as we face the year ahead? If God be for us—and for us in such an unexpected and indescribable manner—who or what can be against us?

FRANCIS C. ROSSOW

First Sunday After Christmas

GOSPEL   Matthew 2:13 – 15, 19 – 23 (KJV)

Sermon Notes/Introduction

1. The prophecies of God are equivalent to promises. The Scriptures assure us that God cannot lie (Titus 1:2; Heb. 6:18). When God in His Word prophesies or promises, He sees to it that these prophecies are fulfilled, even if He must use supernatural means, such as the directions given in dreams (vv. 13, 19, 22), to overcome apparent obstacles. Consider the events surrounding our text. A Roman emperor, through his decree of

taxation or enrollment (Luke 2:1–7), leads Mary and Joseph to Bethlehem, where Jesus is to be born according to prophecy (Matt. 2:4–6). A star guides the Wise Men to Jerusalem and then to Bethlehem, and God warns them not to return to Herod in order to protect the promised Messiah (Matt. 2:12).

2. There are two references to prophecy in our text. "Out of Egypt have I called My Son" (v. 15) is a reference to Hosea 11:1b. "He shall be called a Nazarene" (v. 23) seems to present a problem, for there is no reference to Nazareth in the Old Testament, and Matthew does not quote unwritten prophecies. Note that Matthew writes, "which was spoken by the prophets," not "the prophet." In *The Gospels*, Ylvisaker comments:

> The evangelist ... has no definite prophecy in mind. And so the difficulty disappears immediately. Nazara is the feminine of Nezer, a twig, a young shoot. The name of the city is a result, no doubt, of its humble origin. When Jesus was called a Nazarene because he hailed from the city of Nazareth, and the evangelist finds in this circumstance a fulfillment of the Old Covenant prophecies, he evidently has reflected especially upon Isaiah 11:1. Messiah, the Son of David, should come up, as a twig or a tender plant, from the root of David's tree. This thought is also expressed in Is. 53:2; cf. Jer. 23:5; 33:15; Zech. 3:8; 6:12. The term "shoot," employed in these passages, reminds us of the lowly and despised origin of the Messiah. He should appear without any outward evidence of greatness or dignity, and should descend from the humbled household of David. This prophetic conception is to Matthew accomplished as he visions Jesus growing from childhood to manhood in Nazareth, this despicable little village. So it is that Jesus came to be called the Nazarene. (Joh. Ylvisaker, *The Gospels* [Minneapolis: Augsburg Publishing House, 1932], p. 102)

Sermon Outline

Why do we come to church? To worship God, of course, and to thank Him for all He has done for us—for our redemption from sin, death, and hell; for the sanctified lives He has given us; for His preservation and loving care for us. We come to hear the comfort of His Word in order to be strengthened for living the life He would have us live.

Particularly if we have difficulties and problems (and who doesn't have many of these?), we want to hear how God will solve these problems, how He has promised to solve them.

God has given us many promises in His Word, and He will

keep them, for He cannot lie. His Word cannot be broken (John 10:35).

THE COMFORT OF PROPHECY FULFILLMENT

I. God prophesies or promises. He does this even in great detail (cf. Is. 53). The activities of our text and the events surrounding it are examples of detailed prophetic utterance.

II. The fullness of time comes (Gal. 4:4). According to human judgment, it would seem that the time for the birth of Christ was not a good time. Israel was not at the height of its power. There was no national unity. Israel was a conquered nation, subject to foreign powers and evil rulers. The difficulties that present themselves in our text point to a less than ideal world situation. But God's ways are much wiser than men's ways (Is. 55:8 – 9), and He knows the best time for action. We must trust His decisions and understand that His ways are best.

III. God directs the fulfillment of prophecy. Our text shows the scrupulous care with which God effects the fulfillment of His promises. Even the details (Egypt, Nazareth) are fulfilled. Obstacles are met head on and are even used to fulfill rather than impede the will of God. God coordinates many unusual details and even negative events so that we may be redeemed and receive adoption as sons (Gal. 4:4 – 5). The Wise Men had to be guided by a star (Is. 60:3); bloodthirsty Herod had to be evaded by a flight into Egypt (Hos. 11:1); and Joseph's fear of brutal Archelaus had to be taken into account so that Jesus, born in Bethlehem, might reside in Nazareth and be called a Nazarene (Matt. 2:23). God does direct the fulfillment of prophecy.

Because God cannot lie, He will direct the fulfillment of all His promises to His dear children in Christ. He promised them eternal life in Christ before the world began (Titus 1:2). He promised them eternal safekeeping (John 10:28). He promised them eternal mansions (John 14:1 – 3). He promised that "all things work together for good to them that love God" (Rom. 8:28). He promised forgiveness to the repentant (Is. 1:18 – 20). He promised cleansing from all sin through the blood of Christ (1 John 1:7). Many other examples of God's promises can be cited from the Scriptures for the comfort of believers.

ALFRED FREMDER

Second Sunday After Christmas

EPISTLE   Ephesians 1:3 – 6, 15 – 18 (RSV)

Sermon Notes/Introduction

Christmas is a time for celebration. We celebrate with family reunions as we come together for the holidays to share our unity. We celebrate through the exchanging of gifts as a symbol of our love. We celebrate with parties to generate the feeling of "good will to men." But these are only worldly reflections of our real cause for celebration in this festive season. As we are still in the near shadow of the Feast of the Nativity, in which we celebrated our Lord's incarnation, let us continue our festive mood this morning by saying with Paul, "Blessed be the God and Father of our Lord Jesus Christ, who has blessed us in Christ with every spiritual blessing in the heavenly places" (v. 3).

Sermon Outline
LET US PRAISE GOD FOR CHRIST'S BIRTH AND OUR ADOPTION

I. Christ's birth and our adoption have their roots in the past.
   A. The Father in eternity chose His Son to be the Savior, and He chose us in Him (v. 5). He destined us to be His sons through Jesus Christ.
      1. The Father foresaw that Adam and Eve would plunge the world into sin and that human beings would be helpless to save themselves.
      2. The Father proclaimed the remedy, first to Adam and Eve (Gen. 3:15; Ps. 22; Is. 53).
   B. The Father in eternity chose us to be His children (vv. 4 – 6; Rom. 8:28 – 30).
      1. Our election took place before the foundation of the world was laid (v. 4), before we were born (Rom. 9:11).
      2. Our election was motivated by love (v. 5; John 3:16).
      3. Our election was effected by grace (v. 6), God's compassion toward us apart from any merit of our own (2 Tim. 1:9; Eph. 2:8 – 9).
II. Christ's birth and our adoption became realities in time.
   A. At God's appointed time, the Word became flesh (John

1:14; Gal. 4:4 – 5). *Illustration* (Kierkegaard): A prince, after visiting a village in his kingdom, found a maiden he wanted for his wife. Should he take her by force or impress her with his royalty? No, he decided, the girl would be his but she might never love him. Rather, disguised as a common laborer, he went and worked in that village and won the girl's love.
1. Christ came into the world as an infant, born of the Virgin Mary. Irenaeus: "He (Christ) came to save all persons by Himself; all, I mean, who by Him are regenerated (baptized) into God; infants and little ones, and children, and youths and elder persons. Therefore He went through the several ages: for infants being made an infant, sanctifying infants, to little ones He was made a little one, sanctifying those of that age, and also giving them an example of godliness, justice, and dutifulness; to youth He was a youth," etc. (*Against Heresies* XXII. 4).
2. He grew to manhood to keep the Law perfectly in our stead (Heb. 7:26).
3. He suffered, died, and rose again for our salvation.
B. In God's appointed time, He became flesh so that we might receive adoption as sons (v. 5).
1. We came into the world of sinners, deserving eternal death (John 3:5 – 6; Rom. 5:12; 6:23; James 1:15).
2. By grace, through Baptism, we became the adopted children of our heavenly Father (vv. 3 – 4 Phillips; Rom. 3:14 – 15; 1 Cor. 6:17 – 18). *Illustration:* As a judge declares an infant the child and heir of his adoptive parents (without any merit or conscious acknowledgment on the infant's part), in like manner we are declared God's adopted children through Baptism.
III. Christ's birth and our adoption should be celebrated now and through eternity (vv. 15 – 18).
A. We celebrate the birthday of Christ with praise and thanksgiving.
1. With festive voices we remember His birth in our yearly celebration of Christmas.
2. With grateful hearts we proclaim the love of God through Christ to others and pray for their salvation and other needs (vv. 16 – 17).

B. We celebrate our adoption through confession and service.
   1. Through eyes of faith we confess the hope that is in us (v. 18a).
   2. Through hands of faith we serve our fellow man (v. 15).

RONALD IRSCH

Second Sunday After Christmas

GOSPEL   John 1:1 – 18 (KJV)

Sermon Notes/Introduction

"In the beginning God created the heaven and the earth" (Gen. 1:1). "In the beginning was the Word, and the Word was with God, and the Word was God. The same was in the beginning with God. All things were made by Him; and without Him was not anything made that was made" (John 1:1 – 3). Genesis begins at the creation of heaven and earth by God. John's gospel takes us back into eternity before the world was made to point out the eternal existence of the Word, who made the world (John 1:10).

John trumpets clearly and proclaims majestically the deity of the Word made flesh who "dwelt among us" (John 1:14). There is no doubt that Jesus, the incarnate Word, is God. John states this boldly and then proceeds to give a partial record of the "signs" that Jesus did in the presence of His disciples (John 20:30)—turning water into wine (chap. 2), healing a nobleman's son (chap. 4), feeding a multitude of five thousand with five barley loaves and two small fish (chap. 6), giving sight to a man who was born blind (chap. 9), and raising Lazarus from the dead (chap. 11)—"signs" that indicated, underlined, and verified the deity of Jesus in order "that you might believe that Jesus is the Christ, the Son of God; and that believing you might have life through His name" (John 20:31).

Not only does John declare the Word to be God (v. 1), but he also declares that the Word was made flesh (v. 14), that Jesus is true man, and then he proceeds to give evidence of this. He shows Jesus weary and exhausted, sitting by the well of Jacob (chap. 4). He shows Jesus weeping with those who are weeping (chap. 11). He shows that Jesus' soul is troubled at the thought of His impending death (chap. 12). It was necessary that Jesus also be a true man so that He might be under the Law, that He might suffer and die *as our substitute* (Heb. 2:14).

Sermon Outline

Jesus, true God, also became true man so that you and I may receive the gifts of the Word.

THE GIFTS OF THE WORD

I. The Word gives life (John 1:4). It is true that God gives us physical life, but "man does not live by bread only" (Deut. 8:3). You and I deserve "the wages of sin," death; but "the gift of God is eternal life through Jesus Christ our Lord" (Rom. 6:23). Eternal life is a gift secured through faith in Jesus, our Savior (John 5:24; 6:47). The incarnate Word is the only source and the generation of our spiritual life (John 1:12–13; 1 John 5:12).

II. The Word gives light (John 1:4, 9). Spiritual darkness is opposed to Jesus, "the Light of the world." Jesus says: "He that follows me shall not walk in darkness, but shall have the light of life" (John 8:12; cf. Is. 9:2). Men are condemned for rejecting that light, for loving darkness rather than light (John 3:19). The incarnate Word, the true Light, gives light that shines in the darkness (John 1:5), a gift that is not always accepted and that can only be accepted through the power of God (vv. 12, 13). John the Baptist came to bear witness to the true Light (vv. 6–9) so that "all men through Him might believe" (v. 7).

III. The Word gives fullness (v. 16). We know that in Christ dwells "all the fullness of the Godhead bodily" (Col. 2:9). For us to be filled with all the fullness of God is "to know the love of Christ" (Eph. 3:16–19), to be rooted and grounded and growing in the love of Christ, a gift of pure grace from the incarnate Word (John 1:16).

IV. The Word gives grace (vv. 14, 16–17). Grace is the unmerited mercy of God in Christ toward us sinners. We are justified by His grace, not by anything we have done or can do (cf. Eph. 2:8–9; Rom. 3:24; 11:6; Titus 3:4–7). We are also sanctified by His grace (2 Cor. 9:8).

V. The Word gives truth (John 1:14, 17–18). Jesus is truth (John 14:6). The incarnate Word declares the Father (John 1:18) and bears witness to the truth (John 18:37). He asks us to hear and believe His witness (John 18:37), and He empowers us to do this (John 1:12–13).

The incarnate Word, true God and true man, bestowed all these precious gifts on us so that we may "be His own, and live under Him in His kingdom, and serve Him in everlasting righteousness, innocence, and blessedness." Therefore, "walk in love, as Christ also hath loved us, and hath given Himself for us an offering and a sacrifice to God for a sweetsmelling savor" (Eph. 5:2). Walk in love! (Here specific applications may follow.)

ALFRED FREMDER

The Baptism of Our Lord: First Sunday After the Epiphany

EPISTLE   Acts 10:34 – 38 (KJV)

Sermon Notes/Introduction

The context should be noted. Peter is speaking in the house of Cornelius, a Gentile. Peter receives a previous vision on his housetop. Later he reports his presence in Cornelius's house at Jerusalem. Thus this event marks a critical juncture in the development of the early church.

Sermon Outline
JESUS, SAVIOR FOR ALL HUMANITY

I. The unique *person* of Jesus as Savior for all humanity.
   A. "Lord of all" (v. 36) implies His deity.
   B. The unique Triune God is taught in v. 38.
      1. Jesus was "God's anointed."
      2. He was anointed "through the Holy Spirit."
      3. "God [the Father] was with Him."
   C. The unique person of Jesus was needed for the salvation offered to all humanity.
      1. God is "no respecter of persons" (v. 34).
      2. Before God in His justice, all people are in need of redemption, regardless of nationality, race, or color.
      3. Jesus was sent to bring "peace" to all humanity (v. 36).
   D. The baptism preached by John (v. 37) pointed to the need for repentance and a Savior also in legalistic Judaism.
II. The unique *work* of Jesus as Savior for all humanity.
   A. Jesus showed His deity through His power over the forces of evil, or the devil, by healing the ill (v. 38).
   B. The physical healings of Jesus are parallel to His spiritual healing of humanity as the agent of "peace" with God (v. 36).

C. People from all nations may receive the benefit of Jesus, our Redeemer (v. 35). The phrases "fearing God" and "working righteousness" must be construed in the context of the latter part of Peter's sermon (vv. 39–43), which refers to Jesus' death and resurrection and concludes: "Through His name whosoever believeth in Him shall receive remission of sins." Forgiveness is a forensic act of God.

III. Application.
  A. As Gentiles we are thankful that God sent His Son as Redeemer for all nations.
  B. Mindful of our baptism, each day we are to confess our unworthiness and rely only on Christ's redemption.
  C. With the peace from Christ in our hearts, we should follow the example of Peter in promoting the spread of the Gospel message throughout the world.

ROBERT G. HOERBER

The Baptism of Our Lord: First Sunday After the Epiphany

GOSPEL   Matthew 3:13–17 (RSV)

Sermon Notes/Introduction

1. Now that Christmas is past and the Messiah is here, what is His mission all about? At His "inauguration" Jesus is baptized by John and thus begins His walk from Galilee to Golgotha. Not to be confused with *Christian* Baptism, which Jesus would later command, Jesus' "washing" clearly establishes Him as the Messiah, God's Son sent to suffer.

2. John's baptizing meant repentance and forgiveness, but the sinless Savior would seem to have no need for that. John recognizes his own subordinate role and "wanted to prevent" Jesus, the sense of the conative imperfect *diekoluen*. Instead, the humble sinner John has the real *need* to be baptized. But Jesus' mission was not to die for His own sin; rather, He took on Himself the sin of Adam and all who have lived since. In His baptism Jesus identifies Himself as the "second Adam," as the rightful representative of all men, who are sinners in need of repentance and forgiveness.

3. Jesus also identifies Himself specifically with God's covenant people, Israel. Ritual washing meant initiation, inclu-

sion; indeed, the children of Israel were saved and established by their "baptism" through the Red Sea (1 Cor. 10:1–2), and they were brought into the Promised Land by a "washing" in the Jordan. It was the same with Jesus. As the true Son of Israel, the Messiah was now to bring to fulfillment the Old Covenant, to "fulfill all righteousness." In general, "righteousness" is the whole redeeming activity of God, salvation through imputing Christ's righteousness to man. *Dikaiosunē* translates not only the Hebrew *sedekah* but at times also *chesed* (e.g., Ex. 15:13; cf. also Ps. 103:17, where they are paralleled), linking its understanding more closely to God's covenant love and plan of salvation, which culminate in Christ (Rom. 1:16–17; 3:21–22).

4. But at the time of Jesus' baptism, His mission is only beginning; there is more to come. Jesus' use of the aorist imperative, "let it be" (v. 15), accents the "for now." John's baptizing is still "Old Testament"; the kingdom is only "at hand."

5. Both Fatherly approval and Messianic definition are indicated by the "voice." The identity of God's begotten Son of Ps. 2:7 is combined with the "chosen servant" of Isaiah 42, whom God has declared "acceptable" (*rasah*). The Hebrew word is often used in reference to a sacrifice that itself is "accepted" by the priest and by which the worshiper is "made acceptable" through forgiveness of sin. The mission of that servant in Isaiah 42, however, is to bring forth "justice" (justification) through humble suffering, as is brought out especially in the fourth "Suffering Servant Song," Is. 52:13–53:12. Jesus Himself realizes a greater baptism coming in His own life, and from now on He is distressed "until it is accomplished" (Luke 12:50; cf. Mark 10:38). It is that baptism of His death in which we participate and by which we enter into the "New (fulfilled) Covenant" (Rom. 6:3–4) when God declares us "acceptable" by His grace and favor.

Sermon Outline

The few weeks since Christmas are short compared to the approximately 30 years between Jesus' birth and His baptism by John. Yet many (in our world) have already forgotten why His birth was so important. Others, as in Jesus' own day, wait with eager or curious expectation to see what His mission in life will be. The baptism of Jesus "begins" His public ministry. Like an "inaugural address," this text outlines the credentials and anticipated "program" for the coming years.

SO WHO... AND WHAT... IS THIS CHRIST?

I. The Messiah identifies with the past.
   A. He identifies with all people from Adam to John, who "need" to be baptized for forgiveness.
   B. He claims a heritage with God's covenant people, Israel; indeed, He is Israel (and all God's people) "reduced to one."
   C. Thus His mission involves forgiveness—not for His own sin but for the sin of all others.
II. The Messiah identifies with the present (at His time).
   A. In the baby of Bethlehem God has sent "His Son" (Ps. 2:7).
   B. This Messiah is also the "chosen servant" foretold by Isaiah, with whom God is "well pleased," that is, whom God has accepted by grace to be His sacrifice for sin.
   C. Jesus is baptized "to fulfill all righteousness" ... "for now." The fulfillment of God's plan has begun, but Jesus' mission moves from the Jordan to Jerusalem.
III. The Messiah's mission points to the future.
   A. He has come primarily to suffer and die so that by repentance and forgiveness through His righteousness, the kingdom of God may come.
   B. In our (Christian) baptism, we participate in the death of Christ (Rom. 6) and identify with the "New Israel," saved by baptismal grace.
   C. As the Epiphany season stands between our celebration of Christ's birth and His Passion, we remember that He came to manifest God's good favor (grace) by humbly offering Himself for the sins of the world.

ANDREW H. BARTELT

Second Sunday After the Epiphany

EPISTLE   1 Corinthians 1:1–9 (KJV)

Sermon Notes/Introduction

1. Like the Series A Old Testament Reading for this Sunday (Is. 49:1–6) and the Gospel (John 1:29–41), our text emphasizes the activity of God in Jesus Christ (compare most any verse with Is. 49:1, 5, and John 1:29–34) and the church's mission outreach (compare v. 2 with Is. 49:6 and John 1:40–41), both of them familiar Epiphany themes.

2. Note how the pericope bombards the reader throughout with the truth that whatever good things happen among Christians, it is God who does them through Jesus Christ. His is the power and the glory! It is God who wills Paul's apostleship, and it is God who calls Paul to the apostleship (v. 1). It is God who calls and sanctifies the congregation at Corinth (v. 2). Grace and peace are from God (v. 3), an idea repeated in part in v. 4. Enrichment in the gifts of utterance and knowledge comes from God (v. 5). It is God who confirms the testimony of Christ in the Corinthian Christians (v. 6) and gives them spiritual gifts (v. 7). It is God again who confirms us in our faith and keeps us blameless until Judgment Day (v. 8). And, lest we forget, all depends on God's faithfulness (v. 9), that same God (to clinch the point) who called us into the fellowship of His Son. Furthermore, this stress on divine rather than human activity, explicitly stated again and again in this pericope, is reinforced by frequent use of the passive voice. The point is that we don't achieve salvation and sanctification but that rather they *are achieved* in us by God through Christ.

3. Note in verses 1 and 2 the common denominator between Paul and his readers. Both are called by God, he to his apostleship, they to their membership in the Christian church.

4. There is an interesting play on words in verse 2. First, God "calls" people to be saints; then people, in response, call on the name of Jesus. The second kind of calling (worship) is the result and the evidence that the first kind of calling (conversion) occurred.

5. Parallel to God's confirmation of the Corinthian Christians in the past (v. 6) is His confirmation of them for the future (v. 8). God's faithfulness in the past is a solid basis for our trust in His faithfulness for the future.

6. The words in verse 8, "that ye may be blameless in the day of our Lord Jesus Christ," are meant in a forensic sense; that is, God, by grace and because of the merits of Jesus Christ, *declares* us blameless even though in behavior we aren't—and, as is obvious from the remainder of this epistle, the Corinthians weren't either. Even on Judgment Day our salvation depends 100 percent on this incredibly gracious declaration of God, not on the actual righteousness of our everyday lives. Yet the fact remains that where God declares us righteous, He makes us righteous as well. Day by day through Jesus Christ He renders us more and more blameless in actuality, an activity He means to get as far as possible with before we die. And in heaven we

shall be perfected in actuality! This is one of the many joys of heaven to which we look forward.

Sermon Outline

Like the Corinthians, we have both personal and congregational problems. The good news of our text is that the solution to these problems lies not in our own feeble efforts but rather in the power and faithfulness of God, who saved us through Jesus Christ.

THANKS BE TO GOD, WHO DOES IT ALL!

I. God through Christ did everything in the past (vv. 1–2).
II. God through Christ does everything in the present (vv. 3–7).
III. God through Christ will do everything for the future (vv. 8–9).

How fortunate we are that everything—our salvation and our sanctification—depends entirely on God's faithfulness in Christ rather than on our own faithfulness. Let us rejoice in this God, who is "the same yesterday, and today, and forever"—"Our God, our Help in ages past, Our Hope for years to come."

FRANCIS C. ROSSOW

Second Sunday After the Epiphany

GOSPEL John 1:29 – 41 (RSV)

Sermon Notes/Introduction

John's account in the text avoids two extremes: (1) an overemphasis on human effort as in the "I found it" religious experience and (2) an emphasis on God's determining everything in such a fatalistic manner that people become apathetic toward witnessing.

Here is authentic human searching for a more profound relationship to God in Christ. God uses the questions raised by John the Baptist and by his disciples to lead to a discovery of Christ.

Sermon Outline
GOD LEADS US TO DISCOVER CHRIST

I. He is the Son of God.

- A. Christ ranks above the prophets such as John the Baptist (John 1:30).
- B. John the Baptist said, "He was before me" (v. 30, Christ's preexistence).
- C. We need a Savior who tenderly approaches us in our needs but who also has the divine power and love to raise us up through our problems.

II. He is the Messiah.
- A. The priestly office of Jesus was revealed to Israel by John (v. 31).
    1. John said, "For this [purpose] I come baptizing with water" (v. 31).
        a. John preached repentance.
        b. He preached the urgency of the kingdom of God.
        c. He preached the forgiveness of sins.
    2. The purpose of Christ's coming was "that He might be revealed to Israel" (v. 31) and later to us.
- B. The priestly office of Jesus consisted in offering Himself up as the Lamb of God in our place (vv. 29, 36).

III. He is the One chosen by the Spirit (v. 33).
- A. The disciples address Him with honor as "Rabbi" (v. 38).
    1. Their question, "Where are You staying?" (v. 38), indicates a searching-finding process.
    2. The answer, "Come and see" (v. 39), invites the inquiring potential disciples to learn from the greatest prophet of all.
- B. The function of the Holy Spirit in leading people to Christ is seen in "He on whom you see the Spirit descend and remain ..." (v. 33).
    1. The Holy Spirit finds seekers through the witness of "brothers."
    2. Those whom the Spirit has found then follow Christ by witnessing to Christ. Through this witnessing the Holy Spirit leads others to Christ.

As I was writing this outline, I answered the telephone. A woman responded to my advertisement about the formation of Bible study groups. "Who are you? Are you one of those sects that don't believe in the Trinity?" "No," I said. "I belong to a church that teaches the authentic message of the New Testament, according to which God works through Jesus Christ and the Holy Spirit." "Good," she said. "Your group can meet in my living room and I'll furnish Bibles for study and cake and coffee for refreshments." Thus began another encounter in which people came to God through Christ. God led new brothers and sisters to discover Christ.

HAROLD H. ZIETLOW

Third Sunday After the Epiphany

EPISTLE 1 Corinthians 1:10 – 17 (RSV)

Sermon Notes/Introduction

If the general theme of the Epiphany season is "God's revelation (or manifestation) of the Christ," then the Series A Epistles from 1 Corinthians offer a contrast to the expected topics of "light" and "glory" that are illuminated in the Old Testament and Gospel readings. Perhaps a short sermon series could be unified under the heading "So This Is Christ?"

Sermon Outline

The Epistle for Epiphany 3 might suggest the following title:

SO THIS IS CHRIST: A CHURCH DIVIDED?

Most congregations (and church bodies!) will provide many examples of quarreling and bickering, not to mention dissension and division, somewhat analogous to the situation Paul confronted in Corinth. The text implies that the Corinthians identified with various factions on the basis of whoever baptized them, thus turning the unity given in Baptism into disunity and discord. One should ask, Is *this* Christ(ianity)? Is the "church militant" to be weakened by internal strife? The problem is typical, because it results from man's own nature. The solution lies in the power of the cross.

I. The problem is with man, even within the "household of faith." Although the Corinthian congregation was "not lacking in any spiritual gift" (v. 7), it still managed to hinder the work of Christ.
   A. Man's method involves a selfish search for identity. He wants to be in the right group, the "in crowd." He may trace his "roots" to someone important, as though identifying with another makes himself special. Pride and ego have a field day.
   B. Man's goal is his own glory. He boasts in himself.

C. The result is strife and contention.
   1. Man is never happy; he must always be "one up" on others.
   2. Spirituality diminishes. The "spiritual gifts" caused the Corinthians no end of problems. Baptism had become more a means of division than a means of grace.
   3. The "light" and "rejoicing" promised in the Old Testament and Gospel readings are clouded by man's sin.
II. The solution is God's revelation in Christ.
   A. God's method is the cross. He deals with sin, and He offers forgiveness. The message of "light" and "rejoicing" begins with "repent" (Gospel). Pride and ego are transcended.
   B. God's goal is forgiveness and true life.
   C. God's result is Christ and His church ("kingdom of heaven"—Gospel).
      1. We find our true identity in Christ.
         a. Our "roots" lie in Baptism in *His* name.
         b. Our life comes through His death.
         c. The power of the cross is completely independent of man's ideas or "wisdom" (v. 17).
      2. We have true unity only in Him.
         a. Mutual identity means unity, not division. Christ is *not* divided (v. 13).
         b. We are "made complete" or "confirmed" (same word as RSV "equipping" in Eph. 4:12) in one mind and one intention (purpose), e.g., "evangelism" (v. 17).

This *is* Christ and His church, not divided but united. Unified by identity under the cross, the church finds unity also in its purpose to proclaim the cross.

ANDREW H. BARTELT

Third Sunday After the Epiphany

GOSPEL   Matthew 4:12–23

Sermon Notes/Introduction

Jesus' ministry had been inaugurated with His baptism and temptation (Matt. 3:13–4:11). John, the last prophet to operate solely under the Old Testament, was removed from the scene (Matt. 4:12). But John was also the herald of the immediacy of the New Testament kingdom (John 1:29). Now the kingdom was near (Matt 4:17), or better, "rubbing up against you." Jesus had to begin His teaching-preaching-healing ministry (v. 23) in the area of Zebulun and Naphtali (v. 15) to fulfill Is. 9:1–2. He came not only to a certain place but also with a particular purpose (v. 16), thus fulfilling Is. 42:6–7. The urgency of Jesus' mission was conveyed to Peter, Andrew, James, and John, for they all responded immediately (*eutheōs,* vv. 20, 22). The urgency of the call to the disciples contrasts with the more leisurely attitude of Elijah in 1 Kings 19:20. For Jesus, the fullness of God's time had come (Gal. 4:4), and He had to get on with the task. Note that nowhere in Scripture are we told that these professional fishermen ever caught any fish without the direct intervention of the Lord. When they were fishers of men (Matt. 4:19), the Lord worked through them to let His kingdom come and grow.

As the kingdom of God came in Christ's day, so it has continued to come.

Sermon Outline
GOD'S KINGDOM COMES!

I. It comes among us.
   A. It comes where we are (vv. 18, 21).
   B. It comes with a sense of urgency (vv. 18–22).
   C. It comes with divine power flowing from the Gospel message of forgiveness (Matt. 9:5–6).
      1. It heals people in spirit and sometimes also in body (Matt. 4:23).
      2. It calls them out of an old life (vv. 20, 22).
      3. It calls them into a new life (vv. 19, 21c).
II. It comes in many places (v. 16).
   A. In the Old Testament, most of God's saving work was localized. The New Testament work of God (Matt. 3:13–4:11) is worldwide.
   B. Jesus began His work in a place remote from Jerusalem and Judea (Matt. 4:13, 15, 16, 23), thus signaling a wider mission than John had.
   C. Jesus sends His messengers wherever the "fish" are (v. 19).

God's kingdom comes—among us now and in many places through us.

WARREN MESSMANN

Fourth Sunday After the Epiphany

EPISTLE 1 Corinthians 1:26 – 31 (RSV)

Sermon Notes/Introduction

The section between the Epistle for last Sunday and this text is necessary background for Epiphany 4. "Christ crucified" is the "stumbling block" to Jews, who could not accept a suffering and dying God as Messiah, and "foolishness" to the Greeks, whose love for philosophy saw little value in accentuating a criminal's crucifixion. By contrast, the Christians based their entire faith on such "nonsense" and no doubt appeared a bit "weak in the head" to those around them. What is more, many of the early Christians came from the ranks of the poor (and slaves) and were also considered physically and socially "weak." Paul speaks a word of contrast and comfort, highlighted also by the exhortation to humility in the Old Testament Reading and by the Beatitudes in the Gospel.

Sermon Outline

Continuing the series from last Sunday, this sermon might be entitled:

SO THIS IS CHRIST: WEAKNESS AND FOLLY?

To most people in our world, Christians must stand out as being a bit odd. One man has described a Christian as a "well-programmed sucker." The Christian does not participate in the same goals, the same "fun" as the rest of our society. (Compare the situation at Corinth, which was known in its day for debauchery and immorality.) The pressure to "conform" can be very severe on a Christian, until he remembers that strength and foolishness need to be defined in God's terms.

I. Man wants to be strong and wise.
   A. Society emphasizes strength (the hero wins the final fisticuffs) and cleverness (the popular child "puts one over" on the teacher). According to nature, only the "strong" survive.
   B. Man assumes his "wisdom" knows what is best for him, so he seeks materialistic goals of happiness and "fun" (many examples!).
   C. As a result, man must glory in himself; he boasts (ego trip).

II. But man has it turned upside-down.
   A. What he thinks is strength is really weakness; wisdom is folly.
   B. It is a dead end.
      1. Man is on the road to destruction.
      2. What is more, he has no *chance* to understand true strength and wisdom, because he is blinded by his own vanity. Cf. Jesus' saying about the rich man (Matt. 19:23). One who trusts in himself cannot realize that he is weak.
   C. All men (especially the "strong") are *really* weak and foolish.
      1. It is called "sin." We are all sinners. We are all weak.
      2. Man's wisdom is foolishness compared to the wisdom and knowledge of God.
      3. The first step toward strength and wisdom is realizing weakness and foolishness—i.e., repentance, confession. We find strength and wisdom on our knees! The "poor in spirit" are blessed.
III. True strength and wisdom come from God.
   A. "Christ crucified" means power and wisdom (v. 24).
   B. This seems a paradox, but God turns everything around. His foolishness is wiser than the wisest man (cf. 1 Cor. 4:10). Note the antitheses between illusion and reality; weakness/strength; foolishness/wisdom; nonbeing/being; nobody/somebody; death(cross)/life (glory); boasting in myself/boasting in Christ.
IV. Now, consider your (our) calling (cf. also 1 Cor. 1:24).
   A. "Calling" can refer to the state in which we were when God called us, that is, "poor," "weak," "foolish" (before Christ).
   B. "Calling" can also mean the result of God's call—not weak but strong, not foolish but wise.
   C. Thus the rest of the world (still "B.C."), though it thinks it is wise, is not.
   D. We who know "Christ crucified" have true strength and wisdom, which is defined in terms of "justification," "sanctification," "redemption."

If anyone wishes to boast, then let him boast as a *humble* witness to the power of the Lord (v. 31). This *is* true strength (in "weakness") and true wisdom (in "folly"), because we have the strength and wisdom of God. This *is* Christ!

ANDREW H. BARTELT

Fourth Sunday After the Epiphany

GOSPEL   Matthew 5:1–12

Sermon Notes/Introduction

The initial verses of the Sermon on the Mount serve as a fitting text for the Epiphany season, which commemorates the sharing of the Christmas message with the Gentiles. This season signifies God's desire for the enfranchisement of all people within His kingdom. This fact is additionally underscored by the use of a text from the Gospel of Matthew, the gospel that was addressed primarily to the descendants of Israel. They are invited to abandon legalism and see the fulfillment of their ancient faith in the grace of God as revealed in the redemptive work of Christ.

The Sermon on the Mount has been called the Magna Carta of the kingdom of God. While it is in essence a Law sermon, it is addressed to those whom Jesus has already discipled, the Twelve (v. 1). Thus the Sermon, and especially our text, does not set forth legalistic requirements for faith and salvation but God's expectations of those who are already citizens of His kingdom. The expectations, framed or encased in the center of the Beatitudes, chart the course that must be followed by those who are already regenerate. They spell out the inner spiritual qualities and the external life of love as it is expressed toward our neighbor.

The Beatitudes in verses 3–11 are variously numbered from seven to ten. One view considers the first seven Beatitudes (vv. 3–9) as a unit and the last three verses as a threefold conclusion describing the response of the world to the Christian brand of citizenship. The first seven Beatitudes can be divided into two groups. The first four describe the internal qualities that characterize the citizens of God's kingdom, and the last three the manner in which the inner dispositions express themselves in the Christian's relation to his neighbor.

The requirements of citizenship are not easy. The difficulty and pervasiveness of God's demands make the text hard to implement for the modern Christian, who is accustomed to having the more stringent demands of life alleviated, mollified, or ignored. And so we need to remind ourselves that God does not make known His will for us in vain and that we must dedicate ourselves anew to Him.

Sermon Outline

In America today people cry out for relief from heavy taxation, military service, government red tape, and numerous other burdens of citizenship. While some of these complaints may be justified, it is easy to wistfully wish that we were completely free of all obligations. But the privileges and rewards of living in a modern, advanced state have their price. So it is with the kingdom of God. God's requirements of the faithful are always stringent. He desires a total commitment from those who have responded to the call to follow Him. Yet those requirements seem light when we remember the price He paid for our redemption and when we consider the great glory that awaits those who persevere.

THE DEMANDS AND REWARDS OF CITIZENSHIP IN GOD'S KINGDOM

I. Citizenship requires a change of heart.
   A. We must recognize that man, by nature, is completely destitute of all qualities that might merit God's mercy (v. 3).
   B. We must be grief-stricken because of the sin and misery of the world and the resultant alienation from God (v. 4).
   C. We must turn the other cheek to all who injure us and forgive them as Christ forgave those who crucified Him (v. 5).
   D. We must ardently crave the righteousness of God, the righteousness that is imputed to us by faith (v. 6).
II. Citizenship requires a change of life.
   A. We must reflect the mercy of God toward others (v. 7).
   B. We must establish a relationship with others that is characterized by honesty and integrity of both mind and heart (v. 8).
   C. We must promote the peace that God wills should prevail on earth (v. 9).
III. True citizenship brings both hardships and rewards.
   A. In all ages Christians will experience the persecution of rejection and opposition from the world (vv. 10–11).
   B. Ultimately, Christians, like the rejected prophets of old, will receive the reward of heaven (v. 12), a gift of God's grace through Jesus.

Centuries ago the Roman poet Horace wrote, "Dulce et decorum est pro patria mori" (*Odes* 3.2.13). Glorified citizenship has always had its price. True citizenship, whether in God's kingdom or in the world, is never easy. But without it the rewards of life and of society are short-lived. And so God asks us to live according to His will, but always in the light of those rewards that He has already given us in Jesus Christ and that He is still anxious to bestow on us. Christian life must always be a grateful response to what God has done for us in the redemptive work of Christ Jesus.

QUENTIN F. WESSELSCHMIDT

Fifth Sunday After the Epiphany

EPISTLE							1 Corinthians 2:1 – 5 (RSV)

Sermon Notes/Introduction

Corinth, from all descriptions, was a highly cosmopolitan city. Yet according to 1 Cor. 1:26, the Christians there were not noble, wise, or mighty by the world's standards. They had a different kind of wisdom—Jesus Christ (1:30). Paul urges them not to be swayed by the diversions that Corinth offered. His confidence in the facts put forth in 1:27 – 28 led him to preach Christ and Him crucified rather than human wisdom.

In 2:4 Paul offers a contrast between the persuasive words of wisdom and the demonstration of the Spirit and of power. The contrast stresses the difference between learned rhetoric and the Holy Spirit. Language devices may be used to give a message power and appeal, but to rely solely on such devices is dangerous for preaching and disastrous for the Gospel. Verse 4 may also be seen as irony or sarcasm on Paul's part. He refused to preach to the Corinthians with "persuasive words of wisdom." He could well have tried to impress the Corinthians with his preaching style. He chose, however, to impress their hearts with the power of the cross.

The central thought of the text is that through the power of God—through the preaching of Jesus and the cross—comes faith that endures. The goal of the sermon is that the hearer will rest his faith in the power of God rather than the wisdom of man.

A power struggle involves two or more people attempting to exert their power on each other. The outcome is predictable. The person or group with the most power or influence always emerges on top. The power of one group gives way to the power of the other. Because we Christians face trials and other situations in which the devil, the world, and our sinful flesh seek to overpower us, it is necessary that our faith be based on a power that will not give way to another. We need God's power as the basis for our faith.

Sermon Outline
IS OUR FAITH BASED ON GOD'S POWER?

I. It is not based on God's power if it is based solely on "superior" speech and wisdom.
   A. There are many who offer such a basis.
      1. In Corinth there was much pseudointellectual pride. Fine words could tempt the Christians to follow a new way.
      2. We often look more at the form in which the message comes to us than at the message itself. Not just rock music or suave politicians catch our ear. Often we are captivated by "good preachers" who nevertheless fail to preach Christ and Him crucified.
   B. Such a basis for faith is shaky at best.
      1. God has made the world's wisdom foolish (1:26–27).
      2. Faith founded on the wisdom of man cannot endure the tests of life.
II. It is based on God's power if it is based on Jesus Christ and Him crucified.
   A. This is the central tenet of Christianity.
      1. Although Paul could have come with persuasive words, he determined to know nothing but "Jesus Christ and Him crucified" (2:2).
      2. The message of Christ's death and resurrection is God's way of coming to us.
   B. With this message come the Spirit and power of God.
      1. Paul's preaching found its power here (cf. Rom. 10:17; 1 Cor. 12:3).
      2. Such a power will not falter or fail. The message of God's redemption of the world through Christ's death on the cross is all that is needed to bring us to God. A faith based on that message is faith based on God's power.

Conclusion: When your faith rests on God's power, you can be assured of strength in time of weakness. God's power is being offered to you now through the cross of Christ. It is a power that will not let you down.   DAVID L. BAHN

Fifth Sunday After the Epiphany

GOSPEL Matthew 5:13 – 20

Sermon Notes/Introduction

Latent within all celebrations of the Epiphany season is a remembrance of the long and arduous journey of the Magi, under divine guidance, from the East to the manger of our Savior. Their journey, and all that it entailed, shows complete openness and dedication to the call of God, willingness to be at His disposal, and the joy of being His instruments.

The opening verses of the text (vv. 13 – 16) mandate the public expression of our faith for the benefit of the world and of Christians themselves. The difficulty of this injunction is that it runs counter to the attitude of much of society, including members of the church. Our contemporary world is characterized by blatant individualism, excessive selfishness, minimal involvement that verges on personal isolationism, and extreme fragmentation along ethnic and interest lines. Ours is not a society that is willing to have sacrificial concern for others. The famous line of the Roman dramatist Terence, "homo sum, humani nil a me alienum puto" (*Heaut.* 77, later expressed in John Donne's "No man is an island"), is not characteristic of people in our time. For the modern Christian to shoulder the burdens of faith and God's kingdom, he must stand apart from his social context and often be at loggerheads with it. To respond to the mandate of this text in a society that in a contradictory way encourages individualism within cliquish group identity (fashions, cosmetics, sport preferences, etc.) is not an easy task.

The Scripture's concept of the kingdom of God is one of growth and universal outreach. The idea of growth is indigenous to the text if we take into account the preceding verses (vv. 3 – 12), according to which the Christian matures in terms of his own spiritual development and in his personal relations to others (compassion, purity of heart, peacemaking). His responsibility takes on the more dramatic dimensions of being a beacon and example of God's truth to the world (vv. 13 – 16).

Lest the Christian think that once he has become a disciple of Christ (who has vicariously fulfilled the Law for man) his responsibilities are at an end, Christ reiterates the necessity of keeping the Law in His statement of the theme of the Sermon on the Mount (vv. 17 – 20). However, it is no longer a keeping of the Law in order to earn salvation; rather it is a joyful response to the God who has already won our redemption.

Sermon Outline

God has never promised that the life of faith would be easy. Its difficulty is often increased by the ethical and attitudinal conditions of the world in which we live. However, we find courage to live an active life of faith in the knowledge of what God has already done for us and in what He still promises to do through us.

NEW DIMENSIONS OF CHRISTIAN FAITH

I. The seasoning of society. In verse 13 the Christian is described as the salt of the earth. His responsibilities toward the world are to be understood in terms of the various qualities of salt, such as strengthening, flavoring, preserving, purifying, etc. The world needs the Christian for its betterment. Yet the Christian has a responsibility to retain the saltiness of his own faith and commitment by the use of Word and Sacrament. Otherwise, he will soon lose his usefulness to the world in which he lives.

II. The light of the world. The Christian is the light of the world. Only the Word of God, as communicated by Christians, can dissipate the darkness of sin and the satanic world. Not only does the world need to hear the verbal message of Christianity, but it also needs to see the embodiment of that message in human life and actions. The faith that is hidden in the valley of our own concerns and nonassertiveness is pregnable, just as the faith that does not express itself is soon snuffed out.

III. The new understanding of the Law. In verses 17 – 20 Christ presents the theme of the Sermon on the Mount. The Law does not function as the basis for salvation. Salvation has been accomplished by Christ's fulfillment of the Law for us and by His suffering and death. Christ here urges that the Law be put in its proper perspective. The keeping of the Law is again tied to citizenship in the Kingdom. God demands a righteousness that is superior to the outward righteousness of the scribes and Pharisees.

The Christian does not act under the Law in order to satisfy the demands of a just and righteous God, but he lives gladly in harmony with the Law because God has made him and enables him to be a responsible member of His people, who want to see the Kingdom embrace all mankind. Man, still vested in his humanity, needs the direction of God's will. A life in harmony with God's will is possible only with the strength and power of the Holy Spirit.

QUENTIN F. WESSELSCHMIDT

Sixth Sunday After the Epiphany

EPISTLE   1 Corinthians 2:6 – 13 (NASB)

Sermon Notes/Introduction

The proper interpretation of this text hinges on how one understands the words "those who are mature" (v. 6). Some commentators suggest that this expression refers to those Christians among the Corinthians and especially in other congregations who were more mature in their faith and knowledge of God. The majority of commentators, however, understand Paul to be referring to all Christians. That appears to be the most plausible interpretation. Accordingly, "wisdom" (v. 6) is not higher knowledge of God and deeper understanding of His ways but simply Christ and Him crucified (note 1:24).

The *de* of v. 6 ties the text to Paul's immediately preceding thoughts, in which he distinguishes between the wisdom of man and the power of God. Now he assures the Corinthians that he does indeed speak wisdom to them, the wisdom of God, predestined for their glory (as shown by the final clause of v. 7).

Verse 8 presents a paradox. God's wisdom was to have Jesus crucified for the sins of the world. Yet had those who crucified Jesus known what they were doing, they would not have crucified Him. Here we see the humiliation and the exaltation of Jesus side by side—the Lord of glory crucified.

V. 9: "But just as it is written" is to be combined with the "we speak" of v. 6. Thus v. 9 describes the wisdom that Paul and the other apostles speak (the most likely meaning of the plural "we" in vv. 6, 7, and especially 10 and 12, where it is emphatic, is "the apostles").

V. 10: The Spirit, who has revealed the mysteries of God—His wisdom in the cross—can be trusted. He who "searches all things, even the depths of God" has revealed these things to the apostles. No one can know the things of God ("thoughts") except the Spirit of God. The Holy Spirit is the only One who can reveal God's nature. And the apostles have received no other spirit than the "Spirit who is from God" (v. 12).

The central thought of the text is that the mystery of God's wisdom taught by Paul and the other apostles is not understood by human wisdom but by the Holy Spirit. The goal of the sermon is that the hearer will recognize the uniqueness of God's wisdom in the cross of Christ and not in the events of the world.

Most of us like to consider ourselves mature. We strive to grow and learn in our daily lives so that we can meet each new challenge in a mature way. We want others to consider us mature. In our text Paul uses the term *mature* to describe Christians.

Sermon Outline
GOD'S WISDOM IS FOR MATURE PEOPLE

I. God's wisdom is not grasped by the immature of this age.
   A. It is hidden from them.
      1. We cannot see God's nature on our own. We do not know what God is like without His revelation. Our natural knowledge is limited. This limitation manifests itself in self-righteous attitudes and in despising God and His way.
      2. Those whose thoughts are entirely centered in this age will not see this wisdom.
   B. Even when God's wisdom is seen, it is not always recognized.
      1. Those who crucified the Lord of glory did not recognize God's wisdom. They did not know what they did. Had they known, they would not have crucified Him.
      2. We did not crucify Christ; we were not there. Yet our sins were laid on Him, making His death even more painful. Still we wonder why Jesus had to be crucified. We doubt the wisdom of God in the face of adversity.

Transition: If you are looking to the world for confirmation of God's wisdom in Christ and the cross, then you are looking in the wrong place. Often we find ourselves doing that. That is why it is important to hear God's wisdom—Christ and His cross—again and again so that we would grow in this wisdom.

II. God's wisdom is embraced by His mature people.
   A. God's wisdom is predestined for our glory.

1. God's purpose in this wisdom is not to confuse and confound us. He has not predestined this wisdom merely to impress us with His greatness.
2. God's wisdom is for our glory. It is not just an inwardly turned contemplation but an outwardly turned love.

B. God reveals His wisdom to us.
1. No one knows God as God's Spirit does. He searches even the depths of God's nature. Then He tells us about God through the Scriptures. His knowledge is trustworthy.
2. Paul and the apostles received this Spirit. Through them we too may know God. We may possess this wisdom. God wants us to embrace this wisdom by faith and to enjoy its blessings.

Conclusion: When we look to the world, we will not see or enjoy the blessings of God's wisdom. God has revealed to us a different and better kind of wisdom. The wisdom that centers in the cross of Christ makes and keeps us spiritually mature.

DAVID L. BAHN

Sixth Sunday After the Epiphany

GOSPEL   Matthew 5:27 – 37 (RSV)

Sermon Notes/Introduction

A house eaten by termites and beginning to sag may look better with a fresh coat of paint, but it is still a rotting house. The problem lies on the inside and must be dealt with there. In like manner, Christian morality is not simply doing things that appear good to other people; it has to do with God. Sin is, first of all, an "inside job." The heart of the matter is a holy heart, and that is what this pericope is all about.

Textual notes: Four preliminary observations: (1) Jesus speaks the words of this pericope to His *disciples* (Matt. 5:1 – 2). (2) Three times He declares, "But I say to you." We note the divine *authority* with which He addresses men and also that *Jesus* speaks, the One who came to live for us a life dedicated to His Father's will and to die in payment for our sins. (3) Jesus was speaking in the context of rabbinic legalism, which through casuistry and compromise had externalized God's law, thereby evading its full intent and excluding God's claim over every aspect of life. (4) This pericope is primarily a

Law text directed to a disciple's old Adam and setting forth a pattern for his life.

Vv. 27 – 30: By giving prominence to the outward act, the scribes tended to externalize the command forbidding adultery. Jesus directs the Law to the root of the sinful impulse, the heart. The Sixth Commandment calls for a pure heart that keeps even the eyes pure. The strong words point to the strenuous effort necessary to master sexual passion; Jesus is not recommending successive amputations.

Vv. 31 – 32: The scribes had reinterpreted the prescription of Moses to permit all manner of divorce and thereby to evade the intent and will of God. One rabbinical tradition at the time of Jesus permitted divorce for the love of another woman or for causes as trivial as inferior cooking. We cannot substitute human regulations for the divine requirement. Every severance of marriage, apart from death, violates God's commandment.

Vv. 33 – 37: The scribes had a great deal to say about which oaths were binding and which were not, concluding that any oath that avoided using God's name was not binding (e.g., swearing by heaven, earth, Jerusalem, or one's own heart). The logic was that if God's name was not used, He had nothing to do with the transaction. Jesus declares that no man can keep God out of any segment of life; you cannot exclude His demand for truth by substituting something less sacred for the divine name. For the disciple whose heart is pure and who always speaks the truth, there is no need for oaths. In civic life, however, because of the untruth in the world, the state, which has to deal with all men, must often require oaths.

In the area of Christian morality Jesus makes clear the heart of the matter.

Sermon Outline
THE HEART OF THE MATTER

The heart of the matter is a holy heart wholly intent on doing God's will in every aspect of living.

I. Jesus has made us His disciples.
    A. Jesus came to seek and claim disciples.
        1. Discipleship is a gift of His grace.
        2. Discipleship places His claim of grace on us.
    B. Jesus has authority to make disciples.
        1. He lived a life of wholehearted commitment to God's will for us.
        2. He gave His perfect life in payment for our sins.

3. Through His Spirit He gives us new hearts intent on doing God's will.
II. Jesus calls for a holy heart as the source of a life in keeping with our discipleship.
  A. Jesus condemns the scribes who externalized God's law (e.g., the Sixth Commandment is a matter only of the outward act and not of the heart).
  B. Outward piety is not enough; our hearts must be pure. No matter how pious we appear to others, God sees and judges our hearts.
  C. We continually need to have the Holy Spirit at work in our hearts.
III. Jesus calls for a heart wholly intent on doing God's will.
  A. Jesus condemns the scribes who interpreted the Law so as to evade its full intent (e.g., their casuistry with regard to divorce).
  B. Original sin clouds our judgment; human rationalizing is no substitute for the divine requirement (e.g., situation ethics in which "love" determines "right and wrong"). "Do your best" is not good enough, no matter how acceptable it may be to the world around us.
  C. After all, it is because Jesus was "wholly intent on doing God's will" that we are His disciples today.
IV. Jesus calls for a heart that does God's will in every aspect of living.
  A. Jesus condemns the scribes who sought to exclude God's claim over every aspect of their lives (e.g., their casuistry with regard to oaths).
  B. We cannot compartmentalize our lives and exclude God from any area of our speaking and doing. What we say and do on Saturday night (or Monday morning) is as much under the claim and judgment of God as what we say and do on Sunday morning.
  C. He died for us that we might live for Him (2 Cor. 5:15). "So, whether you eat or drink, or *whatever you do,* do all to the glory of God" (1 Cor. 10:31—emphasis added).

"Unless your righteousness exceeds that of the scribes and Pharisees, you will never enter the kingdom of heaven" (Matt. 5:20). We have that exceeding righteousness in Jesus Christ. Let's live it!

ROGER J. HUMANN

Seventh Sunday After the Epiphany

EPISTLE 1 Corinthians 3:10 – 11, 16 – 23 (RSV)

Sermon Notes/Introduction

As the church encounters the evil forces of the world, conflict results. Church workers begin fighting one another instead of their common enemy. This same tendency shows itself when morale collapses as a team gets behind in a contest. St. Paul wants us to transcend this human tendency. He draws attention to the functions of the persons of the Holy Trinity in the task of empowering, sustaining, and encouraging us in building up the church.

Sermon Outline
BUILDING UP THE CHURCH

I. God commissions us to build up the church.
   A. He commissions the architectural plans.
   B. He commissions the contract for the building process.
      1. A skilled master builder is in charge of each task.
      2. He provides instructive guidelines on how one is to build.
II. Jesus Christ provides the foundation for building up the church.
   A. All other foundations are excluded.
      1. We are to exclude personality cults.
      2. We are to exclude perishable foundations.
   B. Jesus Christ provides an imperishable foundation.
III. The Holy Spirit dwells in those who build up the church.
   A. He helps Christians to live as the holy people they are.
      1. We are to get rid of futile worldly wisdom.
      2. We are to get rid of short-sighted craftiness.
   B. The Holy Spirit builds up the church builders.
      1. He relates us to our work in an encouraging way, saying, "All things are yours"—world, life, death, present, future.
      2. He makes us the possession of Christ.
         a. Christ takes a deep and personal interest in us.
         b. In Christ God sees us as wise and good.
         c. Our Spirit-given relationship to Christ sustains us through all of the process of building up the church. HAROLD H. ZIETLOW

Seventh Sunday After the Epiphany

GOSPEL   Matthew 5:38 – 48 (RSV)

Sermon Notes/Introduction

When the lawyer asked Jesus, "Who is my neighbor?" (Luke 10:29), he was trying to find out who were the guys he did not have to love. In a sense we can understand that. There are some people we don't even like; how can we love them? Others have treated us so badly that they don't deserve our love. Where can we draw the line? What are the limits on love? In this pericope we hear Jesus tell His disciples that for the children of the heavenly Father there is no limit to love.

Textual Notes: Vv. 38 – 42: "An eye for an eye"—this is a sound principle of civil law; its original aim was the limitation of vengeance, indicating how a judge in the court must assess punishment and penalty. In the Mishnah a money payment in lieu of an eye, tooth, etc., is taken for granted. Jesus does not condemn the principle that legal justice is a set of limited revenges. Rather, He removes every impulse for retaliation and desire for vengeance from the hearts of His disciples.

The examples he gives are arranged in descending order of severity—acts of violence, legal proceedings, official demands, simple requests. "Strikes you on the right cheek"—perhaps a backhanded blow that would be a deliberate and contemptuous insult. "Coat ... cloak"—the tunic, or undergarment, and the outer garment that doubled as a blanket at night. Jewish law permitted a man's tunic to be taken as security, but not his cloak; see Ex. 22:26 – 27. "Forces you to go"—a Persian word that came to mean enforced service by an occupying power, for example, Simon of Cyrene (Luke 23:26). "Begs ... would borrow"—nuisance requests.

Vv. 43 – 48: The Law did not include the words "and hate your enemy," but this was the result when the scribe sought to find areas where a person was not explicitly required to show love. "Love your enemies"—Jesus removes every limitation from love. Such love (*agape*), which actively seeks the highest good ("pray for those who persecute you") for those who treat us the very worst, involves something of the will as well as the heart. It is like the action of God's love in the world, which is unwearied in its benevolence toward all people. This love has its source in the adoptive love of the Father. "Father," as a name for God, occurs first in the Sermon on the Mount, where we find it 17 times.

"Perfect" (*teleios*) often means "totality"; the disciples of Jesus should be "total" in their love, including their enemies within its compass. Such perfection is also functional, that is, a disciple is "perfect" to the extent that he reproduces in his life the forgiving, sacrificial love of God which made him a son. The pattern and power of this lived sonship is Jesus Himself. The Gospel makes people the children of God and enables them so to live.

Sermon Outline
NO LIMIT TO LOVE

I. Jesus won't let us limit our love.
   A. We want to limit it.
      1. By nature we have an inclination for vengeance.
      2. God restrains and regulates this impulse through civil courts.
   B. Jesus' words remove every limitation from love.
      1. "Love your enemies" removes every limit.
      2. Rather than vengeance, we are to seek their highest good ("Pray for those who persecute you").
II. This is because God's love, which made us His children, knows no limit.
   A. God's love knows no limit.
      1. We can observe it in His unwearied benevolence in the world.
      2. We see it in the sending of His Son. "While we were yet sinners Christ died for us" (Rom. 5:8).
   B. This love has made us God's children.
      1. He has adopted us.
      2. He wants us to be "perfect" children by demonstrating His kind of love in our lives.
III. Therefore, as our heavenly Father's "perfect" children we show love without limit.
   A. We bear insults and personal abuse without resentment or retaliation ("turn to him the other also").
   B. We do not insist on our right ("let him have your cloak as well").
   C. We put ourselves out for the other person ("go with him two miles").
   D. We are willing to be put upon ("do not refuse him").

ROGER J. HUMANN

Eighth Sunday After the Epiphany

EPISTLE					1 Corinthians 4:1–13

Sermon Notes/Introduction

Ministers are not to be magnified unduly, for they are servants (*hupēretas*) of Christ (v. 1). But neither are they to be unduly depreciated, for they are stewards (*oikonomous*), higher slaves or dispensers of God's mysteries, of truths once hidden but now revealed. As such, ministers are responsible to the Lord, and their appeal, if they are despised and misjudged, is to Him (v. 2). God does not require of His ministers brilliance or eloquence or profound knowledge but only faithfulness. Judgments of man's faithfulness must be left to God, who alone looks into the heart (v. 3). Paul is not aware of unfaithfulness on his part, but God sees with clearer eyes than his (v. 4), and therefore Paul is content to leave the judgment of his ministry to God (v. 5). God's commendation, not human praise or blame, is finally what matters.

Because factions in the Corinthian congregation were exalting Cephas, Apollos, and Paul unduly, Paul reminds the Corinthians (vv. 6–13) to keep their thoughts about men within the lines marked out in Scripture so that zeal for one man does not result in despisal of another. Glorification of one and depreciation of another spring from a sitting in judgment, and that is inappropriate. Even if they had the ability to judge correctly, such ability would be a gift for which to thank God, not to boast about (v. 7). In verse 8 Paul uses irony to contrast the self-satisfaction of the Corinthians with the humiliation endured by the apostles. He goes on in verse 10 to contrast the pseudowisdom of the Corinthians with the contempt the world has for the apostles. In vv. 11–13 Paul describes still more graphically the abject condition of the apostles to impress on the Corinthians that Christians are not to expect the world's approbation nor to think they can escape its hatred. The servant is not above his master. Yet the Master (Christ) will honor His servants.

We judge people as to their competence and trustworthiness, and people judge us. The judgment of others can upset and disturb us. But there is One whose judgment is true and final.

Sermon Outline
IT IS THE LORD WHO JUDGES US

I. His judgment is not based on human standards.
 A. He does not use human standards of achievement.
  1. The Corinthians made judgments based on the learning and eloquence of Paul and Apollos (v. 6; 3:4).
  2. We are prone to judge pastors and others on the basis of their intellect, education, and communication skills.
 B. He does not use human standards of position.
  1. It was disconcerting to the Corinthians, who prized worldly positions of honor, to be reminded that Paul and Apollos were considered the refuse and offscourings of the world (vv. 10–13).
  2. We are prone to regard high-paying, influential positions as honorable and low-paying, more humble occupations as less honorable.

The Lord's judgment of us is not based on human standards of achievement and position.

II. His judgment is based on what Christ has done for us.
 A. Because we belong to Christ by faith (3:23), God judges as acceptable all that we do to serve our fellow human beings.
  1. He gives all of us gifts with which to serve (v. 7).
  2. He asks us to be faithful in the use of any gift we have (v. 2).
  3. God alone can judge accurately how faithful we have been. When the Lord comes, we shall all have to rely on Christ's faithfulness to cover any unfaithfulness on our part (v. 5).
 B. God for Christ's sake judges us rich and wise (vv. 8, 10).
  1. It doesn't matter how meager our income or how ordinary our job.
  2. No matter in what disrepute the world holds us, God judges us as very special people in Jesus Christ.

Conclusion: There is no need to engage in morbid introspection when other people judge us. There is One alone whose judgment is final and true. It is the Lord who judges us. We can leave our judgment with Him.

GERHARD AHO

Eighth Sunday After the Epiphany

GOSPEL					Matthew 6:24 – 34 (RSV)

Sermon Notes/Introduction

"You can't work for me and him too!" explodes an employer when he learns that one of his employees is also trying to hold a full-time job with his archcompetitor. It is ludicrous; it cannot be. That sort of thing is what our Lord has in mind when He states that a disciple of His cannot "serve two masters." He points out that worry is a test of our allegiance. If God comes first, we will trust Him completely. Worry indicates that someone or something else is in the top spot—namely, mammon.

V. 24: "No one can serve two masters." The disciple cannot have a divided loyalty; there is no room for competing masters. The alternative to God, who has come to us in Jesus Christ and claimed us as His disciples, is "mammon." Mammon is wealth—material possessions—personified. It is a false god that demands exclusive loyalty as God demands it. The meaning is not "You cannot serve God and have riches," but rather "You cannot be faithful to God and make an idol of wealth."

V. 25: "Therefore"—the extent to which we "fear, love, and trust in God above all things" is evident by the amount of worrying that we do. Anxiety with respect to earthly goods is evidence that we are serving mammon. Food and clothing represent basic earthly needs. Can we not trust Him who gave us the greater (body and life) also to give us the lesser (food and clothing)?

V. 26: The birds work, but they do not worry. *V. 27:* No amount of worry can add the shortest span to life. *Vv. 28 – 30:* God, who is so lavish with the short-lived flowers, will not forget His disciples. Worry is evidence that we do not trust God above all things; it points to the littleness of our faith.

Vv. 31 – 32: To make the provision of food and clothing an object of anxiety is to live like the pagans, whose primary allegiance is to the accumulation of earthly goods—mammon. *V. 33:* If, however, our primary allegiance is to God, our primary concern will be for His rule in our lives. The assurance ("shall be yours as well") of the needed material goods implies that the main quest—God's kingdom and righteousness—will be secured. *V. 34:* Trust lives one day at a time.

Sermon Outline
WORRY OR TRUST: A TEST OF OUR ALLEGIANCE

I. God demands our complete allegiance (v. 24).
   A. God is the Owner.
      1. He claims us in order to benefit not Himself but us. He became a slave to serve us; cf. Phil. 2:6–8.
      2. He demands our complete allegiance. We should fear, love, and trust in God above all things.
   B. Mammon is a false god, which also demands our exclusive loyalty.
      1. Mammon is wealth personified. The goods entrusted to us by God become the god in whom we trust.
      2. When mammon holds sway, our primary concern becomes the accumulation of earthly possessions.
   C. Divided allegiance is impossible. "No one can serve two masters."

II. Worry gives evidence of mammon's sway (vv. 25–30).
   A. Mammon says, "Get more!"
      1. We worry that we will not have enough.
      2. That is so unlike the birds; they work but never worry about accumulating for the future.
      3. It is also pointless; worry cannot prolong our lives a moment.
   B. Mammon replaces God, who has already given us "more."
      1. He has given us life and body, which is "more than" food and clothing.
      2. He has given us His Son that we might live with Him forever, body and soul.
      3. Should we not trust Him for the food (we are of more value than the birds) and clothing (we are more important than flowers) we need?
   C. Worry, therefore, is evidence that we do not trust God above all things; it points to the littleness of our faith.

III. God is to hold sway in our lives (vv. 31–34).
   A. We live as children of a heavenly Father.
      1. The primary concern with material goods is a pagan trait.
      2. We trust the heavenly Father, who provides for all our needs.
   B. We seek God's rule and righteousness.
      1. Our primary concern is for these spiritual needs.

    2. We trust God to provide them.
  C. We live one day at a time.
    1. We experience God's help to meet today's problems.
    2. We trust Him for tomorrow's needs.

ROGER J. HUMANN

The Transfiguration of Our Lord: Last Sunday After the Epiphany

EPISTLE   2 Peter 1:16 – 21

Sermon Notes/Introduction

The transfiguration of our Lord, the occasion when He permitted the inner circle of the disciples to witness a glimpse of His majesty in the presence of Moses and Elijah, is a fitting culmination and climax to the season of Epiphany, during which the Christian community has traced the glories of Christ's grace as He manifested Himself as Son of God, as Word made flesh, as Fulfiller of all the promises of God.

Yet one might ask what relevance the Transfiguration has for our faith and life. How is it possible to relate this event, so bound up in experiences beyond our participation, to our living the life of faith and hope? Apart from historic commemoration, what can we do with the Transfiguration?

It would seem that one way is to view it in the same light as the apostles who experienced it did. For them it served to underscore that in Jesus of Nazareth all the promises of God found their yes and Amen! For us it shows that in Jesus Christ we find the prophetic Word made more sure.

Sermon Outline
THE PROPHETIC WORD MADE MORE SURE

I. The Transfiguration centers in the power and coming of our Lord Jesus Christ.
  A. The promise of a Savior is given to suit our need for salvation. Only the full proclamation of our separation from God, our lostness, and the hammer of the Law against us can convince us of our need for rescue and deliverance.
  B. Only in the Savior, whom God has designated, is there forgiveness and life. Throughout the Old Testament—

represented by Moses and Elijah—God gave the promise of a Deliverer and a Rescuer, through whom He would impart forgiveness of sins and life for death.
    C. In the Transfiguration God designates Jesus of Nazareth as His beloved Son, with whom He is well pleased, as the one through whom and in whom all His promises find their yes and Amen!
II. In the Transfiguration the disciples were confronted with the prophetic Word made more sure.
    A. In relating the power and coming of the Lord Jesus, they had not followed cleverly devised myths.
    B. The disciples were eyewitnesses of our Lord's majesty; they were with Him on the holy mountain; they heard the voice that bore witness to Him. The same role is given them in His death and resurrection. They had the Word of prophecy made more sure in its fulfillment.
III. We have the Word of prophecy made more sure.
    A. We have not only been to the Mount of Transfiguration but also to the mount of crucifixion. We have seen all our sins laid on Jesus.
    B. We have heard not only the voice of commendation for the beloved Son but also the voice of rejection in the *"Eli, Eli"* of Good Friday, as the Savior suffered the pangs of hell for us.
    C. In our baptism we have died and our life is hid with Christ in God. The Word of promise has been fulfilled in our very lives.
IV. We do well to give attention to that Word made more sure.
    A. It is the light that shines into our darkness. Because of the old man of sin, we live surrounded by the cloak of darkness. The cares and troubles of life becloud our vision. The light of the Gospel of Christ alone can dispel the gloom and darkness of sin. The Gospel must be central in our lives because it is the Word made sure.
    B. The Gospel is the light that points to the bright day of our Lord. The time will come when by God's grace we will be transfigured before our Lord to shine as the stars forever. That hope of the morning star arising in our hearts sustains us on our pilgrimage to glory.

Until that day dawns for us, we have in the Gospel of Jesus Christ the prophetic Word made more sure. The word of forgiveness, pardon, comfort, and hope is made sure in the death and resurrection of God's beloved Son, in whom He is well pleased and by whom we are also His own and well pleasing to Him.

WILLIAM J. SCHMELDER

The Transfiguration of Our Lord: Last Sunday After the Epiphany

GOSPEL Matthew 17:1 – 9 (RSV)

Sermon Notes/Introduction

V. 1: "Six days" after what? Most likely, it was after Peter's confession at Caesarea Philippi (Matt. 16:13 – 20).

V. 2: The word *metemorphōthē*, "was changed, transfigured," denotes a metamorphosis, a change of the abiding form rather than merely a change of the external appearance (see 2 Cor. 3:18; Rom. 12:2). Luke does not use the word (Luke 9:29). Matthew alone in his description of the "metamorphosis" has "His face shone like the sun." This is an important addition that indicates for Matthew the glory of the exalted "Son of Man" (see Rev. 1:16; 10:1; Acts 7:56; Dan. 7:9 – 14).

V. 3: There is some evidence that in Jewish popular expectations, Moses and Elijah would appear in connection with the coming of the Messiah. Moses, it was believed, like Elijah did not taste death but was translated and would accompany Elijah on his return (see Mal. 4:4 – 6; Matt. 17:10 – 13; John 1:19; Rev. 11:3 – 13). Whatever the tradition, it is clear that the appearance of Moses and Elijah is an important part of the interpretation of the lordship and the glory of Jesus Christ as the Son of Man.

V. 4: Peter's suggestion to erect three tabernacles indicates a desire for a permanency of glory apart from the suffering of the cross (see Matt. 16:21 – 23).

V. 5: The voice from the cloud is reminiscent of the voice in Matt. 3:17 at Jesus' baptism. As at the beginning of His ministry, so now in view of His coming Passion and the glory to follow, the confirmation of the heavenly Father is present.

V. 9: No reason is given for the command that the disciples should not tell of their experience until after the resurrection. Mark's mention of the failure of the disciples to understand Jesus' reference to the resurrection may give us a clue (Mark 9:9 – 10). Matthew uses the word *horama*, "vision, visionary experience," to define the event, a word used in the New Testament only of God's communicating with man. What the disciples had seen was a message from God concerning the glory of the Son of Man, which they would understand only after the resurrection.

Sermon Outline

It is not by accident that the church has chosen the pericope of the Transfiguration as a concluding text to the Epiphany season and as a transition from the glorious light of the Epiphany to the darkness of the Passion of its Lord. The church's mission is the proclamation of the saving presence of the Lord Christ in the Gospel. But this mission is carried out in the midst of suffering. The church proclaims the Gospel while bearing the cross; it proclaims life while facing and experiencing death. And what should encourage the church in its trial and tribulation is the picture of the exalted Christ, the confirmation of the victory of the cross. The church, inspired by the Epiphany Gospel, prepares for Lent, for carrying out its mission in suffering by viewing the exalted Lord Christ. But it can see the exalted Lord only through His suffering and death.

The Transfiguration is rightly seen as the high point of our Lord's earthly ministry, for it is through this glorious event that the ministry and death of Jesus must be viewed if it is to be correctly interpreted. The church is reminded by the Transfiguration that while it is the church of the cross, it bears the cross by means of a triumphant faith, and by such faith it is thus also the church destined for glory.

THE EXALTED CHRIST PREPARES HIS CHURCH FOR MISSION

I. Failure to see that the Christian pilgrimage to glory is only by way of the cross endangers the mission of the church.
   A. A theology of glory fails when it ceases being the hope of faith and becomes instead a reality, a realized promise and goal of the present (see Heb. 11:1; Rom. 5:1 – 6; 8:24 – 25).
   B. The promise of a present glory bypasses the theology of the cross both in the Christian's faith and in his life of service in the church's mission (see Matt. 16:21 – 27; Rom. 8:18 – 25; 1 Pet. 4:12 – 13).
II. The glory of the transfigured Christ shows the Christian the heavenly glory that results from the victory of Jesus' death and resurrection.

A. The cross of Jesus Christ is the victory of the Christian over sin, death, and hell.
   B. Through the Gospel message of sins forgiven, the Holy Spirit instills in the heart of the believer the hope of everlasting glory with Jesus Christ in heaven.
   C. A theology of the cross that comforts and sustains in the midst of suffering is also a theology of glory, for it points to the glory of Christ as a certain hope of faith.

The church's mission is the proclamation of the cross and resurrection of Jesus Christ in the midst of its own suffering. The church is comforted, sustained in, and empowered for its mission by a theology of glory that is realized by faith alone in the suffering and death of Jesus Christ.

LOUIS A. BRIGHTON

First Sunday in Lent

EPISTLE   Romans 5:12 – 19

Sermon Notes/Introduction

The First Sunday in Lent is dominated by the invitation of our Lord, "Behold, we are going up to Jerusalem." From the high point of the Mount of Transfiguration, the church has descended to the plain, to Ash Wednesday, and to the journey that will end at the cross.

For many, the journey to the cross is a sentimental one; Jesus is portrayed as the poor man who died for His convictions, and the minor characters of the Passion are held up for minute examination.

The church needs to remember that its journey in Lent is not to a cross but to an empty tomb, not to defeat but to victory, not to death but to life, not to sorrow but to celebration.

Sermon Outline

We are helped to that end by a text that contrasts the trespass and the free gift.

THE TRESPASS AND THE FREE GIFT

I. The trespass brought death into the world.
   A. Sin came into the world through one man. It has its origin in man and in his act of disobedience (original sin).

B. Sin brought death into the world. Death is the wages of sin, the consequence of man's disobedience. Death is an intruder into God's creation.
C. Death spread to all because all have sinned. No one is exempt from the judgment of death. Its universality underscores the universality of sin.

II. By nature we all stand under the sentence of death.
A. We are born in sin and share in the sin of Adam.
B. We are born under the condemnation that sin brings—no fear of God, no trust in God, and every evil inclination.
C. We too must die.

III. God's free gift brings life.
A. The free gift came into the world through one man, Jesus Christ. In Him alone God chose to act; in Him alone all the fullness of God dwells bodily; He came in fulfillment of God's time.
B. The free gift abounds for all. God loved the world that He created. He died for all. His blood is for many. All the ends of the earth shall see the salvation of our God.
C. The free gift is not like the trespass.
 1. It brings justification.
 2. It brings righteousness.
 3. It brings acquittal.
 4. It brings life.

IV. By God's grace we are recipients of His free gift.
A. All that Christ has done is for us and for our salvation. He was delivered for our offenses and raised for our justification. The chastisement of our peace is on Him, and with His stripes we are healed.
B. God gives us the free gift in the means of grace.
 1. In Baptism we are buried and raised with Him.
 2. In absolution His word forgives.
 3. In the Word of the Gospel His work is applied to our sin and guilt.
 4. In Holy Communion we receive His body and blood for the forgiveness of our sins.

Our purpose in Lent is not just sorrow over sin, not just remorse over the enormity of our guilt. That will, of course, be present as the Law does its work. But our purpose in going up to Jerusalem is to be saturated with the Gospel, to know that where sin abounded, grace did much more abound, to be renewed in faith and invigorated for life precisely because the free gift is not like the trespass.

WILLIAM J. SCHMELDER

First Sunday in Lent

GOSPEL   Matthew 4:1 – 11 (KJV)

Sermon Notes/Introduction

1. It may seem strange that in a season commemorating the closing events of Jesus' career there should be an appointed reading treating an event that took place at the very start of His ministry. Yet there is a close connection between the happenings on that barren knoll outside Jerusalem and the happenings in the barren wilderness described in our text, even though chronologically these events are far apart. For had Jesus not overcome the temptations in the wilderness, there wouldn't have been a cross. The very point of Satan's temptations was to persuade Jesus to avoid the foolishness of the cross, to entice Him to try attractive shortcuts to achieve His mission—shortcuts that would have turned out to be dead ends.

2. Connected with the Old Testament Reading (Gen. 2:7 – 9, 15 – 17; 3:1 – 7) and the Epistle (Rom. 5:12, 17 – 19) for this Sunday, our text obviously underscores the role of Christ as second Adam. The first Adam, when tempted by Satan, fell; in, with, and under his defeat we too were defeated. The second Adam, Christ, when tempted by Satan, conquered; in, with, and under His victory we too are victorious. Both Adam and Christ were representative men, whose respective acts had universal impact. But what a difference in the kind of impact! Adam's fall brought death and damnation to the whole human race, while Christ's triumph provided life and salvation for all people.

3. Note how the first two temptations are logically connected via contrast. (a) In respect to Jesus' relationship with His Father, Satan in the first encounter was tempting Jesus to *a lack of trust* in God. (Will God really take care of You in this wilderness? Better take matters into Your own hands and turn stones into bread!) But in the second encounter Satan was tempting Jesus to *an abuse of trust* in God. (Go ahead! Do what You please. If You wish, jump down from a high pinnacle of the temple, and God will surely take care of You.) (b) In respect to

Jesus' saving mission, Satan was suggesting in the first temptation that the way to a man's salvation is through his stomach (provide him with enough bread) and in the second that it is through his intellect (dazzle him with impressive credentials).

4. "Bread" (v. 4), as in the Lord's Prayer also, is an instance of metonymy, of one thing standing for another. In this case bread stands for everything we need to sustain life—food, clothing, shelter, etc. Note that Jesus doesn't say that bread is unnecessary. Rather, He says that bread isn't enough. A human being has—or is meant to have—two kinds of life—the life of the body and the life of God. (No wonder Jesus told Nicodemus in John 3:3 that a man must not only be born but also be "born again"!) To sustain the first kind of life, the life of the body, a human being needs bread, to be sure. But since there is another dimension to his life, a spiritual one, he cannot live by bread alone (as Jesus reminds us in v. 4). To sustain the second kind of life, the life of God, a person needs "the Bread of life," Jesus Christ Himself (John 6:48 – 51).

5. Throughout the temptation ordeal Jesus was aware of the ancient prophecy that He could crush Satan's head only through the painful process of letting Satan bruise His heel on Calvary. Jesus realized that He could save the world only through the foolishness of the cross. Any other way, whether it was trying to win people by filling their stomachs with bread or by pampering their reason with signs—any other way would not result in people being saved but rather in people falling down and worshiping Satan.

Sermon Outline

(Submitted by a student, Mike Coppersmith)

God's Word creates and sustains our new life in Jesus Christ. But God's Word is not the only word around. There is the word of a fallen and sinful world. Its chief spokesman is Satan. And the world's word tries to snuff out the new life effected in us by God's Word.

WHOSE WORD ARE YOU WILLING TO TAKE?

I. The first word that man hears concerns how he receives God's Word.
   A. Through Satan the world says, "Doubt it" (v. 3).
   B. But God says, "Trust it" (v. 4).
II. The second word that man hears concerns how he uses God's Word.
   A. Through Satan the world says, "Misuse it" (vv. 5 – 6).

B. But God says, "Use it properly" (v. 7).
III. The third word that man hears concerns how he lives out God's Word.
   A. Through Satan the world says, "Disobey it" (vv. 8–9).
   B. But God says, "Submit to it" (v. 10).

Whose word are we going to take—God's or the world's? May we always look to Jesus for our example and for our strength. In life and death He took God's Word and followed it. In this way He brought us grace to do the same.

FRANCIS C. ROSSOW

Second Sunday in Lent

EPISTLE   Romans 4:1–5, 13–17 (RSV)

Sermon Notes/Introduction

In 1941 T. H. White wrote *The Book of Merlyn*. This is the final work in a five-volume series that retells the legend of King Arthur. In *The Book of Merlyn* White argues that man does not so much deserve to be called *homo sapiens* as *homo ferox*. Because the ferocious nature of man is so terrible, the only animals that do not avoid him like the plague are those unfamiliar with his treacherous and murderous ways. White credits man with the following infamous accomplishments: he blinds goldfinches to make them sing; he boils lobsters and shrimps alive, even though he hears their piping screams; he turns on his own species in war and kills 19 million every hundred years (*Harper's Magazine*, September 1977).

Man is familiar enough with himself and his species to know that there is room for improvement. This need for righteousness is an accepted fact in Paul's altercation with the judaizing Christians (e.g., Rom 1:18–32; 1 Cor. 5:1–2, 9–11). The crux of the dispute is not whether man needs righteousness, but how he gets possession of it.

Sermon Outline
RIGHTEOUSNESS IS FROM GOD

I. Man cannot achieve righteousness by himself (Rom. 4:1–2). The converse of this statement was the contention of those Christians in Rome who could not sever themselves from the legalistic principles of their former religion. The fact that men today still hold to this view is amply evidenced in the constant cry for integrity in politics, for effective crime reduction programs, and for consumer activism that demands honesty in business. Constant failure in all of these efforts lends veracity to God's still, small reminder, "None is righteous, no, not one" (Rom. 3:10).

II. True righteousness that is acceptable before God can be received only through faith (Rom. 4:3–5). The wishful concept that there is a spark of the divine in man that can be fanned into a roaring, constructive flame of goodness is debunked not only by Scripture's teachings on original sin and human depravity but also by man's record of his own history. The daily press provides countless examples. If man is to receive righteousness, it must come from outside the human experience. Scripture attests that the only source of righteousness is God Himself. "Abraham believed God, and it was reckoned to him as righteousness" (v. 3).

III. While man's attempt at righteousness brings failure, frustration, and further disillusionment (vv. 13–15), the righteousness of God brings eternal rewards. Most obvious and most longed for is the reward of eternal life. However, the fact that the believing man counts his righteousness as a gift of God is a reward in itself because it keeps us daily dependent on God and outside the realm of pride. There is simply no way in which we can look at our righteousness before God and say, "I've done it."

IV. The doctrine of justification by grace through faith, which is the burden of the entire Letter to the Romans, is crucial (vv. 16–17). Without it the entire framework of God's divine economy collapses into a heap of theological rubble. Faith and works cannot coexist as the source of man's salvation. The message of God to Abraham and to all of his heirs (spiritual as well as racial) has always been a message of grace and faith.

The only hope for ourselves and for our world is that by faith in Jesus Christ and the righteousness that such faith grasps, man, who is by nature *homo ferox,* is also by grace *homo rectus* and *homo sanctus.*

QUENTIN F. WESSELSCHMIDT

Second Sunday in Lent

GOSPEL   John 4:5 – 26 (RSV)

Sermon Notes/Introduction

In asking for a drink (v. 7), Jesus placed Himself on a level with the woman. His request made her willing to listen further to what He had to say. She felt His true, unselfish interest. Her interest was further aroused by the statement: "If you knew the gift of God ..." (v. 10). She was moved to consider Christ's claims (v. 12). Next He made a promise that appealed to conscious need (v. 14). The woman had sought satisfaction all her life, unrestrained in her search by the laws of God or man, but she thirsted still. In every heart there is a thirst, a sense of lack, which Jesus promises to satisfy (vv. 13 – 15). Then came a command appealing to conscience (v. 16). No matter how a person may admit Christ's claims, he will never find satisfaction until the thing that is wrong in his life is made right. Jesus had touched the sore spot in her life. Her answer (v. 17) was half true. Jesus proceeded to reveal her whole life (v. 18) with such divine insight that she called Him a prophet (v. 19). Jesus had also appealed to a religious instinct, which, though dormant, was not dead. But the woman thought of religion only as form and ceremony and imagined that the mistake was in the location of the worship (v. 20). Jesus informed her (vv. 21 – 25) that the problem was not the place of worship but the fact that she had never worshiped at all. Since God is a Spirit, true worship is not a question of place or of form and ceremony but of spiritual reality. Jerusalem had indeed been the divinely appointed place of worship, because of the promise of salvation through the Jews, but the time has come when there are to be no local restrictions to worship. True worshipers will not be concerned with place and symbol. The woman's reply suggested a need for a mediator to give fuller knowledge of God. Now she was ready to hear the supreme word (v. 26). Did she believe? She made no verbal response, but her actions (v. 28) were more eloquent than speech.

The central thought of the text is that Jesus leads lost souls to know the gift of salvation. The goal of the sermon is that the hearers reaffirm Jesus as the gift of God that satisfies.

Sermon Outline
JESUS LEADS US TO KNOW THE GIFT OF GOD

Introductory thought: Although Jews generally avoided Samaria, Jesus did not. He sat down to rest but forgot his weariness when the opportunity presented itself to lead a lost soul to know God's gift. Jesus, who suffered weariness and thirst for us, has come to us and pleaded, "If you knew the gift of God . . . ." He comes to us again today and offers that gift, His own self, to know and to enjoy.

I. Jesus makes us aware of our need for God's gift.
   A. He reminds us that earthly wells cannot quench spiritual thirst (v. 13).
      1. We, like the Samaritan woman, have earthly wells of whose waters we boast (v. 12)—money, success, possessions, ambitions.
      2. There are times when we yearn for something more than the water of these miserable wells (v. 15).
   B. Jesus puts His finger on sin as the cause of our thirst (v. 16).
      1. Jesus condemns as sin actions we may have excused (vv. 17–18).
      2. We can no longer hide or equivocate (v. 19).
      3. What is wrong in our life must be made right if we are to have satisfaction.
      4. Jesus stimulates in us a desire for the gift of God (v. 14).

Jesus leads us to know the gift of God by first bringing us to an awareness of our need for that gift. Then He shows us where to find it.

II. Jesus shows us where to find God's gift.
   A. We find it in the true church.
      1. We may be perplexed as to which church is right (v. 20).
      2. The true church is present where God's Word is taught purely and the sacraments are administered according to Christ's command. There we find the gift of God—salvation (v. 22).
   B. We find it among true worshipers.
      1. They are not bound to any particular place or ritual (v. 21).
      2. They worship the true God in spirit and in truth (v. 23).

a. God is not bound to any outward group or building.
b. Church organizations can cease to exist, but true worshipers, who make up the church, will continue.
C. We find it in the Savior Himself.
1. Jesus reveals Himself to us (v. 26) in the Word.
2. We can have Him now, as we are, in our emptiness and thirst.
3. He is the gift that satisfies (vv. 28 – 29).

Concluding thought: Do you know the gift of God? Jesus says to you, "I who speak to you am He."

GERHARD AHO

Third Sunday in Lent

EPISTLE Ephesians 5:8 – 14 (RSV)

Sermon Notes/Introduction

When the philosopher Diogenes supposedly walked the streets of Sinope with a lantern in his hand looking for an honest man, he was attesting to the light-darkness antithesis that has provided the basis for many philosophical and religious systems. Man has a perennial faith in the notion that light is the solution to difficulties. If you want to decrease nocturnal street crimes, install new and better lighting. If you want to put an end to dishonesty in business or politics, cast on these nefarious deeds the light of public knowledge. If you want to find a cure for troubling diseases, let contributions add more candlepower to the already existing body of brilliant research minds.

Light is also a prominent theme in Holy Scripture. The various lights (the revelation of prophecy, the guidance of chosen leaders, miraculous intervention, etc.) that God shed on a world darkened by sin culminated in the light of the redeeming work of His Son, Jesus Christ. It is this light that leads men to new plateaus in this life and in the world to come.

Sermon Outline
CHRIST IS THE LIGHT OF THE WORLD

I. Christ brings people out of darkness into light (vv. 8 – 9). All of the people with whom Christ came into contact had a darkness of some kind in their lives. (1) Aged Simeon had long years but an unfulfilled life; (2) the palsied man had experienced the frustration and despair of a permanent infirmity; (3) Martha's life was synonymous with a busyness and superficiality that lacked meaning; (4) the thief on the cross looked eyeball to eyeball at a closed future. The entrance of Christ into the lives of these people brought dramatic changes. Nineteen and a half centuries later life is no different for people living in the darkness of godlessness and artificial Christianity. Modern man's problem is that he has filled his life with lights of various kinds (the light of a promising professional future, of abundant materialism, of extensive knowledge, of spectacular entertainment, etc.), yet he often lives in spiritual darkness. To this world of ours Christ comes once more and says, "I am the Way, the Truth, the Life, and the Light." What a change there is in the lives of those who hear Him!

II. The light of Christ brings the responsibility of living a new kind of life (v. 10). The lives of many people do not need direction so much as they need redirection. The rich young ruler who came to Christ had lived with moral directives all his life; however, he was "spinning his wheels" with righteous deeds that could bear no fruit before God. The disciples who disputed over the place of honor in heaven were very much interested in their eternal reward, but they were "barking up the wrong tree" in giving vent to pride and in seeking personal distinction. Like these people, we are rough diamonds who need to be cut with the love of Christ so that a new brilliance can be revealed. Christ has brought to us a new commandment. In regard to this commandment He says, "This do and you shall live."

III. Christ asks us to share His light so that the darkness of others may be exposed and they may join us in the light (vv. 11–13). The earthly life of Christ brought into full view the wretched nature of man. Herod, to hold onto temporal power, exposed his inner self in the gross sin of mass infanticide. The righteous veneer of the Pharisees became more than suspect in the slaying of the innocent God-man. The agreeable Roman officials who could trade justice for short-term civil concord forfeited all claims of being noble. It can only be conjecture to speculate how many of these heinous deeds would have occurred if the perfect light of Christ had not shed light on the imperfect life of man. We have the responsibility of leading God-pleasing lives so that the darkness of others may be exposed in order that they may walk, by faith, in the new light of Christ.

IV. Only Christ can give true light (v. 14). Jesus remarks so ably and so insightfully, "Can a blind man lead a blind man?" (Luke 6:39). Yet man, by psychological analysis, philosophical speculation, and empirical investigation, has led himself to believe that he is forever on the threshold of discovering light for his darkened world. How tragic it is that in his Christless morality and idealism, man has still to learn that he is forever the bridesmaid and never the bride. Our world needs to hear the words of Christ: "I have come as light into the world, that whoever believes in Me may not remain in darkness" (John 12:46).

Man is right in believing that light is a benefit and that it solves problems. But he is wrong in supposing that he can provide his own light. Once again God raises on earth the light of His crucified Son. Let us work diligently and pray that all may see Him.

QUENTIN F. WESSELSCHMIDT

Third Sunday in Lent

GOSPEL John 9:24–41 (RSV)

Sermon Notes/Introduction

The healing of the blind man was a marvelous "sign" and would go far to persuade men to admit the claims of Jesus. His enemies feared this, and so they sought without success to prove that the miracle had not been done. The Pharisees carefully cross-examined the man who had received his sight and also his parents. They summoned him a second time and urged him to admit that the reputed miracle was only a deception (v. 24). The man's answer (v. 25) does not mean that he had no opinion regarding the character of Jesus but that he was willing to leave the theological problems to their superior wisdom. He knew, however, what Jesus had done for him. The Pharisees were indeed in a dilemma; there stood the man before them, his sight perfect though he had been born blind. They must either deny the facts or admit the divine nature of Jesus, which the facts proved. They tried to escape from their dilemma by asking the man to repeat his story, hoping to entangle him in his report. But the man saw their dilemma and asked with bold irony whether their eagerness for more information was due to a desire to become his disciples (v. 27). Now they could only revile him (vv. 28–29), letting abuse take the place of argument. The man heaped on their cowardice the contempt it deserved in the form of an unanswerable argument (vv. 30–33). The Pharisees dismissed the matter by excommunicating him (v. 34). Jesus knew the difficulties the man had encountered in his faith and came to strengthen him (vv. 35–38). He who had first regarded the Lord merely as a man called Jesus and then as a prophet now saw Him as the Son of God. Often the humble who have no wisdom of their own are the first to admit the claims of Christ. But this is no excuse for the wise and learned. The Pharisees' greater privileges and knowledge of Scripture should have made them the first to believe. Their boasted insight was their very condemnation and aggravation of their guilt (v. 41).

The central thought of the text is that the coming of Jesus brings both darkness and light. The goal of the sermon is that the hearers would see Jesus more clearly. The problem is that opposition sometimes blurs their vision of Christ. The means to the goal is Jesus' bestowal and sharpening of spiritual vision.

Sermon Outline
THE PARADOXICAL PURPOSE OF CHRIST'S COMING INTO THE WORLD

Introductory thought: The actions of Jesus are paradoxical: the poor are filled with good things, and the rich are sent empty away; the righteous are declared to be sinners, and sinners are made righteous. To those who laugh He brings weeping, and He gives laughter to those who weep. The last He puts first, and the first last. The wise He shows to be foolish, and to the foolish He gives wisdom. He is the world's Savior, but in our text He declares, "For judgment I came into this world" (v. 39).

I. He came that the seeing may become blind.
   A. The Jewish leaders thought they could see.
      1. Yet they refused to believe that the man had been given his sight (vv. 17–26).
      2. When they could no longer deny the fact, they treated the whole matter with contempt (vv. 28, 34).
      3. They would not admit their blindness. Therefore their guilt remained (v. 41).
   B. Many today think they can see.

1. Skeptics substitute for the religious formula of the Pharisees (v. 16) the axiom that the supernatural cannot exist and that miracles cannot occur.
    a. They try to prove discrepancies in the Gospel story and to accuse Jesus of deception.
    b. Yet they are troubled by the facts.
2. Agnostics lack the moral courage to face the facts.
3. Some in Christendom twist God's Word, deceiving and being deceived (2 Tim. 3:13), and refuse to be instructed by the Word.

Jesus' purpose in coming is to judge all such people. They see Jesus, the Light, but deny Him. Insisting that they see, they remain blind. To them Jesus speaks as to the Pharisees (Matt. 23:16–17, 19, 24). How paradoxical! But there is another side to the paradox.

II. He came that the blind may see.
   A. We are by nature "those who do not see" (John 9:39a).
      1. We cannot discern spiritual things (1 Cor. 2:14).
      2. We are opposed to God (Rom. 8:7–8).
   B. Jesus alone can open our eyes.
      1. He works through the Gospel, which proclaims Him as Savior (Acts 26:18; 1 Tim. 1:15).
      2. The Gospel is the salve of the Spirit, which opens our eyes so that we can say, "I believe" (John 9:38; Rev. 3:18c).
   C. Jesus sharpens our vision.
      1. Obstacles can blur it:
         a. Rational and theological arguments (John 9:24);
         b. Reviling (v. 28);
         c. Persecution (v. 34).
      2. Jesus enables us to confess Him simply and boldly (vv. 25, 27, 30–33).
      3. We see Jesus more clearly (vv. 35–38).

We have seen Jesus and heard Him speak. No more is needed.

Concluding thought: The blessed aspect of Jesus' paradoxical purpose is fulfilled in us who can say, "Mine eyes have seen thy salvation" (Luke 2:30).

GERHARD AHO

Fourth Sunday in Lent

EPISTLE   Romans 8:1–10

Sermon Notes/Introduction

The key word in this triumphant chapter of Romans is *pneuma* (spirit). It occurs 21 times in this chapter, more than in any other chapter in the New Testament; it appears 13 times in all the other chapters of Romans. It is the Holy Spirit alone who can bring the Christian to a certainty of his salvation and keep him in this certainty. Our text begins to develop the subject matter of Romans 8 by drawing our attention to the life that the Christian has in the Spirit, a life that is free from the condemnation of the Law.

Sermon Outline
LIFE IN THE SPIRIT—DEAD TO SIN BUT ALIVE FOR RIGHTEOUSNESS

I. Life outside of the Spirit means death.
   A. Those who are not in Christ face the judgment of the Law. They have to meet its just demands by themselves (vv. 1, 4, 9).
   B. To trust the Law is an impossible hope. It is unable to declare the sinner innocent and deliver him from the judgment of God, because he cannot keep it. The Law can only judge the sinner, not save him (v. 3; cf. Rom. 3:19–20; 7:7–12; Gal. 2:16).
   C. Everyone who lives according to the flesh is not in Christ. He is not led by the Spirit but by his own fleshly desires (*kata sarka*) and thoughts (Rom. 8:4–5). Throughout these verses "flesh" and "Spirit" are in antithesis to each other. To live by one is death. To live by the other is life.
   D. Living according to the flesh results in death because it brings a person under the Law and its judgment (vv. 6–8). The temptation to live according to the flesh is a real and ever-present danger to the Christian. Daily repentance, with an awareness of the fact that sins still cling to the Christian, is in order (cf. Rom. 6:12–14; Gal. 5:16–21; 1 Peter 2:11).

II. Living by the Holy Spirit in Jesus Christ means life.

FOURTH SUNDAY IN LENT

    A. There is no judgment or sentence of death to the one who is in Jesus Christ, because Jesus Christ has met the full demands of the Law in the stead of the sinner (vv. 1, 3 – 4). God visited on His own Son the guilt of man's sin. Jesus Christ through His life and death fulfilled every requirement and demand of the Law. *En tē sarki* in verse 3 refers to the "flesh" of Jesus Christ, not to the Christian's "flesh."

    B. The Holy Spirit through the Gospel brings the sinner into the salvation that Jesus Christ won by His life and death (v. 2) and keeps him in it. Salvation means life, deliverance, and freedom from the judgment of the Law—forgiveness of sins. It also includes a righteousness that avails before God, by which God declares the sinner innocent of sin and its guilt and by which He makes the sinner righteous and pure before Him (Rom. 1:16 – 17). "The Law of the Spirit of life" can be understood as the Gospel. Paul then calls it a "Law" in the sense of an articulated, unchangeable, definite description of what Jesus Christ did for the sinner. It is "Law" in that the message about Christ and forgiveness is set and certain for all time. It is "of the Spirit of life" because in the Gospel the Spirit is always active in bringing a new way of life to the sinner. Or it can be understood as the authority of the Spirit that He exercises through the Gospel. Faith is not mentioned here, but it must be understood as that which receives the Gospel and holds on to it (cf. Rom. 5). The concept of faith is to be understood in the walking according to the Spirit of verse 4.

III. Life in the Spirit is the daily ambition of the Christian.

    A. Living according to the Spirit results in daily denial of the flesh and daily enjoyment of the peace and life of God (Rom. 8:6, 10).

    B. By such living in the Spirit, the Christian joyfully subjects himself to the Law and will of God for a life of good works. These good works are motivated by the righteousness of God in the Gospel (v. 10).

Life in the spirit is a life that is dead to sin and alive to God's righteousness.

LOUIS A. BRIGHTON

Fourth Sunday in Lent

GOSPEL   Matthew 20:17 – 28 (RSV)

Sermon Notes/Introduction

Vv. 20 – 21: In Mark's account James and John, not their mother, make the request to Jesus (Mark 10:35). We are reminded of another time that James and John made a request of Jesus; they asked if He wanted fire to come down from heaven and destroy a Samaritan village that did not receive Jesus (Luke 9:51 – 56). This illustrated why the two brothers were called sons of thunder (Mark 3:17).

Vv. 22 – 23: For "cup" as a metaphor of suffering see Lam. 4:21; Is. 51:17; Jer. 49:12; Rev. 14:10; 16:19. In particular, the "cup" dramatically symbolizes the suffering that Jesus would endure, a cup that Jesus speaks of in Luke 22:42 and John 18:11 (both in Gethsemane and both referring to His death on the cross).

Sitting on Jesus' right and left was another matter. Unless one is to think of the two thieves who were crucified with Jesus, which He did not likely mean here, there is no direct indication here or elsewhere of what He had in mind. It could, however, be a general reference to all those who will inherit the kingdom of God, all those for whom it has been prepared (see Matt. 25:34).

V. 24: The statement that the 10 "were indignant at the two brothers" suggests that all 12 disciples were on the same moral level of a self-seeking ambition.

V. 28: The thought of this verse not only serves as a theme and objective of Jesus' ministry, but it is also, as Bengel called it, the *summum exemplum,* the supreme example for the church to follow.

Sermon Outline

Our text is introduced by the third prediction of Jesus' death and resurrection. This introduction serves as a stance from which to interpret the request of James and John. The text is then fittingly concluded with what can be called the theme of Jesus' ministry and Passion—His life a ransom for many.

The context sets the scene. It is the last journey of Jesus to Jerusalem, where He will suffer and die. Just before this incident, Jesus tells the parable of the workers in the vineyard (Matt. 20:1 – 16). This can help us to understand that an attitude of the heart that wishes to be first in the kingdom of God, an attitude that James and John exhibited by their request to Jesus, is the same attitude that demands more pay, more recognition for more work done in the kingdom. It is an attitude that desires work in the kingdom of God for the sake of one's own glory and advancement rather than for the sake of the cross. How sharply our Lord points out the error of this attitude when He points to Himself and to His own attitude and goal for His life (v. 28).

Immediately after our text is the story of Jesus' healing the two blind men at Jericho (vv. 29 – 34). An attitude of self-service and self-aggrandizement indicates a total lack of understanding of the ministry of the church. It is a blindness of heart that only Jesus can remove and must remove if one is to follow Him and serve in His kingdom.

A LIFE OF SERVICE IN VIEW OF THE CROSS

I. The seeking of honor and privilege in the church is a denial of the Gospel.
   A. The sin of self-seeking obscures the view of the cross, one's need for forgiveness, and the need and blessings of the cross for others.
   B. Such a sin places self in the seat of honor rather than Christ. It becomes the sin of idolatry, the worship of self, and subverts the true mission of the church.

II. Selfless service to others adorns the Gospel.
   A. Jesus Christ gave His life in service to others that all might be set free from sin, death, and hell.
   B. The Gospel message of the ransom that Jesus Christ gave for all is the hope and life of the world.
   C. The mission of the church is the proclamation of this life-saving Gospel, supported and attended by selfless service to others.

The "cup of suffering" becomes the role of the church as it ministers to the world the message of "Christ crucified."

LOUIS A. BRIGHTON

Fifth Sunday in Lent

EPISTLE   Romans 8:11 – 19 (KJV)

Sermon Notes/Introduction

V. 11: "If": the if of reality. "The Spirit ... dwell in you"

(John 14:16 – 18, 23). "Quicken your mortal bodies": see 1 Cor. 15:53 – 57. We are wholly redeemed, body and soul; cf. John 6:39 – 40, 44 – 45. "By His Spirit": because of the Spirit. Note that the three persons of the Trinity are mentioned. *V. 12:* "Debtors": people under obligation. "Flesh": the flesh viewed as a power. We are debtors to the Spirit (Gal. 3:26). *V. 13:* "Die": to die forever. "Through the Spirit": through the new spiritual nature. "Mortify": if you keep up this killing, you will continue to live (Gal. 5:24; 1 Cor. 9:27). *V. 14:* "Spirit of God": the efficient cause. "Sons": sons by adoption. *V. 15:* "Fear": the slavish dread of punishment. "Spirit of adoption": our spirit (Gal. 4:6), the new spiritual nature. "Cry": exclaim, like a boy in distress who cries, "Father!" "Abba": Aramaic for father. *V. 16:* "The Spirit ... beareth witness" through the written Word. "Children of God" are born in regeneration. *V. 17:* "Heirs": cf. Gal. 4:7. Our inheritance is what God has promised, eternal life. "Joint heirs": coheirs. Christ is the supreme heir, who has entered His inheritance; cf. 1 Cor. 15:23. "Suffer with Him": suffer for His sake (Matt. 10:38; 16:24; Gal. 6:12). To evade the sufferings is to refuse to bear the cross (Mark 8:34; Luke 9:23). *V. 18:* "Which shall be revealed": which is about to be revealed. "Sufferings of this present time": suffering in general (Heb. 12:4 – 12). "Not worthy": the idea is that of weight. The glory outweighs the suffering (1 John 3:2). *V. 19:* "For the creation watching with outstretched head is waiting it out for the revelation of the sons of God" (author's translation). "With outstretched head": intently. "The creation": the creature world.

Plastic surgery is a modern wonder. It can recreate a face marred in an automobile accident. We have been recreated spiritually.

Sermon Outline

YOU ARE A NEW PERSON

I. We are children of God.
    A. We have received the Spirit of adoption (Rom. 8:15).
        1. By nature we could only be afraid (v. 15) because we were sinful and deserved punishment.
        2. The Holy Spirit regenerated us through the Word (Titus 3:5; John 3:1 – 15; Rom. 1:16 – 17).
    B. Now we have a new spiritual life.
        1. The Spirit bears witness with our spirit that we are the children of God (Rom. 8:16; 5:5).

2. He pours into our hearts holy desires, like prayer (Rom. 8:15; 7:22).
C. Now we have the call to live like children.
1. We are not debtors to the flesh (Rom. 8:12).
a. Our sinful nature tempts us (Rom. 7:18).
b. To live to the flesh brings death (Rom. 8:13).
2. We are to mortify the deeds of the body (v. 13; Gal. 5:24; 1 Cor. 9:27).

Application: Rejoice in being a child. Live like a child.

II. We are heirs.
A. Now we may have to endure suffering (Rom. 8:17–18).
1. Much of our suffering is self-inflicted.
2. The Lord chastens those whom He loves (Heb. 12:6).
3. We suffer at times also for His sake and the Gospel's (Matt. 10:10–39).
B. Yet we have the hope of glory (Rom. 8:18).
1. All creation looks forward to it (v. 19).
2. We shall receive it.
a. Our souls will be with Christ.
b. On the last day our bodies will be raised and glorified (v. 11; 1 Cor. 15).
c. The glory shall outweigh the suffering of this life. We shall be forever with the Lord (1 Thess. 4:17).

Application: "Fight on, my soul, till death shall bring thee to thy God."

Conclusion: Remade indeed! Thanks to the Spirit we are children and heirs.

HENRY J. EGGOLD

Fifth Sunday in Lent

GOSPEL John 11:47–53 (KJV)

Sermon Notes/Introduction

1. That our text records more than a plot of men, that there was also—and above all—a plan of God, is evident not only from verses 51–52 of the text but also from the incident described in the post context (John 12:1–9). Verses 51–52 depict the "above the scene" activity of God ruling over the

"behind the scene" machinations of Caiaphas and his cohorts. And the post context makes clear from Jesus' reaction to Mary's costly anointing of Him ("Against the day of My burying hath she kept this") that He was fully aware of the death in store for Him and was willingly proceeding toward it. Jesus was not simply the hapless victim of human evil hurriedly concocted. He was, above all, God's appointed agent to work out a plan of salvation designed from eternity.

2. Our text contains a celebrated example of a device common in Greek and Elizabethan drama (and surprisingly frequent in the Bible as well) called dramatic irony. Two ingredients are usually present in dramatic irony: (a) the speaker's words are true in either a greater or different sense than he intends them—he has no idea how truly he speaks; (b) the listener or reader is better aware of certain circumstances than is the speaker—he knows something the speaker doesn't. Thus when Macbeth, having just successfully accomplished the murder of Banquo, expresses the wish that Banquo were present for the dinner he is hosting, his hypocritical wish is true in a way he doesn't realize when he voices it, for Banquo *is* present, if not in body at least in spirit—as a ghost—a presence Macbeth is about to discover to his horror. What's more, the reader of Shakespeare's play knows something that Macbeth doesn't, that the ghost of Banquo has occupied an empty seat at the table just before Macbeth speaks. Hence there is irony, a most dramatic irony indeed.

So it is in our text. When Caiaphas asserts that "it is expedient for us, that one man should die for the people, and that the whole nation perish not," he means something nasty and selfish—that it would be to the political advantage of the Jewish nation if Jesus could be sacrificed to the Roman overlords, that Roman attention to Jesus would take the heat off the chief priests and Pharisees. But as verse 51 helps us to realize, Caiaphas was not aware of the full import of his words. His sinister suggestion turns out to be glorious prophecy! It *is* "expedient," advantageous—spiritually advantageous—that one person, Jesus, has died for the people—all the people of the world—and that because He did, no one need perish in hell. As the spiritual heirs of Jesus' life-giving death, we know something that Caiaphas didn't—hence the dramatic irony.

3. For other possible instances of Scriptural dramatic irony, see Ps. 88:9–12; Matt. 27:24–25; Luke 24:13–35; and Acts 28:3–6. What is at stake, of course, in all these

Biblical instances is more than the mere recognition of a familiar literary device; the reward in each instance for the reader of the Bible is the growing realization that a powerful and gracious God is ever at work bringing His good out of man's evil, accomplishing His wisdom despite (or through) man's ignorance. Biblical dramatic irony always dramatizes the plan of salvation! It is blessed rather than cruel.

Sermon Outline

(Define dramatic irony and provide an instance of it from secular literature.)

DIVINE DRAMATIC IRONY

I. What went on "behind the scene" was a sinister plot (John 11:47–50, 53).
   A. The motive for the plot.
      1. Envy of Jesus' growing success after His raising of Lazarus.
      2. Fear of the political consequences to the Jewish nation if Jesus' growing success should arouse the attention of the Roman overlords.
      3. Basically, the culmination of growing hostility between Jesus and the church leaders throughout the Savior's earthly ministry.
   B. The nature of the plot.
      1. Death to Jesus: a nuisance eliminated (v. 53).
      2. Political advantage to the Jewish nation: the heat is off (v. 50).
II. What went on "above the scene" was a divine plan (vv. 51–52).
   A. God turns plotter into prophet (v. 51).
   B. God turns an evil scheme into a divine plan.
      1. Jesus dies, not for a nation, but for the whole world.
      2. His death is "expedient," advantageous, not in a political sense but in a spiritual sense.
         a. His death effects our eternal salvation (v. 51).
         b. His death effects Christian unity: to a high degree here on earth and to a perfect degree hereafter in heaven (v. 52).

Let us praise and worship our God, who through His Son, Jesus Christ, so powerfully and so graciously guides human history to achieve our eternal welfare.

FRANCIS C. ROSSOW

Palm Sunday: Sunday of the Passion

EPISTLE Philippians 2:5 – 11 (KJV)

Sermon Notes/Introduction

V. 5: "Let this mind": keep minding the one thing, namely, lowly-mindedness. "In": in the case of. "Christ Jesus": His office and person. He is subject of all that follows in vv. 6 – 11. *V. 6:* "He who existed in God's form" (John 1:1). "Not robbery": not a thing of snatching, a thing for self-glorification, a prize for display (Col. 2:9). *V. 7:* "Made Himself of no reputation": He emptied Himself (2 Cor. 8:9), namely, by taking a slave's form when He came to be in men's likeness. "Likeness": In the incarnation Christ did not cease to be God. Even in the midst of death He had to be the mighty God. "Slave's form" refers to the humiliation. *V. 8:* "In fashion": Christ was truly human, except for sin (John 8:46; Heb. 4:15; 7:26). "Humbled": abased. "Obedient" refers to voluntary obedience. "Death of the cross": death of one accursed of God (Deut. 21:23; Gal. 3:13; 2 Cor. 5:21). *V. 9:* "Exalted Him": Only the human nature could experience the exaltation. The full use of the divine attributes communicated to the human nature at the incarnation constitutes the exaltation (John 17:5). "A name which is above every name": see Eph. 1:9 – 10, 20 – 24. "Name" equals revelation, that by which God and Christ alone can be known. *V. 10:* "Every knee": heavenly ones, earthly ones, subterranean ones. The devils and unbelievers shall bow not with joy but with dismay; cf. Col. 2:15; 1 Peter 3:18 – 20. *V. 11:* "Confess": acknowledge. "Glory of God the Father": the glory of His grace (Eph. 1:6, 12, 14).

The world does not rate humility very high. It says, "Blessed are the strong who can hold their own." Jesus says, "Blessed are the meek" (Matt. 5). "God resisteth the proud but giveth grace unto the humble" (James 4:6).

Sermon Outline
A TIME FOR HUMILITY

I. Christ humbled Himself.
   A. He was in the form of God (John 1:1 – 14).
      1. He claimed to be God (John 10:30; John 1:1).
      2. He demonstrated by His miracles that He was God; He predicted His passion.

3. He confessed His deity before Caiaphas (Matt. 26:64) and Pilate (Matt. 27:11).
  B. Yet He served (cf. the Old Testament Reading).
     1. He did not always use the divine qualities He had.
     2. He became obedient unto death.
        a. He willingly suffered (John 10:11; Is. 53:7).
        b. He suffered for us (1 Peter 3:18; Is. 53:4–5).
  C. "Let this mind be in you."
     1. Greatness in the kingdom comes through humble service.
        a. We regard others above self (Phil. 2:3).
        b. We serve one another (Matt. 20:26–28).
     2. Arenas for humble service are manifold.
        a. The home (Eph. 5:24–6:4).
        b. The congregation (2 Cor. 13:11).
        c. Society (Rom. 13:1–10).
     3. The greatest service we can render to anyone is to share the Gospel (Acts 1:8; Matt. 28:18–20).
II. Christ was exalted.
  A. God raised Christ from the dead.
     1. He showed His acceptance as a sacrifice (Rom. 4:25).
     2. He declared Christ to be the Son of God (Rom. 1:4).
  B. God set Christ at His own right hand (Eph. 1:20–23; 4:10).
     1. He has a name above every name: King of kings and Lord of lords (1 Tim. 6:15; Rev. 17:14; 19:16; Is. 9:6–7).
        a. The God-man is exalted.
        b. He is head of all things for the sake of the church (Eph. 1:22).
     2. Before Him every knee shall bow.
        a. The devil and all who were enemies of the cross in this life shall do so reluctantly.
        b. Christians shall do so joyfully throughout eternity (Rev. 7:9–14).
     3. Every tongue shall confess that Jesus Christ is Lord.
        a. We do that now already in worship and witness (Matt. 21:1–9).
        b. In heaven we shall join the angels in singing: "Worthy is the Lamb that was slain" (Rev. 5:12).

C. We shall be exalted.
1. Our exaltation to eternal life is God's gift to us (Matt. 25:34).
2. This hope encourages us to live lives of humble service (Matt. 25:34 – 36; 1 John 3:3).

How great our hope is in Christ! What an incentive His love for us is! We can be humble servants of our Lord by sharing with others the Good News of Christ, our King, who once came in meekness but now reigns as King of kings.

HENRY J. EGGOLD

Palm Sunday: Sunday of the Passion

GOSPEL   Matthew 26:6 – 13 (RSV)

Sermon Notes/Introduction

According to John 12:1, it was six days before the Passover when Jesus came to Bethany. The verses (Matt. 26:3 – 5) immediately preceding the text express the hatred of Jesus' enemies, but the supper and the anointing described in the text are tokens of love. The devotion of Jesus' friends and the exuberant love of Mary are in striking contrast to the sinister plans of the Jewish leaders. The man in whose house the supper was given (v. 6) had been leprous and had been made well by Jesus. He wished to show his gratefulness to the Master. According to John 12:3, the woman (Matt. 26:7) was Mary, the sister of Martha and of Lazarus. Now she wished not only to receive from Jesus but also to give a token of her esteem. The ointment she poured on Him was very expensive (v. 7). Her deed was inspired by her ardent love for Christ. The disciples' displeasure was instigated by Judas (John 12:4). "Why" (Matt. 26:8) is a word of censure and cutting reproof. They considered Mary's act senseless extravagance and in questionable taste. She remained silent and Jesus stepped into the breach in her defense (v. 10). The love of the Lord is beneficent. Even luxury and embellishment are permissible when done to the glory of God. We cannot be sure whether Mary knew that Jesus would die in Jerusalem, nor that she now intended to anoint Him for His burial (v. 12). It is more likely that Jesus construed her active devotion as much richer and greater than she had supposed. He thought so highly of what Mary had done that He held her act up (v. 13) as a model for all good deeds for all times.

The central thought of the text is that Mary performs an

exemplary good deed. The goal of the sermon is that the hearers will be active in good deeds. The problem is that we sometimes disparage good works because we are not saved by them. The means to the goal is Jesus' acceptance and commendation of good deeds.

Sermon Outline

DEEDS THAT HONOR JESUS

Introductory thought: We are entering Holy Week, when so much evil was done to Jesus. But a week before His death He must have been cheered by a very good thing done to Him. He holds up what Mary did as an example for us. Her act is a model for all time.

I. They are the fruit of faith.
   A. Externally good deeds that spring from motives other than faith do not honor Jesus (Heb. 11:6).
   B. Mary's faith moved her to act (Matt. 26:7; John 12:3).
      1. Her faith was created and sustained by Jesus' Word (Luke 10:39, 42).
      2. Faith in Jesus always produces good deeds (Matt. 7:17; 12:35; 1 John 3:3; Gal. 5:6).
      3. Only the believer can do good deeds according to God's standard. Unbelievers can do outwardly good deeds, deeds of civil righteousness, which are indeed commendable, but God looks at the heart.
II. They reflect love for Christ.
   A. Deeds done to reflect love of self, to gain recognition and praise, do not honor Jesus.
   B. Deeds of *agape* are needed (1 Cor. 13:2, 13).
      1. With them we show love for Him who died for our salvation (Matt. 26:12).
      2. With them we honor Christ's body, the church.
III. They represent effort on our part.
   A. Mary gave the best she had.
      1. The ointment was "very expensive" (v. 7).
      2. She could have used the money for herself.
   B. There is a correlation between goodness and sacrifice.
      1. We must sacrifice the claims of the self—squelch the flesh with its desire for self-indulgence.
      2. How much have we sacrificed (Mark. 12:44; 2 Cor. 8:2–3)?
      3. Think of how the church would be blessed and Christ honored if we gave our best.

IV. They receive the Lord's commendation.
   A. Some do not commend them.
      1. Hypocritically, some find fault (Judas—John 12:4–5).
      2. Others thoughtlessly join in (Matt. 26:8): "Why spend so much for missions, the upkeep of the church and ministry, etc.?"
   B. Deeds that honor Christ have abiding value.
      1. Faultfinders will pass away.
      2. Good deeds are a perpetual memorial (v. 13; Rev. 14:13).
      3. Therefore we can leave our vindication to Jesus.

Concluding thought: Are we engaged in ugly faultfinding or in doing beautiful things that honor Jesus?

GERHARD AHO

Maundy Thursday

EPISTLE   1 Corinthians 11:23–26 (RSV)

Sermon Notes/Introduction

The Lord's Supper is a feast, not a sacrifice—a feast in which the offering is eaten. At this supper the Lord is the host. The Lord's Supper is not merely a commemoration; it is a feast of union with the Lord and a communion with the other participants (1 Cor. 10:17). Jesus gave thanks for the bread and the wine as vehicles for the nourishment and strengthening of the spiritual life. With this blessing He consecrated the bread and the wine for a new and holy purpose in the Sacrament; the elements were to be the bearers of the body and blood of the Lord. Jesus' words in the text are His last will and testament. It is the duty of a testator to use plain and simple words, avoiding terms that are misleading. The beneficiary has the right and also the duty to abide by the literal interpretation. Accordingly, we believe that when we receive and eat the bread, we receive and eat Christ's body, and when we receive and drink the wine, we receive and drink Christ's blood. Bread and wine, body and blood are all present. This is a deep mystery.

When Jesus instituted the Lord's Supper, He called it a "new covenant." A covenant is ordinarily a contracted agreement between two parties. The Lord's Supper, however, is a unilateral contract in the sense that Christ instituted it for no other reason than that He loved us.

Sermon Outline
THE NEW COVENANT OF JESUS CHRIST

I. It is a clear covenant.
   A. There is no indication that Christ intended His words (1 Cor. 11:24–25) to be understood in any but a literal sense.
      1. He did not say that the bread and the wine represent His body and blood.
      2. He did not say that the bread and the wine change into His body and blood.
   B. We believe what Christ said even if we do not understand how it is possible for His body and blood to be present.
      1. The human mind is limited even with regard to earthly things; e.g., we do not fully understand what electricity is, how the body transforms food into energy, how a seed produces a plant.
      2. It should not surprise us to find things beyond our understanding in God's ways with us.

II. It is a gracious covenant.
   A. Jesus offers us Himself.
      1. Since we receive His body given for us on the cross and His blood shed for our sins, we can be sure that we are also receiving forgiveness and salvation.
      2. Christ's real presence is a powerful assurance of His grace.
   B. Jesus offers us fellowship with God.
      1. The barrier of sin between us and God has been removed.
      2. No sin need disrupt our relationship with God.
   C. Jesus offers us fellowship with one another (1 Cor. 10:17).
      1. We are one body in Christ.
      2. Our participation in this covenant testifies to a unity of faith.

III. It is a responsible covenant.
   A. We are to partake as believing people.
      1. We believe that Christ is really present.
      2. We believe that we receive in and with the bread and wine His true body and blood for the forgiveness of our sins.
   B. We are to proclaim His death until He comes (1 Cor. 11:26).

1. We live as forgiven people.
2. We are His instruments through which He carries out His work in the world.

In His new covenant Christ is saying to us: "I am your Lord. I gave Myself for you. Now I give Myself to you." Let us respond by saying, "We are Your people. We believe in You. We want to live for You."

GERHARD AHO

Maundy Thursday

GOSPEL   John 13:1 – 17 (RSV)

Sermon Notes/Introduction

When Jesus sat down, He waited in vain for one of the disciples to perform the customary foot washing. But their minds were filled with a sense of their own greatness and dignity. So Jesus gave them a memorable object lesson to remind them that greatness is measured by service. John describes the incident from the viewpoint of Christ's great love (v. 1). Even though Jesus knew that the resolution to betray Him had already formed in the mind of Judas (vv. 2, 11), and even though He was fully conscious of His own dignity (v. 3), He performed the menial service of washing His disciples' feet, even those of His betrayer.

His act was interrupted by a dialog with Peter that reveals the spiritual significance of the act. Peter's sense of Jesus' dignity was the compelling motive in his refusal (vv. 6, 8a). The Lord, the Son of the living God, should not wash the feet of a sinful man. But Peter did not grasp the importance of this act (v. 7). If it were not done, Peter would have no part in the friendship of Jesus and in all that Jesus would impart that night to His disciples (v. 8b). Now Peter, typically, went impulsively to the other extreme (v. 9). Jesus' answer (v. 10a) obviously refers to a spiritual cleansing.

The foot washing portrays spiritual purification from daily sins. Having been justified by faith, the believer is indeed cleansed from the impurity of sin. But since the believer's sinful flesh still leads Him into evil ways, he needs cleansing or forgiveness from the guilt and stain of sin each day. The foot washing is also a token of mutual service and helpfulness. The disciples are to imitate Jesus in loving, lowly service (vv.

12–16). They need not literally wash each other's feet on every occasion, but they are to bear one another's burdens in the spirit of love. Christ calls such service blessed (v. 17) because it is done in a spirit quite different from the love of glory shown by the disciples in their strife about who would be the greatest.

The central thought of the text is that Jesus reveals His unfailing love by washing His disciples' feet. The goal of the sermon is that the hearers will be renewed daily, both inwardly and outwardly, by the love of Christ. The problem is their tendency merely to admire the love of Christ. The means to the goal is that Christ in His unfailing love daily cleanses us from sin.

Jesus kept on loving His disciples despite their self-seeking (v. 1b). Even though He knew one would betray Him (v. 11), and even though He was conscious of soon entering the glory from which He had come (v. 3), He performed for His disciples, even for His betrayer, the menial service of foot washing. In that act He showed His love in all the beauty of its perfection.

Sermon Outline
THE UNFAILING LOVE OF JESUS CHRIST

I. It is a love that makes us clean.
   A. The foot washing portrayed Christ's loving work of spiritual cleansing (v. 10).
      1. Peter did not understand the real significance of the act (vv. 6–8a, 9).
      2. Though justified by faith and thus purified from sin, we still sin daily.
         a. Flesh and blood lead us into evil.
         b. We need daily cleansing from daily defilement.
      3. We are assured that Jesus is ready and able to give this cleansing when we see Him stoop to wash His disciples' feet.
   B. If our feet are not washed, we have no part in Jesus (v. 8b).
      1. We confess we need to have our feet washed when we pray daily, "Forgive us our trespasses."
      2. He is faithful and just to forgive our sins and to cleanse us (1 John 1:9).
      3. We have a part in all that Jesus earned for us by His suffering and death.

We are daily made clean all over. The love Jesus showed in washing His disciples' feet does not fail us either.

II. It is a love that makes us humble.
   A. The foot washing provides us with a pattern for humble service (John 13:12 – 15).
      1. Christ's act is a picture of His voluntary humiliation whereby He stooped to save (Phil. 2:6 – 8).
      2. But literally washing one another's feet will not bring us any nearer to the mind of Christ.
      3. We follow Christ's example when we bear one another's burdens (Gal. 6:2).
         a. We are concerned for their physical comfort.
         b. We aim to secure their spiritual and moral cleansing.
   B. The love of Jesus enables us to "wash one another's feet."
      1. That love transforms our hearts so that we get rid of arrogance, envy, and anger.
      2. That love guides us in a spirit of lowliness and helpfulness.

Blessed are we when we let the unfailing love of Jesus move us to imitate Him (v. 17).

The love of Jesus will not fail. He who washed His disciples' feet will cleanse us daily and empower us to humble service.

GERHARD AHO

Good Friday

EPISTLE   Hebrews 4:14 – 5:10

Sermon Notes/Introduction

After exhorting and warning in Heb. 4:11 – 13, the author takes up the main argument of the book, already alluded to in 1:3; 2:17 – 18; and 3:1—namely, the priestly work of Jesus as superior to that of the Levitical line (4:4 – 12:3). *V. 14:* Jesus has passed through the spheres of the created heavens (perfect active particle of *dierchomai* indicating a state of completion) into heaven itself; that is, He is before the face of God (9:24). Unlike the Levitical high priest, who passed through the veil to the earthly symbol of eternal glory, the "great High Priest" passed through the heavens to the eternal glory itself. Since they have such a high priest, the readers are exhorted to "hold fast" both their inward faith and their confession of it before men. The present active subjunctive (*kratōmen*) means to keep on clinging to tenaciously. *V. 15:* Even though Jesus is such a great High Priest, He can still sympathize with our weaknesses and understand our trials. Even though Jesus did not sin, it does not follow that He could not in His human nature have personal experience of temptation. Jesus felt the power of the tempter to seduce. *V. 16:* We can keep on coming to our High Priest, confident that we will receive mercy and well-timed help.

According to the opening verse of chapter 5, Jesus has the necessary qualities of a high priest, for He was chosen from among men and appointed by God. *V. 2:* The Levitical priests were able to show compassion to the erring because they themselves experienced weakness, infirmity (*astheneian*). *V. 3:* Their sin offering for themselves, first of all, was a prominent part of the ceremonial of the Day of Atonement (Lev. 16). *V. 6:* The quotation from Ps. 110:4 shows that Christ's entry into His kingly priesthood, a priesthood that would never end, was prefigured by Melchizedek, who prior to the Aaronic priesthood united in himself the office of priest and king. *Vv. 7 – 8:* Christ was prepared and consecrated for the eternal priesthood, which He entered after the human experience of suffering. *V. 9:* Having been made perfect (*teleiōtheis*, aorist passive participle), having completed the process of training, He was forever after the author not of a mere ceremonial cleansing or temporary remission of guilt but of eternal salvation. His one oblation of Himself on the cross "at once consummated His consecration to the priesthood and effected the atonement." He offered one sacrifice for sins forever (10:12), and after His resurrection He entered His eternal office of mediation on the basis of that one sacrifice.

The goal of the sermon is that the hearers will experience Christ's involvement as the great High Priest in their daily lives. The problem is that Christ as the great High Priest is often viewed more intellectually than experientially. The means to the goal is Christ's sympathy and sacrifice for us.

Good Friday impresses on us Christ's intimate involvement with our existence. His death, as well as the suffering that preceded it, testifies that He is what the text calls Him, a priest.

Sermon Outline
JESUS IS OUR GREAT HIGH PRIEST

I. He sympathizes with us as no other can.
    A. He knows our weaknesses (4:15).
        1. The Old Testament priest was able to sympathize with people in their weakness because he himself

was beset with weaknesses (5:2).
2. Although Jesus had no sin, He felt temptation's seductive power as it worked through His human fear, desire, indignation, hope, and joy.
3. He knows how severe temptation can be for us.
B. He knows our sufferings.
1. In Gethsemane and on Calvary He endured suffering far greater than that endured by any Old Testament priest or anyone before or since (v. 7; Matt. 26:39; Luke 22:44–45).
2. He pleaded with God to help Him and then was obedient to His Father's will.
3. No matter what kind of suffering we go through—spiritual, mental, or physical—we can be sure that He sympathizes with us and will help us before it is too late (Heb. 4:16).

The temptations Christ faced and the suffering He endured culminated in the cross.

II. He offered a sacrifice no other could.
A. It was a sacrifice to end all sacrifices.
1. The Old Testament priest had to offer sacrifices continually for his own sins and for those of the people (5:3).
2. Christ offered the sacrifice of Himself not for His own sins but for ours (7:26–27). His resurrection and ascension proved the completeness of His sacrifice (4:14).
3. There is no need for us to do anything to make up for our sins. Christ took care of sin once and for all on the cross.
B. His sacrifice is the source of eternal salvation.
1. God Himself designated Christ to be a priest whose sacrifice is eternally valid.
2. He is the source of salvation for us as long as we obey Him, that is, believe in Him as our great High Priest (5:9).

God may sometimes seem far removed from us in our sin, temptation, and suffering. Yet we know that Jesus is our great High Priest, whose sympathy sustains us and whose sacrifice renews us.

GERHARD AHO

Good Friday

GOSPEL   John 19:30b (RSV)

Sermon Notes/Introduction

Jesus summons His waning strength, lowers His head, and cries with a loud voice the words from Ps. 31:5 (reported in Luke 23:46), "Father, into Thy hands I commit My spirit!" He dies with Scripture, even as He dies according to Scripture. With this word He summons death. The power of death does not take away life from Him who had life in Himself. He enters death of His own free will, just as He willingly let Himself be bound as a prisoner. He came to death, as the church fathers have put it; death did not come to Him. Calling out with a loud voice, He proclaims that truth to all. Here is an awesome mystery: The Son of God died. John's expression, "He bowed His head and gave up His spirit" (John 19:30), emphasizes Christ's willingness to die and His consciousness of dying. As the Father's beloved Son, He gives His life into the Father's hands in order to receive it again from Him on the morning of the resurrection. Thereby Jesus teaches us not only how to live but also how to die. Through His death He gives us strength to die as He did.

The goal of the sermon is that the hearers will be confident that in the midst of death they possess life. The problem is that they are often fearful as they think about the death of others as well as their own. The means to the goal is that God through death destroyed death.

"God isn't dead" was a bumper sticker response to the death-of-God theology some years ago. Of course, God isn't dead; God cannot die. And yet today we are brought face to face with an awesome fact: God died! What happened on the first Good Friday is incredible.

Sermon Outline
THE INCREDIBLE DEATH OF JESUS CHRIST

I. His death was real.
   A. We cannot fathom how the God-man could die, and yet His spirit left His body.
   B. His body hung lifeless; His lips no longer spoke; His eyes no longer saw; His ears no longer heard.

II. His death was voluntary.
   A. Death comes to us because of something—illness, accident, bodily deterioration.
   B. But Jesus came to death, giving up His spirit when He was ready to, in full possession of His faculties, in full control (John 10:18).
      1. He died only when He had accomplished all things (John 17:4).
      2. He died only when He had finished the atonement.
III. His death was the death of death itself.
   A. He took on Himself the penalty for our sin, which causes death (Ezek. 18:4; Rom. 8:3; 1 Peter 2:24a).
   B. Death could not hold Him; He was sinless and had made a perfect atonement (Rom. 6:4, 9).
IV. His death means life for us.
   A. Death is now but the "shadow" (Ps. 23:4) of its former menacing power, for it is not a step into the unknown (Ps. 118:17; 2 Cor. 5:8).
   B. Death is now the avenue to God's presence, which is eternal bliss (1 Cor. 15:54c, 57).

What an incredible death! Because Jesus died, "It is not death to die." The sting of death has been removed. We can live well—and die well.

GERHARD AHO

The Resurrection of Our Lord: Easter Day

EPISTLE   Colossians 3:1–4 (RSV)

Sermon Notes/Introduction

Paul has shown in the preceding chapter that when his readers were baptized, they died with Christ (Col. 2:20), were buried, and were raised and made alive with Him (2:11–13). In this way they were restored to favor with God (1:21–23; 2:13), cut off from their old life of sin (2:11), and set on the path of holiness (1:22). Now he reminds them (3:1) that they can master the flesh by rising above it instead of fighting it on its own ground through ceremonial rites and ascetic rules. "The things that are above" (*ta anō*), the upward things (Phil. 3:14), are not abstract, transcendental conceptions, for they are where Christ is. His presence gives distinctness to our view of heaven and concentrates our interests there. "Seated" is placed with emphasis at the end of the clause in Greek to indicate the completeness of Christ's work and the dignity of His position. We are to "set" our mind on (*phroneite*)—keep on thinking about—the things above so that things on earth, though we think about them too, do not become our master (v. 2). The source of and power for such heavenly-mindedness spring from the life that came about through having died with Christ (v. 3). The aorist, *apethanete,* denotes the past act, and the perfect *kekruptai* ("has been and is hid"), the permanent effect. The Christian's life centers in Christ. As Christ is hidden, withdrawn from the world of sense yet always with us in His Spirit, so is our life with Him. And if it is with Christ, then it is in God, for "Christ is God's" (1 Cor. 3:23). No hellish burglar can break that combination. The term "hid" (Col. 3:3) points to the mystery of Christ's dwelling in believing hearts. Our life is not only with Christ, but He is our life (v. 4), for He is its source and means and end. Since His ascension, He has been hidden from physical sight, but when He appears, that is, whenever He is manifested (*hotan ... phanerōthē*, a reference to the second coming), we will see Him in His glory (1 John 3:2), and we will be like Him. Our spiritual life will find organic expression also in a perfect and heavenly body.

The central thought of the text is that life in Christ makes for heavenly-minded living. The goal of the sermon is that the hearers will live on a higher level than the earthly. The problem is that the world is too much with us. The means to the goal is our life in the resurrected and ascended Christ.

The Gospel for today assures us that Jesus lives. "Because I live," Jesus promises, "you will live also" (John 14:19)—not just in a physical, earthly way, but in a higher, heavenly way.

Sermon Outline
WE CAN LIVE ON A HIGHER LEVEL

I. We have died to sin (Col. 3:3a).
   A. Our sinful nature was buried with Christ in baptism (2:12a; Rom. 6:3–4).
      1. Since we are not yet rid of sin in our bodies, we continue to feel its effect.
         a. We may become preoccupied with things earthly—making money, acquiring things, getting ahead.
         b. Our minds may dwell on evil rather than on good—on envying, lusting, and coveting.
         c. We sometimes forget that evil thoughts, as the

ancient collect for the Second Sunday in Lent puts it, do "assault and hurt the soul."
   2. Yet we can consider ourselves dead to sin (Rom. 6:11a).
      a. When Christ rose, He destroyed sin's control over us (Col. 2:12).
      b. Our baptism enables us to crucify the sinful flesh (Rom. 6:6).
   B. Christ's power is available to us to put down sin in our bodies.
      1. The same power that He displayed in His resurrection He now uses fully at God's right hand (Col. 3:3b). As the living, ascended Lord, He gives us power to live on a higher level.
      2. We do not have to set our minds "on things that are on earth" (v. 2). Nor do we have to occupy our minds with what is sensual and mean. Rather we can think on those things that are good and right and noble and true. Our thoughts are important. "As a man thinks within himself, so he is" (Prov. 23:7 NASB).
II. We have been raised with Christ.
   A. We were made spiritually alive in our baptism.
      1. We live through faith in the forgiveness that Christ's resurrection guarantees us (Col. 2:12–13).
      2. We are now sensitive to God's thoughts toward us.
   B. Our life is hid with Christ (3:3).
      1. Christ is withdrawn from the world of sense, yet He is with us always.
      2. It is a mystery that we can be in Christ and He in us.
      3. Christ in us (Gal. 2:20) draws us to Himself and enables us to think His own thoughts (2 Cor. 5:14; Rom. 12:2; 1 Cor. 2:16).
   C. Our life will be manifested when Christ appears (Col. 3:4).
      1. Our living Lord will come again, and then we shall be like Him in glory (v. 4; 1 John 3:2).
      2. Our life in Christ will have perfect bodily expression (1 Cor. 15:35–49; 2 Cor. 5:1–5).

GERHARD AHO

The Resurrection of Our Lord: Easter Day

GOSPEL   John 20:1–9 (KJV)

Sermon Notes/Introduction

V. 1: Women were the last at the cross and the first at the tomb. Mary may have reached the tomb before the other women (Matt. 28:1). *V. 2:* Mary made her own deduction. She should have followed the Scriptures. "We know" implies that Mary came with the other women. *V. 5:* John respected rabbinic law and did not go into the sepulcher. Peter did. *V. 7:* The grave clothes were laid aside with apparent care. This would not have been the case had Jesus' body been stolen. *V. 8:* "He ... believed," i.e., Mary's report, or that Christ had not been taken away by others from the grave. *V. 9:* What John saw brought all the prophecies of the Old Testament together, e.g., Ps. 16:10; Is. 53:10–11. Furthermore, Jesus predicted His resurrection (John 2:19; Matt. 20:18–19). "They knew not the Scripture": They were blinded by overwhelming emotion.

Sermon Outline
HE IS RISEN

Introduction: The resurrection of Christ is the cornerstone of our faith (1 Cor. 15:17–20).

I. Faith looks at the evidence.
    A. Mary had the evidence but drew the wrong conclusion.
    B. Peter and John had the evidence but were blinded by overwhelming emotion (v. 9).
    C. We have conclusive evidence.
        1. The Old Testament prophecies (Ps. 16:10; Is. 53:10–11).
        2. The predictions of Christ (John 2:19; Matt. 20:18–19).
        3. The testimony of the angel at the open grave.
        4. The testimony of Jesus' enemies.
        5. The postresurrection appearances of Jesus (John 20:11–18, 19–31; Luke 24:13–35; 1 Cor. 15:1–8).

The evidence of Christ's resurrection is overwhelming, and faith rejoices in it.

II. Faith rejoices in the consequences.
   A. Jesus is indeed the Son of God (John 2:19).
   B. Jesus is with us as our living Lord (Matt. 28:20).
   C. The Father has accepted the sacrifice of Christ (Rom. 4:25; Phil. 2:5 – 11).
   D. Christ's resurrection is the pledge of our resurrection (1 Cor. 15:20 – 23; John 11:25 – 26; John 14:1 – 3).

What treasures there are for us in the empty tomb! "Thanks be to God who gives us the victory through our Lord Jesus Christ."

Henry J. Eggold

Second Sunday of Easter

EPISTLE   1 Peter 1:3 – 9

Sermon Notes/Introduction

This pericope lends itself very well to the continuing celebration of Easter. While our joy in the resurrected Christ is tied ultimately to our own resurrection from the dead to eternal life, our celebration of new life takes place in the world already now. We have learned with believers of all ages that we do not have smooth sailing. Our faith is put to the test regularly. This reading leads us to recognize trials as a part of our lives until the end comes. It explains the purpose of these unpleasant events, but above all, it offers power in the risen Christ to stand the test.

The resurrection of Jesus from the dead brought to an end the power of our common enemies—sin, death, and Satan. Life for the people of God should be pleasant, a mere step away from heaven. The victory is complete, and it is ours, but the battles continue to rage in the form of tests that God permits to come our way. Our Father did not show the power of the resurrection only in an empty tomb. That power is dramatically seen in every believer's life as it provides aid in time of trial. We must not feel cheated that trials come to us, but we can be comforted, strengthened, purified, and even downright delighted with them because through Christ we stand the test.

Sermon Outline
YOUR LIFE IN THE RISEN CHRIST IS BEING TESTED
I. Life in the risen Christ is a gift of God.
   A. God raised Jesus from the dead.

SECOND SUNDAY OF EASTER

   1. The Gospel for today continues to proclaim the joyous, astounding resurrection of Jesus.
   2. Through this act our enemies have been defeated for us by Christ (Rom. 4:25; John 14:19).
  B. He gives us a new life of hope.
   1. God mercifully connects us to Christ by giving us a new birth (1 Peter 1:3).
   2. This new birth qualifies us for an indestructible, undefiled, unfading inheritance in heaven (v. 4).
   3. This fact fills us with unspeakable joy through believing (v. 8). We get what we are looking for by faith (v. 9).
II. The tests in this new life can be severe.
  A. Every Christian has them.
   1. The people to whom Peter wrote were scattered because of persecution. They suffered the burdens of refugees along with continued attacks on their faith (v. 6).
   2. Today Christians suffer the same age-old trials; only the details are different. (Here the preacher may elaborate on conditions that currently try to pull people away from Christ.)
  B. The purpose of these tests is to strengthen and purify (v. 7).
   1. We do, to be sure, deserve punishment for the ever-present sins for which we should and do repent. But forgiven people are not punished to "pay for sin."
   2. As we exercise our faith during tests, we strengthen our spiritual muscles.
   3. Tests also burn away impurities. In times of stress we learn what is valuable and what is not (v. 7).
  C. These tests are temporary (v. 6).
   1. Many trials that people have do not last all their lives.
   2. God mercifully sets boundaries on the length and severity of trials (cf. Job).
III. The new life in the resurrected Christ stands the test.
  A. We are protected by God's power.
   1. The same power that raised Jesus from the dead protects believers.
   2. This protection is given during the fight to guard us from losing our grip on Christ. We are not kept out

of the trial; we are in it—yet safe. To be beaten by adversity means that we have deliberately done something that allows us to be overcome (like a soldier who takes off his helmet during combat).
B. We will receive commendation when Christ comes again (v. 7).
 1. Christ will praise and honor us on the Last Day because we endured through His gifts. That is His will.
 2. We will accept His praise because He wants us to have it. His praise of us complements His mercy toward us.
C. Until then, our lives are filled with joy in spite of tests.
 1. So many feel there can be no joy until they die and go to heaven.
 2. We have joy now. It is the quality of mind and heart that is certain of victory, no matter how dark the days.
 3. We do not strive for joy. We are filled with it by God as He gives us life in the risen Christ.

LOWELL F. THOMAS

Second Sunday of Easter

GOSPEL   John 20:19 – 31 (RSV)

Sermon Notes/Introduction

The text for the Second Sunday of Easter is a most familiar one. It is the Gospel from the historic pericopes for Quasimodogeniti Sunday and is assigned as the Gospel for all three series of the three-year lectionary. The versification of the narrative is known in a Latin carol of about 1600, which is familiar in the English dress of John Mason Neale's "Ye Sons and Daughters of the King" and is frequently assigned as the *de tempore* hymn for this Sunday.

There are a number of approaches one might take to the text. The first is to treat it in its entirety. Second, one could treat a single verse. Third, one could take the Thomas incident (vv. 24 – 29) or the summary (vv. 30 – 31) and subject them to individual homiletical treatment. This study will focus on the appearance of the risen Lord on Easter evening (vv. 19 – 23).

A central concept in this pericope is peace. Since the average parishioner thinks of peace only in terms of the absence of hostility and the cessation of war, a study of *shalom-*

eirēnē will help the preacher note the positive accents of well-being, wholeness, and salvation in these words. Peace is central to the covenant God has made with His people (Num. 6:22–27). In Psalm 85 God's favor, forgiveness, pardon, steadfast love, and salvation are bound up with His peace: "Let me hear what God the Lord will speak, for He will speak to His people.... Steadfast love and faithfulness will meet; righteousness and peace will kiss each other" (Ps. 85:8, 10). God's plans for His people are plans for welfare (*shalom*) and not for evil, to give them a future and a hope (Jer. 29:11). This peace reaches its fulfillment in the Prince of Peace, whose coming ushers in the peace that has no end (Is. 9:6–7). Zechariah summarizes the work of the "way-preparer": "to give knowledge of salvation to His people in the forgiveness of their sins, through the tender mercy of our God, when the day shall dawn upon us from on high to give light to those who sit in darkness and in the shadow of death, to guide our feet into the way of peace" (Luke 1:77–79). So the birth of Christ is heralded as the coming of God's peace among men (Luke 2:14). Jesus wept over Jerusalem because the city did not know the things that make for peace (Luke 19:42). The peace that He imparts is not like the peace that the world gives (John 14:27). Christ as our peace receives its fullest treatment in Eph. 2:14–17. We have peace with God through our Lord Jesus Christ (Rom. 5:1). The God of peace, who brought again from the dead our Lord Jesus, equips His people with everything good that they may do His will, working in them what is pleasing in His sight (Heb. 13:20–21). This is a mere sample of the richness of the concept of peace in the Scriptures.

Sermon Outline
PEACE, PURPOSE, AND POWER

I. In Jesus Christ we have peace.
   A. God created man for peace, for wholeness with Him.
   B. Because of sin, man lost his well-being with God; he no longer had peace.
   C. Because of sin, we enter this world at enmity with God.
   D. God sent His Son to restore peace, to bring salvation.
   E. Peace with God is forgiveness of sin for Jesus' sake.

II. In Jesus Christ we have a purpose.
   A. The Father sent the Son for His purpose (Luke 4:18; John 5:30, 36; Rom. 8:3; Gal. 4:4; 1 John 4:9, 14).
   B. The Son sends us into the world for His purpose (Luke 10:3; 24:49; John 17:18).

III. In Jesus Christ we have power.
  A. We have been given the power to forgive sin (Luke 24:47; Acts 2:38; 5:31; 10:43; 13:38; 26:18; Col. 1:14).
  B. We also have the power to retain the sins of the impenitent (Matt. 16:19; 18:15 – 20).

WILLIAM J. SCHMELDER

Third Sunday of Easter

EPISTLE   1 Peter 1:17 – 21 (RSV)

Sermon Notes/Introduction

This is still a Sunday of Easter. The power of the resurrection of our Lord is still the central theme. Peter is writing primarily to Gentiles who had embraced faith in Christ. His basic purpose is seen in 1:13: "Gird up your minds." Who knows what tensions the early Gentile Christians endured? They must have had many hours of uncertainty. In his letter Peter points to the solution to their trembling fear. As Gentiles, they must have had sleepless nights worrying about how to appease an omniscient God. Here we see the elemental contrast between the basic human notion that a man must face his God naked and alone and the truth that God accepts us as we are for Jesus' sake. Where can we find confidence? Peter says: "Have confidence in God" (v. 21).

Sermon Outline
HAVE CONFIDENCE IN GOD!

I. We cannot face God alone with confidence.
  A. God judges each person impartially.
    1. God is *omniscient*. No thought escapes His attention. We rightfully confess: "We have sinned against you in thought, word, and deed." This is no news to God.
    2. God is *impartial*. There is no way in which anyone can bribe God. The Creator of all needs nothing that any human being can offer.
    3. God is *unavoidable*. Whether we invoke Him or not, He is the God whom every human being must face.
  B. We cannot face such a God alone.

1. From the moment of birth we are undone. We have inherited "futile ways" from our fathers (v. 18). Original sin is not an inconsequential stain but a basic inability to face God as He is.
2. To this we all have added actual sins. Our consciences make us aware of this.

The text requires us to face the possibility of standing before an absolutely perfect (He makes the rules) and impartial God in our human nakedness. The sermon should now turn to ask, "How do we handle such a situation?"

II. In Christ we can have confidence in God.
   A. Original sin condemns us, but we have been ransomed from the "futile ways inherited from your fathers" (v. 18).
   B. Who paid the price, and how much did it cost to get God to lift the penalty? There was no human agent, to be sure. It was not done with gold or silver.
   C. Aha! God Himself planned it in eternity. He alone knew how this impossibility could become possible. He "destined" something from eternity (v. 20).
   D. What was His plan? It was to accept the precious blood of His Son, Jesus Christ, as the ransom and nothing less.
   E. How can we "have confidence" that all of this is valid (v. 21)? Look to the open tomb. Why did Easter happen? "God . . . raised Him from the dead and gave Him glory, so that *your* faith and hope are in God" (v. 21).

Where are you grounding your faith, Christian? In your own morality? Don't try. You will always fall short of God's absolute demands for holiness. In bargaining with God? Don't try. God deals impartially and never bargains. In enjoying life and gambling on what comes next? What comes next is not all that uncertain. It is heaven or hell. Can we then live confidently? Yes, indeed. Our confidence is in God, who raised Christ from the dead and in that crescendo of history gave to all who desire it *confidence*. Live or die, in the risen Christ and His marvelous ransom we can face the perfection of God and not only survive but flourish! This alone is of ultimate worth.

RICHARD J. SCHULTZ

Third Sunday of Easter

GOSPEL　　　　　　　　　Luke 24:13 – 35 (NKJV)

Sermon Notes/Introduction

V. 13: Emmaus, the modern Kalonich, was six or seven miles from Jerusalem. This appearance of Christ probably took place between four and six p.m. on Easter Sunday. *V. 16:* "Their eyes were restrained": overcome with sorrow; they did not recognize Jesus. Jesus wanted to give them a lesson in believing the Word. *Vv. 17 – 23:* Our faith and hope are often subject to vacillations and uncertainties. The disciples had the facts but a wavering faith. Jesus' coming changes things. *V. 18:* Literally, the question is, "Are you the only stranger in Jerusalem who does not know?" *V. 26:* "His glory": After the resurrection Christ's human nature shares always and fully in the attributes of His divine nature. *V. 27:* Christ found Himself everywhere in the Old Testament (John 5:39 – 40). *V. 30:* Many feel that this breaking of bread refers to the Lord's Supper, but the idea is debatable. *Artos* was a general name for food, including drink. *V. 31:* "He vanished"—evidence of His state of exaltation. *V. 34:* The appearance to Peter is not recorded in the Gospels, but Paul places this appearance first (1 Cor. 15:4 – 8).

Easter proclaims the living Lord as promised: "Lo, I am with you always, even to the end of the age."

Sermon Outline
THE ABIDING PRESENCE OF CHRIST

I. He is our Companion through life.
   A. The disciples desperately needed Christ as their Companion.
      1. Their spirits were low, and their hopes were shattered.
      2. They had evidences of the resurrection but little faith to accept the evidences.
      3. Sometimes we become so overwhelmed by tragedy that it is difficult to believe God's promises (Mark 4:40).
   B. Jesus joins the Emmaus disciples.
      1. He knows about them, and he knows about us (John 11:11; Ps. 139:1 – 4; Is. 49:15).

2. He joins them, but they do not recognize Him—how much like ourselves when tragedy strikes!
3. He wants them to tell Him all (Matt. 7:7).
4. He points them to the Scriptures.
   a. The Scriptures testify to Him as Savior and Lord (Gen. 3:15; 12:3; Is. 7:14; 9:6; 53:1–12.
   b. Their hearts burn within them as the fire of faith is renewed (Matt. 18:20).

In our anxieties, let us remember that Christ is with us. Let us diligently seek Him in the Scriptures.

II. He is Head of the Christian home.
   A. Jesus enters the home of the Emmaus disciples.
      1. They constrain Him to come in.
      2. As He responds, they are blessed.
   B. Jesus wants to bless our homes, too, with His presence.
      1. Homes are in trouble when Jesus is not there.
      2. We need to constrain Him to be present.
         a. We pray together at meals.
         b. We read and share the Scriptures (John 8:31–32).
         c. Prompted by His love, we confess our faults to one another and forgive one another.

Let us welcome Christ into our homes by seeking Him in the Scriptures and following Him in Christian living.

HENRY J. EGGOLD

Fourth Sunday of Easter

EPISTLE   1 Peter 2:19 – 25 (RSV)

Sermon Notes/Introduction

Some preachers have been diverted from using Christ as an example by those who have held Him forth as *merely* an example. We shy away from speaking about Christ as example because we want to speak about Him as Redeemer, King, and Savior. The fact that some have urged Him *only* as example has made us gun-shy of preaching about Him as our model. Yet we have now preached through the Passion narratives and the resurrection. We need not fear preaching Christ as example. Eph. 4:13 teaches us that we have the likeness of Christ as our goal. The goal of Christ-likeness will not be achieved until we enter eternal life, to be sure. However, the Epistle sets before us

Christ as an example. It gives an opportunity to clear up the whole matter.

Sermon Outline
THE IMITATION OF CHRIST

I. Our Lord—an Example we cannot follow.
   A. He suffered for us. His suffering was efficacious. No suffering of ours could possibly atone.
   B. He committed no sin. In this we cannot follow Him because of the flesh, which still adheres to us. In our stead He led a perfect life.
   C. He bore the penalty for our sins. He bore our wounds. This we could not do.
   D. He is the Shepherd. We are sheep. Sheep can never become shepherds.

II. Our Lord—an Example we can follow.
   A. We *can* follow because His work redeems us and empowers us.
   B. We can follow Him in humility, though the flesh impels us to sinful pride.
   C. We can follow Him in patience, though the flesh impels us to impatience with the sins of others.
   D. We can follow Him in self-sacrificing love, though the flesh impels us to selfishness.

III. Our Lord—the Power for a life that follows Him.
   A. Following Christ is not a moral decision on our part.
   B. Rather, it is a rebirth; we "die to sin and live to righteousness" (1 Peter 2:24). People need and want to hear this practical result of release from the bondage of sin in their own lives.

This text ought to produce a sermon with a joyous note for the Christian who sees the ideal of the Christian life but is beleaguered by the remnants of the flesh. The message is one of hope. It is a "You can't—but Christ can" message. The text clearly distinguishes between the unrepeatable divine acts of the Son of God and the reflective, resultant change in the life of the Christian. The pastor who absorbs the marvelous hope of this text will hardly restrain himself from bounding into the pulpit to share it.

RICHARD J. SCHULTZ

Fourth Sunday of Easter

GOSPEL John 10:1 – 10 (KJV)

Sermon Notes/Introduction

V. 1: The words of the text were spoken in the temple immediately after Jesus healed the man who had been blind (John 9:1 – 41). The sheepfold was a yard with a high stone wall to keep out wild animals and other intruders. The gate was guarded by a porter. On the contrast between true and false shepherds, see Jer. 12:1 – 4; Ezek. 34; Zech. 11:4 – 17. The sheepfold is the church of God. True pastors enter by the gate (Acts 20:29). False teachers climb over the wall (Rom. 16:17 – 18; Matt. 7:15). Luther says: "All who do not preach Christ are thieves and robbers." *V. 3:* The sheep know the voice of their shepherd. He has names for each of them. *V. 4:* Overnight several shepherds may use the same sheepfold. In the morning the sheep heed the call only of their shepherd. "He goeth before them": This is still the custom in the East. *V. 5:* Sheep do not trust a stranger as they do their shepherd. *V. 6:* A "parable" is literally any speech differing from the common way of expression. "They understood not": In rejecting Christ, the Pharisees and scribes become thieves and robbers. *V. 7:* Jesus is still the door because He is the only Savior (John 14:6). *V. 8:* "All that ever came before Me," that is, making themselves doors. *V. 9:* The thief wants to make the sheep his own, not to give them pasture; to sacrifice them to his purposes, not to deal graciously with them for theirs; to destroy, not to give life. The three great blessings the sheep have are (1) deliverance from all enemies; (2) liberty to go out and in, the liberty of the children of God; (3) sustenance. *V. 10:* The thief comes to take away, to use the sheep for his selfish purposes. But Christ has come to give life—true, lasting, eternal life in its fullness.

There are various pictures of the intimate relationship between Christ and the Christian: We are branches in Christ the Vine, members of His Body, His bride, stones in the spiritual temple. The most familiar picture of all, however, is that of the Shepherd and His sheep.

Sermon Outline
THE INTIMATE RELATIONSHIP BETWEEN THE SHEPHERD AND HIS SHEEP

I. The Relationship of the Shepherd to His Sheep.

A. Christ is the door.
   1. He came to give His life for the sheep (John 10:11).
   2. He is the only door (John 14:6).
B. Christ gives rich blessings to His sheep.
   1. False teachers are thieves and robbers (Acts 20:29).
      a. The thief wants to make the sheep his own, not to give them pasture (Rom. 16:18).
      b. He wants to sacrifice them to his purposes, not to deal graciously with them for theirs.
      c. He wants to destroy life, not to give it (Matt. 7:15).
   2. In contrast, Jesus is the Good Shepherd.
      a. He calls His sheep by name.
      b. He gives them safety in the sheepfold.
      c. He sustains them by leading them out, and He goes before them (Ps. 23).
      d. He gives them life now and eternally (John 10:28).
II. The Relationship of the Sheep to the Shepherd.
A. They enter by the door through faith (Rom. 3:27; 4:5).
   1. They are deaf to the voice of others.
      a. False teachers (Rom. 16:17–18; Matt. 7:15).
      b. The devil, the world, and their own flesh.
   2. They hear His voice.
      a. The warnings of the Law.
      b. The encouragement of the Gospel.
   3. They follow Him.
      a. In faith.
      b. In Christ-like living.

Let us diligently hear the voice of our Good Shepherd in His Word and seek to follow Him in our lives.

HENRY J. EGGOLD

Fifth Sunday of Easter

EPISTLE   1 Peter 2:4–10 (RSV)

Sermon Notes/Introduction

Today's Epistle follows immediately the section of Peter's letter that urges us to long for the pure milk of the Word, that we may grow by it in respect to salvation. In directing our attention to this matter, the Holy Spirit makes plain for us both the gift and the goal of spiritual growth.

Sermon Outline
THE GIFT AND THE GOAL OF SPIRITUAL GROWTH

I. The Gift of Spiritual Growth. We have spiritual life only as a gift of God for Christ's sake, not as something we deserve of ourselves.
   A. Spiritual growth is *begun* by God's creation of spiritual life.
      1. Once we were no people; once we had not received mercy (1 Peter 2:10); that is, we were by nature spiritually dead.
      2. God sent His Son as the "chosen and precious" living stone (v. 4). He is called the *living* stone because He is the One who died for our sin, rose in victory, and now lives forever, and also because He gives us true and eternal life.
      3. Through faith in this living stone, we become "living stones" (v. 5), rejoicing that God has made us "a chosen race, a royal priesthood, a holy nation, God's own people" (v. 9). "Not pitied" has become "pitied."
   B. Spiritual growth is *furthered* by God's preservation of spiritual life.
      1. It is only because we "are being built up as a spiritual house" (v. 5 NASB) by God that we believe in Christ.
      2. Left to ourselves, we would be numbered with "those who do not believe" (v. 7).
   C. God uses His Gospel and the sacraments of Baptism and the Lord's Supper to begin and further spiritual growth.
      1. "Put away" is baptismal language (v. 1).
      2. "The pure spiritual milk" refers to the Gospel (v. 2).
      3. "Tasted the kindness of the Lord" calls to mind the Lord's Supper (v. 3).

II. The Goal of Spiritual Growth.
   A. The goal is *not* that we may escape dependence on God.
      1. The old Adam tells us it is a shameful thing that we believe in Jesus, trust that His substitutionary work earns for us God's favor, and do not stand on our own two feet (cf. v. 6).
      2. A subtle variation of unbelief suggests that Jesus did His part, and now we must do our part in order to

be saved. To yield to this idea is also to "disobey the Word" (v. 8).
    B. Rather, the goal is that we may make known God's wonderful deeds.
        1. We make them known when we "advertise" (*exaggeilēte,* v. 9) the redemption from darkness and sin that was brought about by Christ's death and resurrection and the marvelous light of God's love and mercy that for Christ's sake now shines on us.
        2. We make them known when, depending on God's grace more and more, we selflessly "offer spiritual sacrifices" (v. 5), which are motivated by our love for God and for our fellowmen (see Rom. 12).

May we always thank God for His undeserved gifts of spiritual life and growth; may we likewise confidently obey His will for our lives and make known to the world His wonderful deeds in Christ.

JERROLD A. EICKMANN

Fifth Sunday of Easter

GOSPEL   John 14:1 – 12 (KJV)

Sermon Notes/Introduction

John 14 is the beginning of Christ's farewell discourse, spoken, no doubt, partly in the Upper Room, partly on the way to Gethsemane. Few passages are more replete with the love of Jesus. "Let not your heart be troubled": That night much would happen to agitate the disciples. The cure for agitation is faith. *V. 2:* He promises the disciples mansions where they will enjoy His presence forever. *V. 4:* His going involved suffering. *V. 5:* Thomas was expressing doubts that others may have had also. *V. 6:* "I am the Way": Jesus prepared the way to heaven. He is the Truth; His every word may be trusted implicitly. The Truth directs the Way. Christ is the Life, the fountain and giver of life. There is no other Way, Truth, or Life. *V. 7:* To know Jesus is to know the Father (John 10:30; Col. 2:9). We know the Father by faith. *V. 8:* Philip felt that if he saw the Father, that would be enough to establish his faith. *V. 10:* Christ's word and works are not performed separately from the Father. The essence of the Father and the Son is identical. *V. 11:* He who refuses to believe Christ's Word has the unquestionable testimony of His works. Jesus repeats what He told the unbelieving Jews (John 10:38). *V. 12:* "Greater works": Converting sinners through the preaching of the Gospel is greater than healing physical infirmities. The reason Christians can perform these greater works is that Jesus is going to the Father, namely, through the cross. The great works of converting men are works of the exalted Christ.

Sermon Outline
REJOICE THAT YOU ARE A CHRISTIAN

I. You have the assurance of heaven.
   A. Jesus promises us heaven.
      1. He is going to prepare a place.
      2. He will come again to receive us to Himself.
   B. Jesus is the Way, the Truth, and the Life.
      1. He prepared the way by a substitutionary death.
         a. He paid the debt of sin.
         b. The way is now open to all.
      2. He is the Truth.
         a. He speaks the truth.
         b. He is faithful to His word.
      3. He is the Life.
         a. He is the true God and eternal life (John 1:1).
         b. He gives life in fellowship with God now and eternally (John 3:16).
   C. By faith life is ours.
      1. No man comes to the Father without Christ (Acts 4:12).
      2. By faith heaven is ours (John 3:17–18; 11:25).

II. You know the Father.
   A. The request: "Show us the Father" (John 14:8).
   B. The response: "He that hath seen Me hath seen the Father" (v. 9; Col. 2:9).
      1. Jesus and the Father are one in essence (John 10:30).
      2. The Father shares in the words and works of Jesus (John 14:10).
   C. Faith sees the Father in Christ.
      1. Faith knows from the words of Jesus that God is gracious (John 1:14–17).
      2. Faith sees in the works of both that Jesus is the Son of God and that God is all-powerful (Matt. 28:18).

III. You can do greater works than Jesus.
   A. Jesus performed mighty works.
      1. He healed the sick and raised the dead.

2. But all those whom he healed finally succumbed to physical death.
  B. By faith we can perform greater works.
   1. We can make disciples of all people (Matt. 28:18 – 20).
   2. We can tell them the Good News that Jesus, our crucified and risen Lord, has gone to the Father to prepare a place for us.

HENRY J. EGGOLD

Sixth Sunday of Easter

EPISTLE   1 Peter 3:15 – 18 (RSV)

Sermon Notes/Introduction

Verse 15 of today's text contains the Greek word *apologia*, from which comes the English word "apology." In the RSV, *apologia* is translated "defense." Such a translation reminds us that one meaning of "apology" is "an explanation, defense, or justification in speech or writing." But "apology" can also mean "an expression of one's regret for having injured, insulted, or wronged another." Keeping both meanings of "apology" in mind, let us learn today through St. Peter about offering a Christian apology.

Sermon Outline
OFFERING A CHRISTIAN APOLOGY

I. Christians should certainly be willing to offer an "apology" (that is, an expression of regret) when they do what is wrong (3:17) and thereby injure, insult, or wrong someone else.
  A. The many passages in 1 Peter that warn us against sinning (e.g., 3:10 and 4:3) make plain that God intends for His people to obey His commandments and be holy in all their behavior (1:15).
  B. If people disobey God, the terms of God's law are very plain: "The face of the Lord is against those that do evil" (3:12). Such divine opposition is a frightful prospect, and who among us can deny that he deserves it?
  C. However, the Gospel is also very plain: "Christ also died for sins once for all (*hapax*), the righteous for (*hyper*, in the place of, as the substitute for) the unrighteous" (v. 18). Such substitutionary satisfaction,

earning for us an entrance into God's gracious presence ("that He might bring us to God"), both saves us from God's anger and enables us to "have unity of spirit, sympathy, love of the brethren, a tender heart and a humble mind" (v. 8) and thus to offer an "apology" (that is, an expression of regret) when we sin against others.

II. Christians should also be prepared to offer an "apology" (that is, an explanation and defense) when they are asked about their "hope" (v. 15).
  A. The "living hope" (1:3) of Christians is beyond the comprehension of the unbelieving world.
    1. The world judges all things according to what it sees, according to externals, and it sees Christians suffering.
    2. The world, assuming that good behavior earns divine approbation and evil behavior calls forth divine condemnation, concludes that a person's suffering is always a punishment for that person's own evildoing, and therefore the world sees no reason for Christian hope in the midst of Christian suffering.
  B. Nevertheless, the lordship of Christ serves as a solid foundation for Christian hope.
    1. In Christ, we see a just person suffer and even die for all of us unjust persons (*dikaios hyper adikōn*, 3:18).
    2. Yet He conquers death, being made alive again (v. 18) and exercising His lordship over the powers of both hell (v. 19) and heaven (v. 22).
    3. Accordingly, to "reverence Christ as Lord" (v. 15) simply means the same as to trust in Him as our Redeemer. (See Luther's explanation of the Second Article of the Apostles' Creed in his Large Catechism for a magnificent treatment of the "lordship" of Christ.)
    4. Even if we suffer for doing what is right (and St. Peter frequently alerts us to that probability: 1:6; 2:19–20; 3:14, 17; 4:16; 5:10), we need fear no lack of God's salvation and blessing, since our Lord is the one to whom "belong glory and dominion forever and ever" (4:11).
    5. Assured of His lordship for us, let us gently and reverently offer an "apology" (that is, an ex-

planation and defense) for our Christian hope (3:15).

By the grace of God, we can confidently offer a Christian "apology," both in the sense of "an expression of regret for wronging another" and in the sense of "a defense for the hope that is in us." May God help us do both.

JERROLD A. EICKMANN

Sixth Sunday of Easter

GOSPEL   John 14:15 – 21 (RSV)

Sermon Notes/Introduction

Many of us have probably had the experience of walking down the tall, narrow aisles of a department store and coming on a little child crying for its mother. With a voice choking with tears, the child cries out in deepest longing: "I want my mommy!"

A child is so much more open than an adult. We may not get lost in a department store and cry out our anguish, but we do, down deep in our souls, express that basic fear: What if I am all alone in the universe? What if no one is there to hear my cry and come to my side to wipe my tears, take my hand, and lead me safely home?

This is our cry when we are lost in grief or trial or spiritual doubt. We may fill our lives with many comforts in order to stop the feeling, but even these fairly shout our fear of being abandoned. In our text for today, Jesus reaches out to His fearful, lonely, hurting followers of all ages.

Sermon Outline
I WILL NOT LEAVE YOU DESOLATE

I. The Spirit will come.
   A. The disciples felt abandoned.
      1. Jesus' words (John 14:1 – 4) bring forth Thomas's troubled question of abandonment (v. 5).
      2. The events in Jesus' life that they would experience—arrest, trial, crucifixion, entombment—furthered a feeling of abandonment.
      3. Soon would come resurrection, ascension, and Pentecost.
      4. And yet they felt the fear expressed in Rom. 8:35—who shall separate us?

SIXTH SUNDAY OF EASTER

   B. We experience the same feelings of abandonment.
      1. We experience trials, sickness, and death.
      2. All our options sometimes seem to be bad.
      3. We live with such rapid change—family problems, jobs that are threatened, nuclear threats, economic problems.
      4. It is then that we know how precarious physical life is and how weak we are.
   C. Jesus understands and promises another Counselor.
      1. He appears on our behalf—a mediator, intercessor, and helper.
      2. The Counselor is the Spirit of truth, the One who can be known and received only by faith, the One who dwells and lives in us.
   D. We are not orphaned!
      1. The helplessness and precariousness of life are ultimate and overwhelming only if we live spiritually alone.
      2. But by God's grace through the Gospel, the Holy Spirit, the Advocate, lives in us.
      3. We are not alone, abandoned, mere objects of fate, or spiritual nobodies going nowhere.
      4. By the indwelling Spirit we can say: "Who shall separate us from the love of Christ? . . . In all these things we are more than conquerors through Him who loved us. For I am sure that neither death, nor life, nor angels, nor principalities, nor things present, nor things to come, nor powers, nor height, nor depth, nor anything else in all creation will be able to separate us from the love of God in Christ Jesus our Lord" (Rom. 8:35, 37–39).
II. Jesus will come.
   A. He spoke of His leaving.
      1. He would soon leave them by dying on the cross.
      2. He would leave them by ascending back to heaven's glory.
   B. But He gave a promise.
      1. "You will see me"—the resurrection and 40 days of Jesus' earthly presence.
      2. "Because I live, you will live also"—the promise of resurrection to all who believe in Christ.
   C. He comes to remove desolation.
      1. He comes to live in us by faith (John 14:20).

2. He comes to shape love and obedience within us (v. 21).
3. He comes to give the daily resurrection of grace and the final resurrection to glory (v. 19).

All of these words were spoken at the supper table on Maundy Thursday. Soon the events that led to Jesus' death on the cross would be put into motion, and the disciples would wonder if Jesus had in fact failed and abandoned them. But on Easter Sunday He came back to deliver on His promises, and the disciples would know that He who was abandoned on the cross would, by the cross, never abandon them. By faith we know that also. The Spirit says so. The living Christ says so. "I will not leave you desolate."

RICHARD G. KAPFER

The Ascension of Our Lord

EPISTLE   Ephesians 1:16 – 23 (RSV)

Sermon Notes/Introduction

V. 16: This verse looks back to v. 15. Paul thanks God because he has heard good things about the Ephesian Christians—their faith in Jesus and their love toward one another. But the verse also looks forward and gives us a clue to the rest of the text. Both the Greek text and the RSV punctuate verses 15 – 23 as one sentence. The central thought is really Paul's intercessory prayer for the church at Corinth, which could well be a pastor's prayer for his congregation. The NEB punctuation is helpful for making an outline of the text.

V. 17: The knowledge of God is the key thought in this verse. Lenski comments that *epignōsis* is "the knowledge which really apprehends God, true realization in the heart and not merely that of the intellect." It should be a knowledge of God like that of Abraham, who "was called the friend of God" (James 2:23). We only know God personally through God the Son, Jesus (John 14:7).

Vv. 18 – 19: Paul moves on from a prayer for personal knowledge of God to knowledge of the hope that belongs to the Christian. NEB: "I pray that your inward eyes may be illumined, so that you may know what is the hope to which he calls you" (v. 18). The hope is in the "inheritance" and the "power." This same inheritance is mentioned in 1 Peter 1:4, and power is granted to the Christian now in this age; see 2 Tim.

1:7. We must be careful not to forget the power that God gives us or let our Christianity deteriorate into mere religiosity; see 2 Tim. 3:5. The living God is with us!

Vv. 20–21: The two complementary aorist participles state how God wrought His power: *egeiras* and *kathisas*. Christ was raised once and for all from the dead, and He was exalted once and for all above everything. His exaltation is also expressed in Phil. 2:9–11. The phrase "far above all rule and authority and power and dominion" (Eph. 1:21) expresses Christ's dominion over the angelic hierarchy, both angels in heaven and fallen angels. His rule is permanent and extends into the age "which is to come."

Vv. 22–23: "He has put all things under His feet" alludes to the messianic prophecy of Ps. 110:1–2, the Old Testament passage most frequently quoted in the New Testament.

On Ascension Day Christ left His disciples visibly. If a pastor knew he would soon be leaving his congregation, we can imagine what his intercessory prayer would be for it. It might well be the same as Paul's intercessory prayer for the church at Ephesus.

Sermon Outline
A PASTOR'S PRAYER FOR HIS CONGREGATION

I. Know God personally (Eph. 1:17).
   A. He is a God of glory.
      1. He is holy (Is. 6:3).
      2. He is love; He sent His Son, Jesus (Luke 2:14).
   B. He reveals Himself in His Son.
      1. There is no other way to know God personally.
      2. Knowing God is the highest wisdom of all (1 Cor. 1:21).
   C. Our friendship with God grows deeper.
      1. Listen to Him through His Word.
      2. Speak to Him through prayer.
II. Know the hope to which God calls you (vv. 18–21).
   A. You have a glorious inheritance.
      1. It is imperishable.
      2. It is kept for you in heaven.
   B. God's power in the Christian is great.
      1. He raised Christ from the dead.
      2. He made Him King of kings.
      3. He dwells within you (2 Cor. 13:5).
III. Know that God's plan for this world is in the hands of the church (vv. 22–23).

A. The church is the body of Christ.
   1. Christ as head of the body is Lord of the church.
   2. Christ has commissioned us to do His work.
B. His desire is to make the whole world the body of Christ.
   1. Christ died for all.
   2. God wants all to know it.

BRUCE J. LIESKE

The Ascension of Our Lord

GOSPEL   Luke 24:44 – 53 (RSV)

Sermon Notes/Introduction

At this time of year high schools and colleges throughout the nation are marking the end of an academic year with commencement exercises. The ending of one period of the students' lives will be noted, and the beginning of a new period in their lives will be anticipated. High school graduates look forward to jobs or college, and college graduates look forward to beginning their careers. They will say farewell to friends they may never see again or see only occasionally. It is a time of ending and beginning.

The ascension of our Lord marks an ending and a beginning also. The earthly ministry of Jesus had been accomplished. Now, as recorded in the closing words of Luke's gospel, Jesus gave final instructions to His disciples. Then He ascended on high to the position of eternal glory that He, the Son of God, had left in order to be our Redeemer. But this ending was truly a beginning, for now He would bestow power on His faithful people.

Sermon Outline
POWER FOR ENDING AND BEGINNING

I. We end and begin with the powerful Word.
   A. Jesus is the fulfillment of the Word.
      1. The sweep of salvation history covers "everything written about Me in the law of Moses and the prophets and the psalms" (Luke 24:44).
      2. Luke's gospel is a record of fulfillment. (Here the preacher will want to review Luke's theme and progression through the life of Jesus. This day provides a good opportunity to summarize Jesus'

life from John the Baptist through the ascension.)
    B. Jesus reveals Himself as the Center of the Word.
        1. He "opened their minds to understand the Scriptures" (v. 45). (Without Christ the Word becomes a mere record of ancient history.)
        2. His death and resurrection are the key that opens up the Word.
    C. The fulfilled, Christ-centered Word must be proclaimed.
        1. The proclamation is repentance and forgiveness in His name.
        2. It is proclaimed to all nations.

Scripture's purpose is not a dead end. It is a new beginning, for it has power through proclamation to bring repentance, forgiveness, and new beginnings.

II. We end and begin with the power of the Spirit.
    A. We are called to be witnesses.
        1. We witness to what the disciples had seen in Christ (past tense).
        2. We witness to what we by faith have seen ourselves (past tense).
    B. But wait! Power will come!
        1. Pentecost would "clothe" the disciples with the power of the Holy Spirit.
        2. We too begin by the power of the Spirit to witness to Jesus Christ.

A witness is one who cannot but speak and live the endings and beginnings that God by grace has bestowed. As we begin, we receive the living Christ.

III. We end and begin under Christ's powerful blessing.
    A. The ending point of Jesus' earthly ministry was the ascension.
        1. He ascended to heaven to receive all glory and honor.
        2. He ascended to bless His Church as its living, present Head through Word and Sacrament.
    B. We are blessed with joy.
        1. The disciples did not mourn Jesus' leaving; they rejoiced.
        2. This is far different from Memorial Day sadness and helplessness.
        3. He who rose is with us, and He will return at His second advent.

So, filled with joy, the disciples waited and "were continually in the temple" (v. 53). We too await the Lord's return not with sadness but with joy, not in weakness but in His power. The ascension is the ending that brought new beginnings. It is power like that of our baptism. Our earthly lives will end but will also begin again with joy and eternal life.

RICHARD G. KAPFER

Seventh Sunday of Easter

EPISTLE   1 Peter 4:13 – 19 (RSV)

Sermon Notes/Introduction

This text continues a theme developed earlier in the letter, namely, that it is the Christian's vocation to imitate Christ in His suffering (1 Peter 2:21). Speaking to people who have apparently experienced firsthand the pressures of seeking to imitate Christ in a not so Christ-like world, Peter points his readers to a recurring Gospel theme, the joy of living *for* Christ right now related to the glory of living *with* Christ later (see Matt. 5:11; Luke 12:32). The present thrust of 1 Peter 4:14 should be noted as Peter asserts the "here and now" blessing for those who are insulted on account of their relationship with Christ ("you are blessed"). The verb "insult" or "reproach" in v. 14 (*oneidizein*) is frequently associated in the gospels with the indignities endured by the suffering Christ (Matt. 27:44). Peter's reference to the Spirit of glory and of God as the cause of the present blessing (1 Peter 4:14) is surely to be taken as the Holy Spirit, who is in fact linked on several occasions in the New Testament with the suffering and persecution of God's people (see Matt. 10:19 – 20; Acts 7:55).

The point is clear: The trials of God's people are grounds for positive joy, since those who suffer for Christ have a present share of the glory of the end. The contrast of 1 Peter 4:15 is plain. Those who practice the wrongdoings listed deserve suffering, but those who suffer simply because of their standing as Christians ("under that name," v. 16) have no need to be ashamed. Significantly, this suffering is part of the glory mentioned above. The ultimate reason for the tribulation of God's people (v. 17) rests with the unfolding of God's plan for the end. As preparation for the close of history, the people of God will be purified by tribulation (see Mark 13:8 – 13). This is not a pleasant picture, but the courage and determination of God's people should be strengthened by the knowledge of what awaits those who do not "obey the Gospel of God" (1 Peter 4:17). The quote from Prov. 11:31 (Septuagint) is sobering (v. 18). If God uses trials and suffering to strengthen us and finally spare us, we can, as Peter concludes, continue our "active well-doing" (*agathopoiia*) and entrust ourselves to the One who is in complete control, the faithful Creator.

The central thought of the text is that the suffering of God's people has both a present blessing and a future glory as the Lord uses tribulation to keep pointing us to His faithfulness. The goal of the sermon is that the hearers will recognize that suffering because of their standing as Christians is not pointless. The problem is that we can often recognize no logical value in Christian hardship. The means to the goal is that our faithful Creator gives us unmistakable glory as evidence that our trials have both a present and final purifying value.

It is a natural tendency to view hardship and difficulties as valueless. They signal lost opportunities and wasted time as people are forced, when they occur, to focus attention on them rather than on positive growth. Proper Christian thinking, however, would dispute the logic of worldly people who view tribulation as something of no value. The Lord uses suffering to prepare and purify His people for the end, as well as to give them blessing and glory right now. This is hardly nonsense, even though Christians may ask how hardship can be called glory.

Sermon Outline
HOW CAN YOU CALL THIS GLORY?

I. Hardship is an imitation of Christ's suffering.
   A. We count it a privilege to suffer at the hands of the world, even as He did.
      1. The world may not kill us, but it despises our trust and love.
      2. The world cannot understand how we can rejoice when we are condemned, because the world cannot understand our willingness by grace to imitate our Savior.
   B. We remember the victory of One who suffered with a purpose.
II. Hardship is an indication of Christ's blessing.
   A. We know that the Lord will be at our side when we are insulted on account of our relationship with Him.
      1. This presence is a great blessing.

            2. This presence brings us glory.
        B. We acknowledge that even though we may experience pain and hardship, our place in the "household of God" (v. 17) will lead us to endure and rejoice.
    III. Hardship is a proclamation of Christ's salvation.
        A. We confess that the trials of this life are part of God's plan of salvation by which He seeks to outfit His people for the life to come.
        B. We rejoice to receive the judgment of our faithful Creator as He prepares us for the end.
            1. This judgment strengthens us so that we can by His grace endure.
            2. This judgment spares us so that we are graciously "scarcely saved" (v. 18).

It is natural to view hardship only in a negative way, but we have the assurance from our faithful Creator that suffering for Jesus' sake is our blessing, glory, and preparation for the end. The world may ask how we can call hardship "glory," but by faith we are convinced that the Lord's special presence and purpose in suffering can lead us to call suffering exactly that—glory!

DAVID E. SEYBOLD

Seventh Sunday of Easter

GOSPEL   John 17:1 – 11 (RSV)

Sermon Notes/Introduction

1. This well-known pericope offers such a wealth of theological themes that the preacher may have difficulty choosing! One unifying idea might be the theme of "glory," so important in John's gospel, as well as throughout Scripture, as a motif expressing God's indwelling "real presence" with mankind. Although Jesus had given up the glory of heaven to come down to man, He nevertheless manifested the glory of God incarnate (John 1:14). Now in this closing chapter of His "final discourse," Jesus asks to be glorified "with the glory which I had with Thee before the world was made" (17:5). However, the purpose of the incarnation and the means of that glorification lie within His present situation—the "hour" of His Passion.

2. Verses 6 – 11 turn attention more specifically to the disciples and all people. Jesus has revealed the "name" of God

to mankind. Throughout Scripture the "name" of God involves much more than a "handle"; it shows insight into the very nature of God Himself. The Gospel of John emphasizes Jesus' identity with the Old Testament name of God ("Yahweh" or the "I Am" of Ex. 3:14) not only through the many "I am" sayings but especially in 8:58, where Jesus claims the name as His own. The "I Am," who began His work in creation, promised a Savior to His Old Testament people, and redeemed Israel from Egypt, now will bring the revelation of His love and justice to fulfillment in the climactic action of redemption in Jesus Christ.

3. Stressed again in verse 7 is the "knowledge" of God, which is eternal life (17:3). "Knowledge" in Biblical thought is much more than facts and figures; it involves an intimate relation, a commitment, a "oneness" (compare Hebrew yd). At the end of verse 8 "they ... know" is virtually paralleled by "they have believed."

4. Finally, Jesus prays for the oneness of His disciples, that they may share in and model the complete oneness of the Father and the Son, based on incorporation into the body of Christ (v. 21), the "one, holy, catholic, and apostolic church." This oneness is something far greater than the formal recognition and external unity so often sought by contemporary ecumenism. Rather, it is based on the deepest level of faith relationship and confession through Word and Sacrament (which Jesus had just shared with His disciples), through knowledge of the Word and His "words" (vv. 7 – 8).

Sermon Outline
THE GLORY OF THE CROSS: OUR SAVIOR'S FINEST HOUR

Many are glory seekers and define glory in any number of ways. As is often the case, God's definition is strikingly different.

I. God's glory is the cross.
   A. Jesus has come as God's "glory" incarnate, as God with us. But now, after the ascension, we remember that Jesus has returned to the glory of His Father in heaven. Like the disciples between Ascension and Pentecost, we may wonder what glory is ours now that Jesus is no longer physically with us.
   B. Yet Jesus says that He has come to share God's glory with us, to reveal God's name to mankind, so that we may know God and have eternal life.
   C. Sinful man could not share in this glory unless sin were

forgiven. No sinner can stand in the presence of the Holy God and live—except by God's grace.

D. Thus God's plan of salvation, of sharing His glory, sends Jesus on a path back to His Father via the cross, where the Lamb of God takes away the sin of the world. This is Jesus' "hour," His moment of accomplishing the work that the Father sent Him to do.

II. Our glory is the cross.

A. Our road to the glory of the presence of God is blocked by sin and by God's just punishment on sin.

B. But in the cross our Savior has already made a way back to God via the forgiveness earned by His death. In Baptism we are buried and raised with Christ and walk that road to the glory of God.

C. In our crucified, risen, and ascended Lord, we have knowledge of God and know His name. We know the Word made flesh and the "words" He gave us: This is eternal life.

D. Our lives, too, are full of crosses, of the evidence of sinful people in a sinful world (note the Epistle).

True glory does not mean seeking what glory seekers want, but rather it means knowing the cross of Christ and believing that the Father sent His Son for us. Even though Jesus has ascended, His cross stands front and center in our lives (and in our churches), and His real presence is with us in the glory of His body and blood, given and shed for the forgiveness of sin.

ANDREW H. BARTELT

Pentecost: The Day of Pentecost

EPISTLE   Acts 2:1 – 21 (RSV)

Sermon Notes/Introduction

Luke is careful to develop the contrast between the believing community ("they were all together in one place," Acts 2:1) and the devout Jerusalem Jews (v. 5). The coming of the Spirit had the effect of bringing these groups together with positive results (see v. 41). The exact nature of the miracle of the Spirit's arrival is hard to describe. Luke uses comparisons—like the sound (noise) of wind and like flames that resembled tongues. The speech of those who received the Spirit was quite intelligible, yet it was foreign to them. Each spoke a meaningful language, readily understood by those who were from the part of the world in which it was used. The word Luke uses for speaking means, according to both Septuagint and classical references, solemn and inspired speech, but not ecstatic utterance.

The miracle of Pentecost should properly be identified as one of both speaking (v. 4) and hearing (v. 6). Words were the vehicle of the Spirit, both as attention-getters (v. 7) and as substance-providers (vv. 14–15), as Peter with the disciples spoke to an attentive audience of the unfolding of God's plan of salvation. The quotation from Joel (2:28–32) about the Day of the Lord was at least partially fulfilled in the events occurring before the crowd's eyes. It is a day of salvation (v. 21); that is the key to Pentecost. The phrase "being saved" has many dimensions. It implies first that a person is in an undesirable state (moral or physical). Then there is relief from this condition by the action of another. And finally, there is a positive change and restoration, enabling the person truly to live.

The central thought of the text is that the miraculous arrival of the Holy Spirit, in all its detail, shows the power of Spirit-directed words in gaining the attention of people, leading them to hear, and helping them to call on the Lord who can save them. The goal of the sermon is that the hearers remember that salvation is a Spirit-wrought miracle of both speaking and hearing, using words and the Word. The problem is that we have too much difficulty both listening and speaking, and even when we hear the Spirit-inspired Word, we forget to pass the message along. The means to the goal is that the Spirit continues to come to us in the spoken and heard Word to assure us of our salvation and to encourage us to speak of it.

Parents often admonish their children for not listening. They have to tell them repeatedly to finish their chores, to eat correctly, to develop good personal habits. Many mistakes on the job are also made because workers have not listened to directions. Too often we abuse words by not listening to them carefully or by treating them too casually. This attitude is spiritually risky because, as the miracle of Pentecost announces, the careful speaking and hearing of the Word means salvation.

Sermon Outline
HEARING IS BELIEVING

I. Spirit-directed words are for hearing.
   A. The Spirit came in a miraculous way to get people to listen.

1. The crowds were attracted by men speaking in their own languages.
   2. Though some mocked, most listened as the disciples spoke the Spirit's words.
  B. The Spirit continues to enter the hearts of people through the ears of people.
   1. God's Word is a spoken and heard Word that is effective only in the Spirit-directed context of a speaker and a listener.
   2. The Spirit opens both mouths and ears. People can never speak or listen without His power.
II. Spirit-directed words are for saving.
  A. The message of the Spirit announces salvation.
   1. His words through Peter proclaim the Day of the Lord as God comes to people.
   2. Those who have heard and call on the Lord by His power will be saved (v. 21).
  B. The work of the Spirit assures salvation.
   1. As He continues to come to people through the Word, the Spirit brings comfort and hope that salvation is sure.
   2. Those who have heard and been saved will joyfully speak the Word and share the Spirit's work of saving.

God's plan of salvation, which has come to us through the Spirit-directed hearing of His Word, includes using us, who have heard, as His mouthpieces to speak, so that others by hearing may also believe.

DAVID E. SEYBOLD

Pentecost: The Day of Pentecost

GOSPEL   John 16:5 – 11 (RSV)

Sermon Notes/Introduction

The inability of Jesus' disciples to understand the necessary course of events in God's salvation plan is the not too surprising undercurrent that affects this text. Often Jesus explained, and often they grasped very little. This occurred even though the Savior was careful to spoon-feed His handpicked followers only as much as He thought they could handle at one time (cf. John 16:4). As the hour of His death and eventual departure approached, however, Jesus knew it was time to tell

His disciples why He had to leave them. Predictably, they did not really understand (v. 5), and in fact, they would not understand until the events that Jesus described finally took place. The incredible miracle of Pentecost surely confirmed exactly what the Lord had told His followers. It was the eventual and dramatic arrival of the Spirit that began the unfolding of the scenario described by Jesus in this text.

The central thought of the text is that the coming of the Counselor establishes the divine continuation of the work begun by Jesus as the Spirit enlarges the task of convincing the world. The goal of the sermon is that the hearers will be involved in the Pentecost miracle by the convincing work of the Spirit in their own lives. The problem is the common failure to understand our need to be convinced, as if our understanding is complete enough and needs no further growth. The means to the goal is the Spirit's power, which can through the Word convince, soften, and bring movement to stubborn and stagnant hearts.

Occasionally situations arise in which people have to admit that they have done as much as they are able and that further efforts would have little effect. This may happen to a physician treating a seriously ill patient or a teacher working with an uncooperative student. In similar fashion Jesus realized that His ministry had a limit beyond which it was important for someone else to keep the message moving. Having the assurance of the successful completion of His task, He could confidently announce to His disciples that, although He would physically depart, the Counselor would be sent to continue the work.

Sermon Outline
KEEPING THE MESSAGE MOVING

I. The Spirit convicts the world of sin.
   A. Faith cannot exist for long in the presence of a defiant, sinful life-style.
      1. Unbelief is to be expected in a sinful environment (v. 9).
      2. The growth of sin effectively crowds out spiritual growth.
   B. Faith can exist in the presence of the kind of convicting work that the Spirit has undertaken.
      1. In the Word of the Law He convicts by accusation.
      2. In the Word of the Gospel He heals by promise.
II. The Spirit convicts the world of righteousness.

A. The arrival of the Spirit was God's announcement that Jesus had completed His work with success and distinction.
   1. He completed His task so that the Spirit could begin His work on a worldwide scale.
   2. Jesus' departure is evidence that what He accomplished is righteous and perfect and complete (v. 9).
B. The arrival of the Spirit was the next step in convincing the world that righteousness has triumphed over wickedness.
C. The arrival of the Spirit provided the opportunity for more people to "see" Jesus than could ever have seen Him physically (v. 10).

III. The Spirit confirms the world of judgment.
A. Because the Spirit came, the judgment against Satan is confirmed (v. 11).
   1. The ruler of this world could not stop God.
   2. He was unable to control God's plan and its movement onward.
B. Because the Spirit came, the victory of Jesus over sin is final and universal.

As Jesus departed and the Spirit arrived, God confirmed that the plan was moving ahead just as He wanted it to. The message was clear: The world is sinful and Satan has been judged. Hope rests alone with the righteousness of the Savior, who defeated sin and Satan, and with the Spirit, who arrived to keep this message moving to all people.

DAVID E. SEYBOLD

The Holy Trinity:
First Sunday After Pentecost

EPISTLE   2 Corinthians 13:11 – 14 (KJV)

Sermon Notes/Introduction

1. The familiar benediction (v. 14), mentioning all three persons of the triune God, is the obvious link between the Epistle and Trinity Sunday and between the Epistle and the other readings assigned for this day.

2. The connection between our text and the preceding context is equally obvious. Positioned at the end of Paul's

second letter to the Corinthian congregation, a letter that frequently deals firmly and bluntly with his readers' problems, our text, by way of contrast, sounds a positive, upbeat note. More specifically, in verse 2 of this last chapter Paul says, "If I come again, I will not spare," and in verse 10 (the verse immediately preceding our text) he says, "Therefore I write these things being absent, lest being present I should use sharpness." In fact, in our text Paul practices what he preaches, using "the power which the Lord hath given me to *edification* and not to *destruction*" (v. 10, emphasis added). In so ending his letter, however, Paul provides more than a literary contrast—he provides us with pastoral precedent, teaching us in our treatment of congregational problems to deal with people evangelically and to deploy the power of the Gospel, ultimately the only solution to all problems.

3. A more subtle link between text and context is the fascinating similarity between the "threeness" of God described in verse 14 and Paul's triple request of God in 12:8 to remove his "thorn in the flesh" and his mention of a contemplated third visit to his readers in 12:14 and 13:1.

4. There is likewise a curious "threeness" in the content of our text: (1) vital greetings within the Corinthian congregation (vv. 11–12); (2) encouraging greetings from the church-at-large (v. 13); and (3) empowering "greetings" from the three persons of God (v. 14)—specifically, "grace" from Jesus, "love" from the Father, and "communion" from the Holy Spirit.

5. The structure of verse 11 is a microcosm of the structure of the entire text—a progress from specific to general, from small to large, from horizontal to vertical. Verse 11 begins with a farewell to Paul's readers and concludes with a benediction from God. The remainder of the text continues in this direction, moving from the "holy kiss" of verse 12 to the trinitarian blessing of verse 14, from the greetings from one another to the "greetings" from God. Might this not suggest two provocative truths? (1) Our majestic, awesome triune God cares about the minutest concerns of our everyday lives (even the very hairs of our head, Matt. 10:30). (2) The horizontal (our relations with one another) depends on the vertical (our relation with the triune God).

6. The relationship between the first and last parts of verse 11 is not that good conduct (first part) receives its reward (second part). Paul is not suggesting that if the Corinthians live

at peace with one another, they will merit a visitation from the God of peace. Rather, the relationship between the two parts is that of goal and means. That is, the Corinthians can live at peace with one another only if they are empowered by the presence of the God of peace. To make assurance doubly sure, Paul repeats this idea in verse 14. That verse is neither a polite farewell nor a pious wish; it is an earnest prayer that the God of all power will empower Paul's readers in the specific virtues he has urged on them. Only His grace, love, and fellowship can make it all happen.

7. Overly familiar as we may be with the words of verse 14, they can still tell us much about the nature of our God. Notice the verse's unusual combination of abstractions and persons. While Paul uses three abstractions ("grace," "love," and "communion"), he makes clear that God is not an abstraction. He is not a personification; rather, He is persons, three of them in fact—Father, Son, and Holy Ghost. Even the Holy Spirit, whose very name may tempt us to associate Him with abstraction, is carefully distinguished from the abstraction "communion" that is associated with Him in verse 14. On the other hand, awesome and majestic as the three persons of God are, they are closely associated, practically synonymous, in fact, with warm and winsome traits: "grace" associated with Jesus, "love" with the Father, "communion" with the Holy Spirit. The point is that love is not God but that God is love. Our God is not a sort of Cloud Nine Deity raised to the nth power. He is a three-person God, whose love has teeth in it, whose love has objects. His love creates. His love redeems. It does things. The Father spares not His own Son for our sakes. The Son enters history to live, die, and rise in our behalf. The Holy Spirit literally comes to us through Word and Sacrament and resides in our bodies.

Sermon Outline
THREE KINDS OF GREETINGS

I. The vital greetings within the local congregation (vv. 11–12).
   A. A pastor gives his members a farewell-greeting (v. 11a).
   B. The members are to greet one another with specific virtues in their everyday associations (v. 11b).
   C. The members are to greet one another with a holy kiss that is symbolic of their unity (v. 12).
II. The encouraging greetings from the church-at-large (v. 13).
   A. They give support with their prayers.

B. They support with their gifts (spiritual and material).
C. They support with their ministry of the Word.
III. The empowering "greetings" from the triune God (v. 14).
A. Father, Son, and Holy Spirit send these "greetings."
B. The "greetings" are grace, love, and communion.
C. The "greetings" can empower our greetings to one another.

FRANCIS C. ROSSOW

The Holy Trinity:
First Sunday After Pentecost

GOSPEL　　　　　　　　　　Matthew 28:16 – 20 (RSV)

Sermon Notes/Introduction

Remembering the great deeds of God for His church on Christmas, Easter, and Pentecost, it is most fitting that we give this day to the praise of the Holy Trinity, the one true God, whom we are taught to worship as Father, Son, and Holy Spirit.

Worship of God is the unique privilege of those to whom God has made Himself known. There are multitudes who seek after God, hoping to find Him in themselves. But all they can find is the echo of their own individual ego. Many seek God in nature. But confusing the works of God (nature) with God must lead either to the proliferation of weird fantasies or to the arrogant pretensions of scientific knowledge built on fictitious assumptions. The God whom we worship is known to us only in Jesus Christ, His Son, our Redeemer: "In Christ God was reconciling the world to Himself, not counting their trespasses against them, and entrusting to us the message of reconciliation" (2 Cor. 5:19). Whatever else can be known of God but has not been revealed to us in the Scriptures we reserve in hope as the joy of the life to come.

But here we worship God, we praise and adore Him, we bless His holy name by means of all the arts at our disposal, and we thank Him because He is our life, our preserver, and our hope for the glorious life to come. Our text gives us sharp and clear directions.

Sermon Outline

IN THE NAME OF THE FATHER AND OF THE SON AND OF THE HOLY SPIRIT

Before His suffering and death, our Lord Jesus had repeatedly instructed His disciples generally (not merely those close to Him) to meet with Him after His resurrection at the mountain location appointed for this purpose (see Matt. 26:32; 28:7, 10; Mark 14:28). This very likely was also the occasion to which St. Paul referred when he wrote that "more than five hundred brethren at one time" (1 Cor. 15:6) saw the risen Christ and worshiped Him and thereby became witnesses of His resurrection.

Suddenly, Jesus appeared among the gathered disciples on the mountain and gave them instructions for the age of grace just now beginning. Possessed of all power, He commanded them to baptize "in the name of the Father and of the Son and of the Holy Spirit" (Matt. 28:19).

I. The Command.
   A. Jesus, the Son of Mary, now uses the plenary power given to Him in His incarnation. In the name of the triune God, Christ's people are to go forth into all the world to make disciples of all nations.
   B. In the name of the triune God they are to teach and baptize.
      1. They baptize so that the Father will be *their* Father, the Son will be *their* Redeemer, and the Holy Spirit will dwell in them for *their* sanctification.
      2. They teach believers to obey or guard (*tērein*) all things that Christ has commanded.
II. The Content of the Command.
   A. The name of the Trinity—Father, Son, and Holy Spirit—is also the missionary power or dynamic of the Christian church.
      1. The name of the Trinity becomes meaningful to the hearer when the character (qualities, attributes) and the work of each Person are known.
      2. The name of the Trinity is the Christian's dearest treasure because he identifies his own life, salvation, and future with this name.
   B. The name of the Trinity—Father, Son, and Holy Spirit—is also important for the Christian's daily life.
      1. It is the content of our worship every Sunday and whenever we gather about Word and Sacrament.
      2. It is the comfort of our days here on earth.

Our Lord's last words on this appearance, "I am with you always, to the close of the age" (Matt. 28:20), are a gracious reminder, as well as an abiding comfort, that "in Him we live and move and have our being" (Acts 17:28). In His promises we are secure, and by His supporting Word we live.

RICHARD KLANN

Second Sunday After Pentecost

EPISTLE   Romans 3:21 – 28 (KJV)

Sermon Notes/Introduction

A careful study of the Pauline epistles demonstrates that in the apostle's mind all time was divided into the "then" and the "now." The "then" was everything that had happened before Christ died; the "now" is everything that is contingent on the death of our Savior. The text for the Second Sunday After Pentecost is a good example of this motif in Paul's thought.

The first two words of the text, "But now ...," introduce a second great division of the Epistle to the Romans that extends from 3:21 to 4:25. The word "therefore" in the preceding verse (20) indicates the conclusion of the first division of the epistle. In that division the sinfulness of man is unveiled, but now in this second division we are to see the righteousness of God as it is revealed in Christ.

Sermon Outline
RIGHTEOUSNESS REVEALED

"*Therefore* by the deeds of the Law there shall no flesh be justified.... But now ..." All the world is guilty before God, "but now" God offers the sinner the free gift of His righteousness. Man has no merit of his own, "but now," since our Lord Jesus Christ has come "to seek and to save that which was lost," sinful man may stand in the presence of God. In other words, Paul speaks about the righteousness of God.

I. The righteousness of God (vv. 21 – 22).
   A. It comes "without the Law" (3:21). The righteousness that avails before God cannot be found in the Law. Our salvation is from God and cannot be obtained by obeying the requirements of the Law.
   B. It was "witnessed by the Law and the Prophets" (3:21). God had this redemption in mind from the beginning. Moses represented the Law, and he depicted this righteousness in direct prophecy and in shadow and type. He recorded God's first promise of

the Redeemer (Gen. 3:15); it was he who first wrote that Christ should come through the nation of Israel and the tribe of Judah (Gen. 12:3). The righteousness of God in Christ was also "witnessed by . . . the prophets," all of whom had one testimony concerning the Messiah, just as Peter said in the house of Cornelius (Acts 10:43).

    C. It is received through faith (Rom. 3:22). The KJV's "by faith of Jesus Christ" is best translated "through faith in Jesus Christ"; the genitive is objective. The righteousness that avails before God is received by faith in Christ Jesus. What does it mean to have faith in Christ? It means to know and accept as true that Jesus, by the shedding of His blood and His suffering and death on the cross, redeemed you from sin, from death, and from the power of Satan, and it means to trust in this Savior for salvation. This gift of righteousness is "unto all . . . that believe."

II. We are justified freely by His grace (vv. 24–26).

    A. "By His grace" (v. 24) enlarges on what this salvation does. When man is clothed in this beauty that is not his own, the beauty of the Lord is placed on him. *Then* the message of v. 24 is realized. That man is justified! Justification not only forgives sin, but it imputes righteousness. The grace of God, which justifies, has been actively manifested in the redemptive work of Christ. The redemption (*apolutrōsis*) is the act of buying a slave out of bondage in order to set him free. Israel's redemption from Egyptian bondage (Ex. 15:13) provides an Old Testament background to Paul's language.

    B. Christ is our "mercy seat" (Rom. 3:25–26). The basis on which God can justify a man is set forth here. "Propitiation" (*hilastērion*) may be taken either as the accusative singular masculine of the adjective *hilastērios* or as the neuter substantive *hilastērion*, used to denote "place of expiation" (*kapporeth*, the "mercy seat"). The death of Christ is the means by which God offers us forgiveness, as at the "mercy seat" God's people of old were offered forgiveness of sins (Lev. 16).

III. Boasting is excluded (Rom. 3:27–28).

    A. "Where is boasting then?" (v. 27). The answer is, "It is excluded." There is no room for spiritual pride. We are saved through faith. No one can boast.

B. "A man is justified by faith without the deeds of the Law" (3:28). Luther underlines "without the deeds of the Law" by adding the adverb "alone" after "by faith."

Paul's "then" and "now" theme is well drawn as he reveals the righteousness that avails before God. The preacher is advised to use appropriate illustrations of this as he again sets before his congregation the truth of this central doctrine.

JOHN F. JOHNSON

Second Sunday After Pentecost

GOSPEL   Matthew 7:21–29 (RSV)

Sermon Notes/Introduction

1. The text is composed of three units of thought that form the conclusion of Christ's Sermon on the Mount. Our text (esp. vv. 24–27) should be understood as Christ's call to respond to His preaching. The emphasis of the first two units (vv. 21–23 and 24–27) is the same: Christ is going to judge all men on the basis of whether or not they really *do* His Word. The third unit (vv. 28–29) records the crowd's response to Christ's sermon—astonishment at His authority.

2. In the first unit Jesus makes plain that it is indeed possible for people to exhibit outstanding outward signs of obedience to God's will—worship ("Lord, Lord"), preaching and teaching, and even casting out demons and performing mighty works (*dunameis pollas*), all in Christ's name (vv. 21–22)—and still have no real relationship to Him.

3. In the second unit, the well-known parable of the two builders, Jesus' point is that only the person who both hears and does (*poiein*) His words has a basis for standing before Him in the judgment. Those who choose another basis are foolish and will fall (vv. 26–27).

4. Doing the will of the Father must be seen from two perspectives. From the viewpoint of the Law, *no one* has a basis for standing before God, since none has ever done God's will (inwardly or outwardly). Thus Jesus' words bring us face to face with our failure. From the vantage point of the Gospel, however, *everyone* has a basis for standing before God since the God-man, in harmony with His own will, perfectly fulfilled His Father's will (both inwardly and outwardly) for us. By God's surprising method of justification, Jesus' perfect hearing and

doing of His Father's will is counted as everyone's hearing and doing. The hearing and doing that Jesus requires is what He also freely gives by grace through faith. His is the doing that counts before God, and it is His gift to all! Miraculously, once one has this gift, he actually begins to hear and do God's will himself in loving response.

5. The goal of the sermon is to move hearers to examine the basis on which they expect to stand in Christ's judgment and to strengthen them in their confidence in Christ's obedience and suffering for them as the only foundation. Thus they will have a firm basis for discipleship.

Sermon Outline
WHO WILL STAND IN THE JUDGMENT?

In the midst of the church year, just after Pentecost, it may seem strange to contemplate Christ's final judgment. That is usually reserved for the end of the church year. Yet as we meditate on our role as disciples, we need to be certain from the outset that we have the right foundation. Thus the Gospel for today raises the question, Who will stand in the Judgment?

I. It is *not* the one who stands on a mere outward performance of Christ's Word (vv. 21–23).
   A. God requires not merely an outward performance of His will but the proper fear, love, and trust in the heart.
   B. Many now say "Lord, Lord," preach and teach in Christ's name, and perform mighty signs to whom Christ will say, "I never knew you; depart from me, you evildoers" (v. 23).
   C. Now is the time for each of us to examine whether the outward performance of our Christian lives is motivated by true fear and love of God.
II. It is *not* the one who stands on a mere hearing of Christ's Word while building his life on another foundation (vv. 24–27).
   A. Only one foundation is acceptable to God—actually doing His will. When Christ preaches His Word, the response He seeks is not just hearing but incorporating the Word at the center of one's life, committing one's eternal destiny to it, and making it one's foundation.
   B. Those who hear Christ's Word but choose another foundation on which to build their lives will be washed away in the deluge of His judgment.
   C. Now is the time for us to probe our hearts to see if we

are merely hearing Christ's Word while building our lives on another foundation.
III. *Certainly* the one who stands on the solid foundation of Christ's hearing and doing (inwardly and outwardly) the will of God for him will stand in the Judgment.
   A. Christ did the will of His Father in heaven. He fulfilled all the requirements of the Law so that all people have a basis for standing in the Judgment.
   B. Christ carried the cross to a rock called Golgotha and there poured out His blood so that all may stand on the rock of His forgiveness.
   C. God the Father has proclaimed that His Son's punishment is completely sufficient and has lifted the sentence of eternal death from every person.
   D. The Holy Spirit now delivers the Father's verdict of "not guilty" in Christ to all hearts through His Good News, offering them the certainty that in Christ they can stand in the Judgment.

TERENCE R. GROTH

Third Sunday After Pentecost

EPISTLE   Romans 4:18 – 25 (RSV)

Sermon Notes/Introduction

Since the Fall our world functions abnormally, and humanity as a whole has run off the track on which God initially set it. At various times we all have to face this reality, which may challenge our hope, security, or joy. Sin takes its toll (health, relationships, world events, etc.). For the believer, there is only one answer to the reality of a fallen world and that is to trust in the promises of God, which are ours through Christ Jesus our Lord. There is hope and power for living when the believer trusts moment by moment in those promises. Trusting in the promises of God is the only answer to the reality of life in a fallen world.

It has been observed that when faced with unpleasant realities, some people dream of castles in the sky, some people live in them, and others comfort themselves by collecting the rent. The question before us this morning is how do we as God's people deal with the sometimes stark and unpleasant realities of the world in which we find ourselves.

Sermon Outline
A FAITH FOR THE REAL WORLD

I. The realities of life may not look hopeful.
   A. The realities of life did not look hopeful for Abraham.
      1. He had to face the reality of no offspring (Gen. 15:1–3).
      2. He had to face the reality of both his and Sarah's ages (Rom. 4:19).
   B. The realities of life have not looked hopeful for many others of God's people.
      1. Examples abound in the Scriptures of believers facing situations that did not look hopeful (Israel at the Red Sea, David facing Goliath, the disciples in the midst of a storm on the Sea of Galilee, etc.).
      2. Contemporary examples also abound of the realities of life that seem crushing. (Here personal examples from one's own life experiences would be appropriate.)
   C. The realities of life may not look very hopeful to you at times, maybe at this very moment. (At this point the preacher should paint with as much vividness as possible the realities that people in the congregation might be facing, such as unemployment, marital or family problems, fears about the economy or world events, guilt, issues concerning old age or loneliness, etc. It is important to be as concrete as possible.)

The realities of life in our fallen world can be stark and sometimes frightening. However, we must never forget that our gracious Father equips us to deal with those realities victoriously.

II. Faith in the promises of God equips God's people to face the realities of life in a fallen world.
   A. Faith in God's promises equipped Abraham to live in the real world.
      1. Abraham, through faith, maintained his hope even in the face of a seemingly hopeless situation (v. 19).
      2. Abraham, through faith, did not "waver concerning the promise of God" (v. 20).
   B. Faith in God's promises will equip you to face the realities of your world.
      1. God, our Father, has made many personal promises to you that become real in your life through Jesus (forgiveness, help in time of trouble, strength

to endure, the prospect of a new world coming, the promise to work for our good in all things, etc.).
2. Let us therefore be persuaded as Abraham was that God can and will deliver what He has promised.
   a. Let our hope be unquenchable.
   b. Let us not stagger at the promises of God; we shall stand strong in Christ.

Trusting the promises of God in Christ will give us the victory in the face of the realities of living in the 20th century and will, in addition, bring into our lives certain other benefits (blessings).

III. Faith in the promises of God in Christ brings wonderful blessings into our lives.
   A. Abraham's faith proved to be a blessing.
      1. His faith was "reckoned to him as righteousness" (v. 22).
      2. It was confirmed and strengthened as God kept His promises, and Abraham witnessed their fulfillment.
   B. Your faith will prove to be a blessing.
      1. Your faith in Christ is the foundation of your relationship with God the Father (Romans 5).
      2. Your faith will be confirmed and strengthened. God's promises are real and certain and will come to pass. You will witness their fulfillment (2 Tim. 1:12; Heb. 10:22 – 23).

In Christ Jesus, our Lord, God the Father has given us marvelous promises to cope with the realities of life that we all face. Let us be persuaded beyond any doubt that even when situations do not look hopeful or are discouraging, faith in God's promises will fully equip us to live victoriously and will bring wonderful blessings into our lives. Truly we can say that trusting in the promises of God is the only answer to the reality of life in a fallen world.

MARK R. OIEN

Third Sunday After Pentecost

GOSPEL   Matthew 9:9 – 13 (RSV)

Sermon Notes/Introduction

To begin sermon preparation the following questions might be helpful to get some insights into this text:

What is the theme of the text for this sermon? How does this theme fit into the overall thrust of the propers? What particular needs or problems of the people can be addressed through the text? What unique Gospel power is available for the people to be strengthened and edified?

When reading this text, one is struck with the simplicity of the call to Matthew and the actions and reactions that follow. There is an echo back to chapter 4, where Jesus said the same words to four fishermen and changed their lives forever. Focusing on the call of Jesus to Matthew, one is impressed with the power of the simple words "Follow Me." The actions of Jesus, who is looking for those who need forgiveness, are probably the highlight of the Gospel message here. One might feel that the second section of the text, beginning at verse 10, carries a much different theme than the first part, but considering that Matthew does follow Jesus, one can see how the ideas mesh. The text would then emphasize the action of the call and the results of its acceptance. The thrust is the exciting Gospel call of Jesus to a notorious sinner, inviting him to a whole new way of life. The sections of dialog that follow serve, therefore, to indicate why the call was issued at all and for whom it was intended, leading to the theme: When Jesus calls to follow, the follower can expect radical change in life.

How do the propers relate to this theme? In the Old Testament Reading (Hos. 5:15 – 6:6), there is talk of illness and healing, distress and comfort, death and life. This fits nicely into the second part of the Gospel text, as does the correlation of ideas between the call of God to His people, expressed in the Matthew reading, and the call of God to Israel in the Hosea text. In the Epistle (Rom. 4:18 – 25), one also sees the bodily illness (mortality) analogy. Abraham in his old age was given a promise that led to a radical change in his life; an old man fathered a baby! The "Follow Me" call (promise) of God demonstrates the grace of God working through Jesus Christ to offer salvation and a radical change of life (see this motif clearly spelled out in the last verses of the Epistle).

There is, therefore, a rather good harmonization of the three readings for this Sunday.

The question about the needs or problems of the people must be answered specifically by each pastor as he thinks of his congregation. Nevertheless, several general needs can still be cited. Is there not in our world today a great premium placed on leadership? What problems arise when the Gospel suggests that a higher calling is to be a follower? Another need of the people is to see the global dimension of the mission of the church in contrast to the self-centered parochialism in congregations, which suggests that the needs in this little place with this group of people are the most important. Therefore, we see two pivotal needs or problems that the people have: (1) their desire to be in control of everything, including their salvation, and (2) their narrowness of view, which prevents an exciting global reaching out to others with the Gospel of the One who calls all to follow Him.

The final question is answered: God is here in His Son, Jesus Christ, showing through a word written particularly for Jewish readers that He would bring all men to Himself. Notice that it is Jesus who confronts Matthew. Matthew asks for nothing. It is God who extends the invitation. It is God who is in action to redeem His people. It is God, addressed as the Creator in the prayer for the day, who would have all creatures brought back to Himself.

Given the above, it should be a rewarding task for each pastor to put together an outline through which he may convey the theme of this text and the power of its Gospel to change lives. What follows might be one way of doing it.

Sermon Outline

I. The call of God to people is evidence of His grace.
II. The radical change in people's lives is the result of the call.

DANIEL H. POKORNY

Fourth Sunday After Pentecost

EPISTLE   Romans 5:6 – 11 (RSV)

Sermon Notes/Introduction

When God's law has done its work, we experience the depth of our sinfulness. Facing the fact of who we are according to our human nature and of who God is according to His perfect and holy nature, we can sometimes get troubled and wonder, Does God really love me? Am I really one of His beloved children, or am I just fooling myself?

There are many possibilities the preacher could pursue with this text. One would be to focus on the depth of our Father's love for us. The love of God in Christ Jesus has broken through into our lives "in spite of" the fact that we were helpless to effect our own righteousness; "in spite of" the fact that we were sinners, who separated ourselves from God and fell in love with the world; and "in spite of" the fact that we were rebels, convinced of the sanctity of our revolution against the true and the living God.

How then can God love us? More specifically, how can God love me, when I find myself a sinner, rebelling against the will of God for my life? The love of God in Christ breaks through it all! The penetrating power of the Gospel is the ground of our unshakable confidence in God's undying love for us. The love of God in Christ breaks through every obstacle.

The great Houdini was a master of breaking out. (A little research on the life of this great escape artist will provide ample material for an attention-getting and interesting introduction.) This morning we want to focus on the greatest master at "breaking in."

Sermon Outline
LOVE CONQUERS ALL

I. The love of God in Christ broke into our lives when we were helpless (Rom. 5:6).
   A. We were helpless to seek the true God—without strength and without desire.
      1. We had totally lost our sense of direction.
      2. We had zero capacity to retrace our steps back into fellowship with the true and living God.
   B. However, "while we were still weak, . . . Christ died for the ungodly" (v. 6).
      1. We were lost, but Christ sought us out. (The parable of the lost sheep would be appropriate at this point.)
      2. The love of God in Christ continues to break into our lives when we feel helpless and have lost our sense of direction.

Not only did the love of God in Christ break into our lives when we were helpless, but Christ broke through when we were still trapped in our sin.

II. The love of God in Christ broke into our lives "while we were yet sinners" (v. 8).
   A. God did not wait until we showed some glimmer of worthiness.
      1. He would have waited forever.
      2. We had long passed the point of no return.
   B. God did not give us a little grace and then sit back to see what we would do with it.

1. God's grace does not come in installments.
2. We were not in a position to accept anything from God. (The cup of reception was tipped upside-down.)

C. "God shows His love for us in that while we were yet sinners Christ died for us" (v. 8). God acted decisively on our behalf on the cross of Calvary and broke through the wall of separation that our sin had built.

D. The love of God is still based on that decisive act in history when Christ died not for the righteous, but for sinners like you and me.
1. The same power of the cross convinces us that "in spite of" our sin we are forgiven and loved.
2. The same power of the cross produces discontent with sin.
   a. We are moved to repentance by the power of the cross.
   b. We are motivated to change by the power of the cross.

As if it were not bad enough that we were helpless and trapped in sin, God had one more obstacle to overcome in His passion to convince us of His love.

III. The love of God in Christ broke into our lives while we were enemies of God (v. 10).
A. We were enemies of God because our human nature, devoid of the Holy Spirit, was at war against God.
1. The natural man feels guilty but believes there is no remedy.
2. The natural man consequently fears God.
3. Therefore, the natural man sees God as the enemy and fights (actively resists) the entrance of God into his life.

B. While we were enemies, "we were reconciled to God by the death of His Son" (v. 10).
1. In spite of our resistance to peace with God, the war is declared over on the basis of Christ's reconciling death on the cross.
2. We are children of God by faith in Christ. We are no longer God's enemies, for we have peace with God.

The love of God in Christ Jesus our Lord broke into our lives when we were helpless, while we were yet sinners, and while we were enemies of God. Can there be any question, any doubt, that the love of God in Christ has broken through every obstacle? Be assured that nothing—nothing will keep the love of God in Christ out of your life. After all, He is the master of all time at "breaking in."

MARK R. OIEN

Fourth Sunday After Pentecost

GOSPEL   Matthew 9:35 – 10:8 (RSV)

Sermon Notes/Introduction

Christ's church can never afford to relax in its mission of disciple-making. Our Lord's words in this text still call us to more fervent activity: "The harvest is plentiful, but the laborers are few" (Matt. 9:36). While careless misapplication of this text should be avoided, the pastor ought to use a text such as this to encourage young men and women to consider professional service to their Lord in the various ways offered in His church.

Textual notes—v. 35: The imperfect verb *periēgen* suggests Jesus' constant activity and also the unfinished nature of it. Of the three participles (*didaskōn, kērussōn,* and *therapeuōn*) note that two of them deal with the Word, which was always primary in our Savior's ministry, which was to be primary in the apostles' ministry (cf. 10:7), and which must also be of primary concern to the Lord's church today. *Tēs basileias* is an objective genitive. The Good News about the Kingdom was the content of the Gospel Jesus was preaching. *V. 36:* The verb *esplagchnisthē* is one of the strongest words rendered "compassion" and is used in the Greek New Testament only of God and His Son; note the periphrastic construction (*ēsan eskulmenoi kai errimmenoi*) emphasizing Israel's hopeless confusion and "lostness." *V. 37:* Note the *men ... de* construction, which highlights the heart-rending contrast between the abundant harvest and the lack of laborers. *V. 38:* The harvest always remains the Lord's and not ours (*autou*), for God "gives His Spirit where and when it pleases God."

However, it is also true that the harvesting of God's elect is directly tied to the use of God's appointed means of grace, as this text clearly shows. Three times in this pericope Matthew very carefully points out that this special "commissioning" was spoken to a select group (the apostles) and not to everyone, reminding us that we should not carelessly imply to people today that they can expect such *exousia* (10:1) over demons and sickness. *V. 6:* The present imperative *poreuesthe* implies that they should keep on going. V. 7: The substance of their preaching is once again *ēggiken hē basileia tōn ouranōn*. What is this "kingdom"? Martin Scharlemann says simply that it is God "active redemptively in order to reestablish His rule over and among men" (*Proclaiming the Parables* [CPH, 1963], p. 45). The perfect verb *ēggiken* suggests that in Jesus the kingdom is here. V. 8: These miraculous works verified the apostles' unique authority, and the signs and wonders done by our Lord's apostles (recorded in the Gospels and especially in the Acts of the Apostles) still serve to authenticate their written word, which the Church proclaims today.

In the past year many Americans have been rightly concerned about unemployment, but our text makes it clear that there don't have to be any unemployment lines in the Kingdom. Our Lord always needs more workers.

Sermon Outline
WANTED— KINGDOM WORKERS!

I. Workers are needed who share His compassion for the lost.
   A. An entire world of confused and lost sinners lies before us (9:36); we were also at one time part of that confused and wandering crowd (*ochlous;* cf. 1 Peter 2:25; Eph. 2:12).
   B. Our Lord's unmerited compassion moved Him to come to our world to seek and to save the lost by dying for the world's sins and bestowing the forgiveness of sins by the Gospel (v. 35); His undeserved compassion moved Him to seek and to find us with His life-imparting Gospel in our baptism.
   C. Our Lord wants His forgiven and renewed people to share His compassion for the lost (v. 38).
II. Workers are needed who are sure of their call and mission.
   A. Just as no one will work without having been hired, so no one will work in God's kingdom without having been rightly called to do so; our Lord carefully called the apostles by name (10:2 – 5); this same Lord has carefully called each of us by name in our baptism.
   B. He gave the apostles careful instructions as to their particular mission (vv. 5 – 6). He has also given us our mission today (Matt. 28:19; Mark 16:15); some He calls to full-time Kingdom work as pastors, missionaries, etc. (Eph. 4:11; 1 Tim. 3:1), but all His baptized people are called to testify to His grace by word and deed (2 Cor. 5:15; 1 Peter 2:9).

III. Workers are needed who have been properly equipped for their work.
  A. Jesus equipped His apostles with their necessary tool—the message about the Kingdom, the Word (Matt. 10:7). It is the same Word about Christ that His church is to take into the world today (Mark 16:15). God's own almighty power always accompanies His Word (Matt. 10:8; Rom. 1:16) and is inherent in it.
  B. Christ gives individual gifts and talents to His people to be used in service to His kingdom (compare and contrast the different apostles, vv. 2–4). So today our Lord gives His people differing gifts and talents (1 Cor. 12). Our Synod has established colleges and seminaries in order to develop those gifts and talents and to equip people for professional service in His church.

There will never be any unemployment problems in Christ's church. Moved by His Holy Spirit, let us eagerly and joyfully serve our Lord in our respective callings, whether professionally or nonprofessionally, as we sing, "Let none hear you idly saying, 'There is nothing I can do.' ... Answer quickly when he calls you, 'Here am I. Send me, send me!' "

STEVEN C. BRIEL

Fifth Sunday After Pentecost

EPISTLE   Romans 5:12–15

Sermon Notes/Introduction

1. Connection with other Series A readings for this Sunday: The Old Testament Reading (Jer. 20:7–13) records the complaint of the writer over God's apparent abandonment of him in his sufferings for the Lord's sake, yet it celebrates God's ultimate rescue of His servant. The Gospel (Matt. 10:24–33) clarifies that the plight of Jeremiah is not unique to him but is representative of God's ministers of reconciliation; disciples are not above their Master, and, therefore, like Him they will experience persecution, but God's providential care will always be equal to—in fact bigger than—man's predicament. The connection of the Epistle with the above readings may not be immediately apparent. Yet there seem to be two possibilities. To begin with, our text deals with the basic cause of the evils detailed in the other readings—original sin. It states the gener-

alization for which the other pericopes provide the documentation. Further, our text, like the other Series A readings, demonstrates that the divine solution is always bigger than the human problem, whatever it may be. Where sin abounds, grace does much more abound.

2. Verses 13 and 14 mention the long interval of time between Adam and Moses not merely to demonstrate the tragic impact of Adam's sin on his descendants, even though the law of God had not yet been formally established through Moses, but also to show that the blessed results of Christ's obedience and sacrifice apply to the people of that era also. If sin and death abounded then (and they did), grace abounded much more—then as well as now.

3. The word "death" of course means death in the fullest sense—spiritual and eternal death as well as physical, the *opposite* of life as well as the *end* of life. The sin we inherit from Adam does more than sever soul from body; it severs us from God forever. Adam's sin does more than dig a grave for us; it prepares a place in hell for us! What the Bible often joins together in the word "death" (loss of the life of the body *and* loss of the life of God), we do well not to put asunder.

4. Adam, according to verse 14, is a "figure" or "type" of Christ. We must be sure to understand the point of comparison, namely, that the effect of each one's act is universal. In Adam's sin all die; in Christ's atonement all live. But here the similarity ends. The text—in fact, the entire chapter—goes on to point out the numerous contrasts between Christ and Adam. Adam, at best, is only a negative and incomplete parallel to Christ.

Sermon Outline
WHERE SIN ABOUNDED, GRACE DID MUCH MORE ABOUND

All the readings for this Sunday realistically display the ugliness of sin, a testimony unfortunately confirmed by the witness of our everyday lives. In today's text we learn not merely the cause of this problem but, above all, God's marvelous solution to it.

I. In Adam's sin we all die.
   A. Adam disobeyed God, his Creator.
   B. His sin became our sin (v. 12).
      1. We inherit the blame for his sin (vv. 12–13).
      2. We inherit his predilection for sin.
   C. His penalty became our penalty (v. 12).

1. In disobeying God, Adam committed spiritual suicide; he lost the life of God.
2. In disobeying God, Adam also committed spiritual murder; in, with, and under his death we too died.
   a. We are dead already in this life. Even though we breathe, move around, eat, work, play, etc., we are "dead in trespasses and sins."
   b. Without God's marvelous intervention, we would have been completely (and horribly) dead in the next life. Physical death would have been the gateway to eternal death in hell—total severance from the life of God.

II. But in God's grace through Christ we all live!
   A. Jesus obeyed God, His Father.
      1. He came to earth to do God's will (Heb. 10:7; John 4:34).
      2. He did God's will perfectly, meeting all the tests Adam had failed to meet (active obedience).
      3. He was "obedient unto death, even the death of the cross" (passive obedience).
   B. His obedience became our obedience (Rom. 5:19).
      1. However guilty we are in fact, we are credited with Christ's own righteousness (2 Cor. 5:21).
      2. However predisposed to sin we are, we receive from Christ power to begin to be righteous in our everyday lives (John 15:5).
   C. His blessedness becomes our blessedness.
      1. We too are sons of God.
      2. We too share in the life of God.
         a. We share it to an exciting degree already in this life.
         b. We share it completely (and ecstatically) in the next life. Physical death, thanks to Christ, is now the gateway to eternal life in heaven—total union with the triune God.

The marvelous things that God through Christ prepared for all men become ours individually through faith in Christ. And wonder of wonders, even this faith in Christ is God's gift to us through the Good News about Christ. Don't we have a wonderful God?

FRANCIS C. ROSSOW

Fifth Sunday After Pentecost

GOSPEL　　　　　　　　　　Matthew 10:24 – 33 (RSV)

Sermon Notes/Introduction

1. A likely theme for relating the concerns of this pericope is fears that interfere with the mission of proclaiming the Gospel (see vv. 26, 28, and 31). The message of Jesus to His disciples is that He is their strength to overcome such fears so that they can proclaim His Word.

2. Verses 26 – 27 suggest one fear that might interfere with the disciples' mission, as well as the resource for overcoming this fear and the response when it has been overcome. Perhaps the disciples may fear that the evil intentions of their enemies will remain *kekalumenon* and *krupton* ("covered" and "hidden") and thus subvert their mission and keep the Gospel *kekalumenon* and *krupton*. In other words, the Gospel mission may fail! Jesus assures the disciples that the evil intentions of their enemies, as well as the Gospel, will be *apokaluphthēsetai* ("revealed") and *gnōsthēsetai* ("made known"). The use of the passives here suggests an effort by someone other than the disciples—namely, by their Master! Since the success of the Gospel is assured, the disciples can get on with the business of being part of its success story—proclaiming publicly ("upon the housetops") the Gospel that they have learned privately (literally, "in the ear").

3. Another interfering fear is suggested in verse 28—fear that the disciples' opponents may kill them. History shows that this fear was not unfounded. Nonetheless, the disciples can take courage from the fact that men have power to kill only the body (*sōma*), while their soul or spirit (*psychē*) will live on with their Lord in eternal life, awaiting the resurrection of the body and soul. With the proper fear and love of God the disciples will proceed on their mission—proclaiming the Kingdom.

4. Verses 29 – 31 provide positive Gospel assurance for a third unstated interfering fear—fear that if proclaiming the Gospel does not cost one's temporal life, it may still cost temporal welfare. Perhaps the disciples will be in want of their "daily bread." By means of two beautiful illustrations, Jesus assures His disciples of their heavenly Father's gracious and certain providence in their lives. Surely the God who is so intimate that He even knows the number of hairs on their heads

and is so protective of His creation that not even a sparrow (worth half a cent) dies without His permission, surely this God will take care of Jesus' disciples, who are the crown of creation (and "of more value than many sparrows"—emphasis by understatement). Once again, the fear is disarmed and the disciples are liberated to "acknowledge [Christ] before men" (v. 32).

5. The goal of the sermon is to expose to hearers the fears that interfere with their proclamation of the Gospel in word and deed and to empower them to overcome such fears by the strength of Christ in the Gospel.

Sermon Outline
JESUS KEEPS FEAR FROM INTERFERING

Have you ever been so afraid that you were kept from doing something you really wanted to do or knew you should do? Has fear ever kept you from expressing in word or deed the message of Christ? In the Gospel for today, St. Matthew records a sermon of Christ to His disciples that shows how Jesus keeps fear from interfering.

I. The Fear of Failure (vv. 26 – 27).
   A. Like Jesus' disciples, we may be tempted to fear that the proclamation of His Gospel in our words and deeds may come to naught.
   B. Jesus overcomes such fear with the promise that His message will not fail. It will be as victorious as was He in overcoming sin, death, and Satan for us.
   C. Therefore, we are liberated to proclaim His glorious message "upon the housetops."
II. The Fear of Death (v. 28).
   A. The fear of bodily death was well-founded for Jesus' disciples. While it may not appear imminent for disciples of Christ in North America today, we would do well to ponder its possibility and our reaction.
   B. Jesus overcomes fear of bodily death with His promise of life eternal with Him and the eschatological promise of the resurrection of our bodies.
   C. Therefore, we are liberated to proclaim Him as the Lord of life and death.
III. The Fear of Want (vv. 29 – 31).
   A. Although we may not be threatened by death, like Jesus' disciples we may be tempted to fear that our proclaiming of Jesus' message may cost us some of the

necessities of life.
- B. Jesus overcomes this fear with His beautiful promise of God's intimate and extensive providence.
- C. Therefore, we are liberated to acknowledge Him before men as the good and gracious Lord, who provided for our ultimate need on Good Friday.

Because Christ overcame all possible threats to His mission for us, we can be confident that He also provides us with His strength and comfort to keep fear from interfering with our discipleship. The ultimate reward of such discipleship is that He will acknowledge us before His Father in heaven.

TERENCE R. GROTH

Sixth Sunday After Pentecost

EPISTLE   Romans 6:2b – 11 (RSV)

Sermon Notes/Introduction

For us who have "died to sin" (Rom. 6:2) to be still living in it is as ridiculous as a physically dead person reacting to stimuli. The dying to sin occurred in our baptism (v. 3), which brought us into union with Christ so as to identify us with Him. To be buried (v. 4), one must have died, which is Paul's way of emphasizing that Baptism so connected us with Christ's death that we died to sin. Then Baptism also has power to effect a new life (v. 4). Walking in newness of life presupposes a resurrection analogous to Christ's. As Christ died and rose again, so we died to sin in order to rise to a new life (v. 5). Because our sinful self was crucified (v. 6), our body is no longer enslaved to the power of sin (v. 7). Christ by His death broke the power of sin and is done with both sin and death (v. 9). So it is with us. Not only have we been delivered from eternal death, but the new man in us has taken over now. We are to live in such a way that sin dominates no longer in our life (v. 11).

The central thought of the text is that in Christ we are dead to sin and alive to God. The goal of the sermon is that the hearers will live as the new people they are. The problem is that we often let sin assert its power in our lives. The means to the goal is our baptism, by which we became partakers of Christ's victory over sin.

Who of us does not want to live right and do what is good? A source of power for such living is our baptism.

Sermon Outline
OUR BAPTISM GIVES POWER FOR RIGHT LIVING

I. Our baptism made us dead to sin.
  A. In our baptism our old self was crucified with Christ (v. 6).
    1. Nothing less than crucifixion could destroy sin's power to control us.
    2. Now we do not have to be enslaved by sin.
  B. It makes no sense to live in sin.
    1. We ought not respond to evil desires when our old self has been "killed."
    2. We ought not play with sin when we are done with it, as surely as Christ is done with it once and for all (v. 10).
  C. While the decisive victory has been won, the battle with sin is not over.
    1. We must live in such a way that sin does not get control of us.
    2. When sin tempts, remember that your baptism has made you dead to sin (Col. 3:9; Gal. 5:24).

But there is a positive as well as a negative side to our living.

II. Our baptism made us alive to God.
  A. In our baptism we were raised with Christ from death to life (Rom. 6:8).
    1. Only God, who raised Christ, could raise us also.
    2. The evidence of this life is the newness of our walk (v. 4).
      a. We bear fruit for God (7:4).
      b. We no longer live for ourselves (2 Cor. 5:15).
      c. We set our minds on things above (Col. 3:2).
  B. It is natural to live as the new people we are.
    1. Good thoughts, attitudes, and actions are an integral part of our new self.
    2. No wonder Christians on the last day will not even be aware of their good deeds (Matt. 25:37).
  C. Yet it will take effort to live as the new people we are.
    1. The resurrection power of Christ given us in our baptism will impel us.
    2. Our aliveness through our baptism will spur us.

Our baptism happened once but has ongoing significance. It is a continual source of power for right living.

GERHARD AHO

Sixth Sunday After Pentecost

GOSPEL   Matthew 10:34 – 42 (RSV)

Sermon Notes/Introduction

Albert Schweitzer agonized long over Matthew 10. He attempted to find a pathological flaw in Jesus' psychological makeup. His search led him to conclude that Jesus was a deranged psychotic, suffering from paranoia.

We do better by affirming Jesus' integrity as the Son of God and also by seeing the prescription of this text as the ongoing condition of the apostolic church. Above all, it emphasizes the total reliance of the disciple on the grace of God in converting us to faith, supplying our needs, and assuring us of our final reward. This is the specific Gospel that every weary worker in the Kingdom wants and needs.

The pattern for mobilizing the saints for service is clearly enunciated. It was prescribed in the Messianic utterances of the Old Testament and fully revealed in Jesus' own Messianic ministry. Not only the Twelve but also all subsequent disciples follow the etchings of His life.

Sermon Outline
ARM YOURSELF WITH THE MIND OF CHRIST

I. A Reminder (vv. 34 – 35).
   A. He brings not peace but a sword.
      1. The Prince of Peace will not have a cheap peace—the peace of compromise with the world.
      2. His peace destroys sin and all love of evil, and it creates the new man in Christ. It is His last will (John 14:27 – 31).
   B. A separation is required that cuts through all relationships.
      1. The church, which has its roots in the quiet privacy of the home, now roots out every sinful relationship, even that between parents and children.
      2. With the divisions of enmity removed, the home is now the most pure church.
      3. This is part of the woes of the daughter of Zion, namely, that the kingdom of peace will be ushered in with the conflict of those who are in close physical union.

II. A Warning (Matt. 10:37 – 39).
      A. What constitutes worthiness?
         1. There is nothing wrong with loving father, mother, son, or daughter per se—this is even commanded, for example, by the Fourth Commandment.
         2. The lesson is the "more than me"—a question of priority. Other loyalties must be defined.
      B. Take up the cross!
         1. The pattern of Christ's suffering is the outline of our ministry.
         2. It tells us that grace alone can make and keep the disciple.
      C. Find life or lose it.
         1. Life, *psychē*, is the life principle. It refers to temporal life and what supports it. To lose that life in contrition and faith is to find eternal life.
         2. This again points to grace—nothing in us but God's enabling power toward us.
   III. A Promise (vv. 40 – 42).
      A. The disciple is the extension and vehicle of Christ Himself.
         1. The persuasive call of the Gospel goes out through us.
         2. The peace of forgiveness rests on those who receive the messengers of God.
      B. The disciple's work is never in vain.
         1. The most menial service (a cup of cold water) rendered to His messengers shall receive a reward.
         2. The blessings of grace are assured to us, and through us they are scattered to others.

G. WALDEMAR DEGNER

Seventh Sunday After Pentecost

EPISTLE   Romans 7:15 – 25a (RSV)

Sermon Notes/Introduction

Man is a complex being composed of contradictory aspects—body and soul, spirit and flesh. Man also has varied reactions to the world, ranging from elation to depression, from courage and determination to fear and trepidation. The Christian adds another dimension of duality in that he is regenerate but has remnants of his former unregenerate state. He is subject to conflicts both in the world outside and in the private universe within.

In our text St. Paul speaks of this conflict and shows how basic it is for all people. However, the Christian realizes even more acutely these antithetical forces within.

Sermon Outline
WARFARE

What Paul says here applies only to the regenerate man; only he can recognize the conflict that exists between the flesh and the spirit, between the sinner and the saint as the Christian engages in his life of constant warfare.

I. The Reason for the Warfare.
   A. We have inherited original sin.
      1. There is nothing we can do to prevent it (Rom. 5:12).
      2. There is nothing we can do to avoid it (6:20).
   B. The will of man is opposed to God.
      1. Sin shows itself in man's will, which when left to itself, always decides to do what is evil and revengeful against God.
      2. Paul was emancipated, but the flesh was still left (7:17).
II. The Conflict.
   A. The Christian is both carnal and spiritual.
      1. The carnal nature makes war on God.
         a. It does not fight against the flesh.
         b. It does not understand the things that belong to the Spirit of God.
         c. It dissents from the Law and would prefer that the Law did not exist.
      2. The spiritual nature fights evil.
         a. It does not intend or desire evil and does not sin deliberately.
         b. It wills to do good but does not always know how.
   B. The whole man, composed of flesh and spirit, is the location of the conflict in our day-to-day life.
      1. "I want" and "I hate" refer to and apply to the spiritual nature.
      2. "I do" refers to the carnal man (v. 15).
      3. Evil lies close at hand. There is an extraneous

power working against the spiritual side (vv. 17, 21).
        4. The inner man delights in the law of God, but another law is warring against God's law and brings him into captivity (v. 23).
III. The Victory.
    A. In the struggle we cry out for deliverance (v. 24).
        1. Only a regenerated man can say this; it is a plea for God's mercy.
        2. It does not refer to our physical body but to the sinful, fleshly body that carries with it spiritual death.
        3. It echoes Paul's statement: "My desire is to depart and be with Christ" (Phil. 1:23).
    B. In victory we cry out in thanksgiving (Rom. 7:25).
        1. The name Jesus points to Him as the Mediator, the God-man (1 Tim. 2:5).
        2. As Christ He is the promised Messiah, whose blood covers all our sins and whose sinless life replaces all our mistakes and shortcomings.
        3. As our Lord He is the sovereign, omnipotent Creator and Ruler of the universe, who sympathetically watches over us and protects us during all the battles of our earthly warfare and guarantees our ultimate victory.

Sin is present and pervasive. We have to deal with all its unpleasant consequences constantly. Christ has overcome sin and reduced its strength and hold over us. The result is that we can grow in sanctification and become more and more saintly as we strive with the aid of the Holy Spirit to overcome evil and perform good. Take courage. This is a painful battle for us now, but our Lord has guaranteed a victory for us forever.

GEORGE S. ROBBERT

Seventh Sunday After Pentecost

GOSPEL Matthew 11:25 – 30 (RSV)

Sermon Notes/Introduction

One of the greatest obstacles facing a person who begins to realize, through the working of the Holy Spirit, that he is a sinner is the opposition of his flesh to the teaching of Scripture that a person can do nothing on his own to save himself from God's judgment and wrath. Sinful flesh and pride also continue to rise up in the life of a Christian and tempt him to ask, Isn't there something I can do to contribute to my soul's salvation? Isn't there some good in me? Am I really any worse than other people whom I can name? Shouldn't I get some credit for the good things I do? In the face of such temptations our text invites us to consider Jesus' words of invitation and promise of refreshment and rest.

Sermon Outline
THE YOKE OF REFRESHMENT AND REST

I. It is hard to accept the implications of original sin and actual sin.
   A. People find it very difficult to accept the implications of original sin, namely, that people born into this world are spiritually dead and even enemies of God (John 3:7; Rom. 8:7).
   B. People find it difficult to accept the limitations of their intellect and of their actions when it comes to satisfying the judgment of God due them because of their actual sins (1 Cor. 2:14).
II. Believers in Christ are still in the flesh.
   A. Human pride continues to gnaw at the believer's conviction that Jesus Christ alone is the basis and source of spiritual life and salvation.
   B. The believer's sinful flesh would like to lead him to think that the observances of rites and ceremonies or acts of service and sympathy toward our fellowmen must somehow be added to what Jesus Christ did for us.
III. We need Jesus' words of invitation and promise.
   A. Jesus invites us daily in the words "Come to Me!" The God-man Jesus Christ reminds us that He made the full and final payment for all of our sins.
   B. Jesus assures us, "I will give you rest." Our Lord reminds us that He paid the full price for our guilt before God and that He rose as Victor over sin and death. Jesus offers us rest and refreshment as He did to the paralytic: "Take heart, My son; your sins are forgiven" (Matt. 9:2). He continues to offer us His personal assurance of full forgiveness through Word and Sacrament. His words also point forward to the re-

freshment and rest that will be ours at the end of days in Christ's Church Triumphant.
C. Jesus promises, "My yoke is easy, and My burden is light." Our Redeemer took the full blast of God's anger on Himself. Through faith in Christ the believer has been freed from the curse of the Law. The follower of the Lord Jesus is refreshed through the Gospel and finds rest in the assurance of the complete forgiveness of sins. He is now free to serve God joyfully and willingly.
D. Jesus encourages His disciples, "Learn from Me." Christian freedom is not license or liberty to live as man pleases but to live as God pleases. In a spirit of Christian freedom and rejoicing, the believer accepts the privilege and responsibility of being a disciple of his Lord.
   1. He tries to learn all that Jesus Himself taught, as recorded in the Holy Scriptures.
   2. He tries to witness to his Lord and Savior by words and actions.
   3. He brings the message of this text and similar passages of Scripture to those who are ill physically and/or spiritually.

God would have all believers in Christ trust and rejoice in the assurance of life and salvation sealed with the death and resurrection of the God-man Jesus Christ, "who for the joy that was set before Him endured the cross, despising the shame" (Heb. 12:2). Jesus Christ, one with the Father, invites us to go to Him, to find full salvation and spiritual rest in Him through Word and Sacrament, and to take from Him the yoke of refreshment and rest so that we may serve Him in true freedom, joy, and gladness here in time and hereafter in eternity.

ARTHUR F. GRAUDIN

Eighth Sunday After Pentecost

EPISTLE   Romans 8:18 – 23

Sermon Notes/Introduction

Everyone has to find some explanation for tragic suffering. People ask why when suffering comes. The best explanation we can find is in Rom. 8:18 – 23. These words of Paul enable us to deal with the questions and emotions that arise in the midst of suffering.

Sermon Outline
GOD GUARANTEES US A GLORIOUS FUTURE

I. God directs our destinies toward a hopeful outcome.
   A. Of itself creation is subjected to futility.
      1. Think of the philosophy of nihilism.
      2. Note the myth of Sisyphus, who was condemned continually to roll a stone up a hill only to have it roll down again.
      3. As a result of the Fall we all suffer frustrations, "thorns and thistles."
   B. By the will of God we are subjected to suffering in hope.
      1. Suffering reminds us that we must live each day in hope of the fulfillment of God's plan.
      2. The hope we now have in God brings motivation to our lives.
II. God will glorify His suffering children.
   A. The sufferings of this present time can be tolerated when we know what the future has in store for us.
   B. The glory that is to be revealed is so majestic and worthwhile that it encourages us to bear the pain of our present suffering.
III. God will reveal a marvelous fulfillment of His plan for His waiting sons.
   A. Creation waits with eager longing for the end that lies in store for it.
   B. God will reveal a dramatic climax of His plan for His sons.
IV. God will free us from the decay of death.
   A. Creation will be set free from its bondage to decay.
   B. We shall all obtain the glorious liberty of the children of God.
V. God will deliver us from travail.
   A. Creation has been groaning in travail until now.
   B. God will redeem our bodies along with the material creation in the new heaven and new earth.

HAROLD H. ZIETLOW

Eighth Sunday After Pentecost

GOSPEL　　　　　　　　　Matthew 13:1 – 9 (18 – 23)

Sermon Notes/Introduction

There can be little debate about the meaning of the parable of the sower because in vv. 18 – 23 of this same chapter, our Lord gives an authoritative, straightforward interpretation of it. The task of the preacher is to enable this clear Word of the Lord to be heard by 20th-century ears. The following outline will primarily center on the good soil and what enables it to bear fruit.

"Mary, Mary, quite contrary, how does your garden grow?" Well, it depends on a number of things, not the least of which is the soil. So it is for the Christian; the condition and attitude of the soil (the heart) are critical to spiritual responsiveness and fruitfulness.

Sermon Outline
GOOD SOIL PRODUCES GOOD FRUIT

I. Good soil hears the Word (Matt. 13:23).
   A. Good soil has heard the converting Word.
      1. The converting Word is God's first intervention in our lives (1 Peter 1:23).
      2. The converting Word transforms us into good soil.
      3. The converting Word is God's power for salvation (Rom. 1:16).
   B. Good soil hears the sanctifying Word.
      1. The sanctifying Word is God's continuous call for us to grow (cf. 1 Thess. 4:3).
      2. The sanctifying Word is God's continuous call to service (Eph. 2:10).
II. Good soil understands the Word (Matt. 13:23).
   A. The Word is understood only through the work of the Holy Spirit.
      1. The human disposition by nature is set against the truth of God in Christ (Rom. 8:7).
      2. The Holy Spirit, by softening our hard hearts and making us into good soil, graciously works understanding (1 Cor. 12:3).
   B. The Word is then understood in the light of the cross.

1. The theology of the cross alone reflects the truth of God in Christ (1 Cor. 2:2).
2. The theology of the cross alone produces the fruit God desires.

III. Good soil lives the Word (Matt. 13:23).
A. The Word is lived through an inward change of attitudes.
1. The inward attitude toward God changes (Rom. 8:15).
2. The inward attitude toward our neighbor changes (Matt. 22:39).
B. The Word is lived through an outward response.
1. The outward response of a Christian toward God is worship (Ps. 26:8).
2. The outward response of a Christian toward his neighbor is service (Matt. 7:12).

MARK R. OIEN

Ninth Sunday After Pentecost

EPISTLE   Romans 8:26 – 27 (RSV)

Sermon Notes/Introduction

After instituting the Lord's Supper, in order to prepare His disciples for what was about to take place, Jesus spoke about the Spirit as Comforter (John 14:15 – 17, 26).

In Romans 8 St. Paul stresses the role of the Holy Spirit, who speaks glorious words of comfort to the children of God. In this chapter Paul refers 21 times to the Holy Spirit and stresses His role in leading us to faith and in nourishing and sustaining us in faith despite our human weakness and the pressures and temptations of our sinful age.

Our text is most intimately connected with the Epistle for last Sunday. Therefore, we need to go back to verse 22 and work through verse 27 to note Paul's wonderfully comforting message in its immediate context.

Sermon Outline

THE SPIRIT'S ROLE IN THE LIFE OF THE CHRISTIAN

I. The Spirit enlightens and strengthens us.
A. The Spirit has enlightened and sustained us.
1. Through His work we have become "sons of God" (Rom. 8:14).

2. Paul speaks of the "firstfruits" of the Spirit (v. 23).
   a. For the meaning of "firstfruits" and its implications in the Scriptural thought pattern, see Num. 18:12–13, Deut. 26:1–15, and 1 Cor. 15:20.
   b. Paul stresses that as "sons of God" we have the firstfruits of the Spirit. In this context Paul speaks of the Holy Spirit as the firstfruits.
   c. Through the ongoing work of the Spirit, we shall receive and experience a certain, eternal hope.
3. Elsewhere Paul elaborates on this as a seal or guarantee to assure us (2 Cor. 1:22; 5:5; Eph. 1:14).

B. We yearn to be freed from evil (Rom. 8:18–23).
   1. We still live in this evil age and face its challenges.
      a. Our present sufferings include our innate sinfulness, temptations to sin, the frailty of the body affected by sin, and misfortunes and trials that are part of our earthly life as followers of Jesus.
      b. Paul stresses that these are not worth comparing with the future glory to be revealed in us.
   2. The Spirit assures us as we eagerly wait to be freed from evil (vv. 24–25).
      a. Christ has won the victory over the Evil One (1 Pet. 3:18–19; 1 Cor. 15:55–58).
      b. The Spirit through Word and Sacrament nourishes the certain hope that in God's time will be revealed in us.
      c. The Spirit empowers us to live out the implications of Christ's victory (1 Cor. 15:58; Rom. 12:1).

II. The Spirit pleads for us.
   A. In our weakness we groan inwardly as we yearn for our adoption as sons (Rom. 8:18–23).
      1. We often lack patience and steadfast adherence to our certain hope.
      2. We are unable to use as we should the means God gives us to strengthen our patience and our hope and trust.
      3. Sometimes we don't know how and for what we ought to pray.
   B. The Spirit intercedes for us (vv. 26–27).

1. The Spirit knows us most intimately, as the Scriptures emphasize (1 Kings 8:39; Ps. 7:9; 23; 139:1–2; Prov. 15:11; Jer. 17:10; Acts 15:8).
2. The Spirit uses our human groanings as He intercedes for us in a God-pleasing manner.
3. This is a source of great comfort, especially as we face the inability to articulate what troubles us.

Of great comfort also is the fact that we have a Mediator at God's right hand in heaven (1 Tim. 2:5–6). The apostle John also stresses the role of Christ as Redeemer and Mediator with the Father (1 John 2:1–2).

ERICH H. KIEHL

Ninth Sunday After Pentecost

GOSPEL   Matthew 13:24–30 (RSV)

Sermon Notes/Introduction

1. "When God is active redemptively in order to reestablish His rule over and among men, this work is like" (Martin H. Scharlemann, *Proclaiming the Parables* [CPH, 1963], p. 45) the puzzling spectacle in the parable of the tares. Yet here is a simple message with "terrifying Gospel" (Luther in one of his sermons on the Gospel of the wedding feast), and it is *Gospel!* "If it is bitter medicine, it is wholesome medicine" (Martin H. Franzmann, *Follow Me: Discipleship According to Saint Matthew* [CPH, 1961], p. 98). Jesus makes sin serve grace. Man's will to master God invokes judgment (now and later); He takes away (Matt. 13:12). But to him who has (does not seek to master God but submits wholly to His Word and working), more is given (a clearer vision of the Kingdom and the Christ). Go from sower to Jesus and this parable enriches you; if not, the same parable judges you. Therefore, "He who has ears, let him hear" (v. 9).

2. The Evil One sows weeds where God sows wheat, weeds that look like wheat. Read Jesus' explanation of this parable (vv. 36–43). (God is His own interpreter, and He will make it plain.) Jesus is the farmer. The field is the world. Good seeds are believing disciples. Weeds are unbelievers. The enemy is the devil. The harvest is Judgment Day. The harvesters are angels. God rules, "the righteous will shine like the sun" (v. 43), and "evildoers" will be thrown "into the furnace

of fire" (vv. 41–42). Wait for the hour of God's judgment, and look forward in patience to the time of your own glory!

3. The pointed purpose of this parable is precisely in the purgeless period of waiting—right now! In the end, the distinction between bearded darnel and wheat will be clear. Now, however, this waiting period is a grace period. Avoid the burning of bundles and see the Bundle Bearer burnt for us on the cross (God's ultimate "parable"). The cross gives to him who has and takes from him who has not. At the cross men say, "Jesus be cursed!" or "Jesus is Lord!" (1 Cor. 12:3).

4. Jesus comes to turn weeds into wheat. We too are weeds—one and all. Surely "all have sinned." But God does not "burn" us; He bears our sins so that as He went from death to life we too may rise and by His power be changed from weeds to wheat. Those deaf to His call will not receive His gift but go to hell. (Cf. also Matt. 13:47–50, the parable of the net. There *will* be a day of sorting good from bad fish.) So man is destroyed by what God sent to save him.

Sermon Outline
WEEDS IN THE WHEAT

I. God sows wheat.
   A. It is good seed.
      1. The seed is the Good News of God.
      2. Grace abounds.
   B. It brings forth sons of the kingdom.
      1. God makes us sons.
      2. His Spirit keeps us (Rom. 8:26–27).

II. The Evil One sows weeds.
   A. The bad seed is sin.
      1. Sin that is sown takes root.
      2. "Overnight" God's greatest gift is poisoned.
   B. It brings forth sons of the devil.
      1. It results in negation and destruction.
      2. It produces faithless people.

III. Wait until the harvest!
   A. This is a grace period.
   B. Jesus takes people who look like weeds and makes them into wheat.
   C. He bundled our weediness, was burnt for us, and rose uncharred to new life.

IV. God sorts the harvest.
   A. His servants do not do the sorting.

1. There is no "Operation Throw Them Out" (Luke 9:55; *note* Western authority addition).
          2. There is no inquisition to destroy (remember Matt. 7:1).
       B. The merciful God in Jesus Christ does the sorting.
          1. He owns the world (13:38).
          2. He is Lord of the angels (v. 41).
          3. He executes the Last Judgment (vv. 41–42).

A simple story? No, it is difficult for those who do not believe in Christ. Yes, it is simple, because it shows that Jesus alone provides the righteousness—the wheatness—for our eternal life with God.

L. Dean Hempelmann

Tenth Sunday After Pentecost

EPISTLE   Romans 8:28 – 30 (RSV)

Sermon Notes/Introduction

The doctrine of predestination is one of God's great gifts to us. It should give great comfort and consolation to the Christian and should therefore be preached to the joy and edifying of Christ's holy people.

Sermon Outline
PREDESTINATION: GOD'S GREAT GIFT TO YOU

I. It is based on the goodness of God (Rom. 8:28, 29).
   A. In everything that happens God works for our good. He even uses the sufferings in our life for our good.
   B. "Called" is the source of our being converted. St. Paul amplifies "according to His purpose" in 2 Tim. 1:9. His foreknowing us is an eternal act of God's will, by which He chose us so that we might "be conformed to the image of His Son." Christ has a glorified body surrounded by majesty; we too will be given this same state of glory in heaven. Christ was the firstborn among many brethren and leads them with Him into glory.
II. It is worked out in the golden chain of God's activities.
   A. As a background for his discussion of predestination, Paul has first presented the doctrines of sin and grace (Rom. 1:14 – 3:20) and justification and sanctification (3:21 – 5:21).

    B. Predestination to eternal life applies to those whom God has called, justified, and glorified.
    C. This election by grace, which is based solely on God's decree in eternity, takes place before faith and is not dependent on man's action in any way. It is, therefore, a source of great comfort to Christians.
    D. Eternal election or predestination always deals with definite persons and individuals.
    E. Foreknowledge is an act of God in eternity. It deals with people who were not yet living but existed only in His plan.
    F. Foreknowledge and predestination describe the same eternal decree of God from different points of view. Foreknowledge sees it from God's perspective; predestination refers to the goal or purpose of God's decree, which is to conform us to the image of His Son.
    G. "Image of His Son"—Christ has a glorified body; every Christian should also bear the image of the heavenly Man (1 Cor. 15:20, 49).
    H. "Firstborn among many brethren"—Christ has entered into glory. He does not remain alone but is the firstfruits and, as Pioneer of our salvation, leads many to glory with Him (1 Cor. 15:23; Rev. 14:4; Heb. 2:10).
    I. "Called"—God called us to Christ, brought us to faith; that is, He converted us and made us believers (Eph. 4:4; Heb. 9:15).
    J. "Justified"—with the call and conversion justification is granted. This means that when He made us believers, He forgave all our sins and declared us innocent (Rom. 5:1; 1 Cor. 6:11).
    K. "Glorified"—to those whom He called He gives the glory of heaven. We do not enjoy it yet, but we have it (cf. Rom. 8:24).
III. This doctrine brings comfort and consolation.
    A. Predestination is God's election, which, in turn, is based on the merits of Jesus Christ. There is nothing in man that is responsible for his election. There is no election in view of faith or in view of merit. Therefore, election is dependent on the gracious God and not on fragile and undependable man.
    B. It is a mystery why some are chosen and others are not. God does not give us a solution; this must wait for the light of eternity. It is no cause for worry or concern to the Christian who lives within the love of God as

manifested by his conversion and God's continued blessings.
C. The knowledge of our predestination and election gives great comfort to the Christian. We are made aware of the great glory of the grace of God. We have a constant motivation to devote all our life to the good works that are fruits of justification. The trials and tribulations of this life are properly seen in their true light and accepted patiently and submissively. (For an example see the story of Joseph, Gen. 50:20.) And finally, we have the absolute assurance of a blessed and completed salvation.   GEORGE S. ROBBERT

Tenth Sunday After Pentecost

GOSPEL   Matthew 13:44 – 52

Sermon Notes/Introduction

Whether we buy a diamond, a pearl, or a simple piece of jade, we take the purchase into the light and turn it around so we can view it from every side and facet. We inspect it for texture, color, flaws, and beauty. We want to make a "perfect" buy.

In the three parables of our text Jesus invites us to take a great treasure—the Kingdom—into the light and look at it from three facets, to inspect it from three points of view.

Sermon Outline
THE KINGDOM TREASURE

I. It is a hidden treasure.
   A. This hidden treasure is Christ.
      1. There is a dire need for this treasure. The world is lost in sin and guilt, "poverty-stricken," spiritually "bankrupt," "broke."
      2. Christ is the treasure because He offers the riches of forgiveness. He is the Way back to God. He is the treasure that gives life.
      3. This hidden treasure has great value. God can give nothing greater than Himself; He does so in giving us His Son.
   B. This treasure is hidden in a field.
      1. The field is our world. The treasure—Christ and His

kingdom—is now in the world, our world. It is now with us and is to be found by us!
    2. The treasure is hidden from natural man (1 Cor. 2:12; Eph. 5:8).
    3. Yet the treasure is intended for all. In the text a man (the Greek word "man" is generic) finds the treasure. God has no favorites. Christ came to redeem all men.
II. It is a singular treasure.
  A. Christ is the pearl of great price.
    1. He is valuable in His person.
    2. He is valuable in His work.
  B. Christ far surpasses all other pearls.
    1. No earthly treasure can compare with Christ. Wealth, education, and success are not equal to Him.
    2. All other pearls are sold. All can be counted as loss compared to Christ (Phil. 3:7).
III. It is a searching treasure.
  A. In His Word Christ seeks us out.
    1. Nets catch things; they are not caught. Just when we thought we had to seek out the treasure, suddenly the treasure finds us. In His Word God seeks us out and calls our attention to the treasure He has prepared for us in His Son.
    2. Through His Word Christ invites the world to the Gospel. Furthermore, His Holy Spirit leads us to faith. His "fishing" is the mission work of the church in the world (Luke 4:43–44; 5:10).
    3. He catches fish of every kind. No one is excluded from the Gospel call. Men of every race and nation are called to Christ the Savior. All are welcome. Christ died for all.
  B. The "catch" is accounted for on Judgment Day. Faith is required. Those who reject what Christ has done for them will be cast aside and abandoned by God. There will be an accounting for the souls of men.

Do we understand what these parables teach us (Matt. 13:51)? Understanding implies faith and trust, not mere intellectual assent. Let our answer be, "Yes, I believe Christ is my Savior. No longer is He hidden. He is my pearl of great price. Because He found me, I shall be in His kingdom forever."

GEORGE R. KRAUS

Eleventh Sunday After Pentecost

EPISTLE   Romans 8:35 – 39 (RSV)

Sermon Notes/Introduction

V. 35: "The love of Christ" is Christ's love for His people, not their love for Him. (Cf. v. 37, "through Him who loved us," and v. 39, "the love of God in Christ Jesus our Lord.") *V. 36:* This is a quotation of Ps. 44:22. Adversity is the lot of God's people in all generations (Acts 14:22; Heb. 11:35 – 38). *Vv. 38 – 39:* Paul develops an antithetical pattern to demonstrate the strength of the love of God. Death—life, things present—things to come, height—depth, angels (good)—principalities (evil) all show the boundless power of God to overcome everything.

Many counselors today are emphasizing the values of a "trial separation." The hope is that the couple will have the opportunity to stand back and assess the situation from a distance.

In the text, Paul is encouraging us to step back and evaluate "trials" that come into every Christian life. Trials usually separate—husband from wife, man from job, parent from child. The emphasis is that no trial, no matter how severe, has the power to separate us from the love of God in Christ Jesus.

Sermon Outline
TRIALS CANNOT SEPARATE US FROM THE LOVE OF GOD

I. Trials are one of the "givens" of the Christian life.
   A. Physical trials for Christians have persisted throughout history (vv. 35 – 36).
      1. Tribulations are the marks of a Christian's struggle (2 Cor. 4:8).
      2. Persecutions, famine, and nakedness were experienced by many (1 Cor. 4:11; 2 Cor. 11:26 – 27).
   B. Spiritual trials befall every Christian (Rom. 8:36).
   C. Death is the final trial through which we all must pass (v. 38).
II. Trials were experienced by Jesus throughout His state of humiliation.

A. He was rejected (Matt. 21:42).
   B. He had no place to lay His head (Matt. 8:20).
   C. He suffered (Luke 24:46).
   D. He felt separated from His Father (Matt. 27:46).
   E. He died (Matt. 27:50).
III. Trials are overwhelmingly conquered through Jesus (Rom. 8:37).
   A. Our ability to overcome is based on His promises.
      1. He will not leave us nor forsake us (Heb. 13:5).
      2. He will not give us more than we can bear.
   B. Our future is secure.
      1. Jesus rose, and so shall we.
      2. Jesus has prepared a place for us.

History has proven that individuals and the church have always been strongest when persecution was most severe. So lift up your head, disheartened father. Keep smiling, pain-racked mother. Do not lose heart, grief-stricken spouse. Be strong, grandfather facing death. You are winners! You are conquerors through Jesus Christ, your Lord.

WAYNE A. POHL

Eleventh Sunday After Pentecost

GOSPEL   Matthew 14:13 – 21

Sermon Notes/Introduction

1. To restrict oneself to this miracle text without reference to the fullness of Scripture may lead to a barren and even mistaken sermon: "As Jesus fed the five thousand, so He takes care of our physical needs." We need not even restrict ourselves to what the text *implies*. Our authority for moving into the realm of spiritual feeding is given by Jesus in John 6.

2. This is a miracle text, but Matthew does not call it a miracle. He uses the term *terata* only for the wonders of false prophets, as in Matt. 24:24. Jesus' miracles are simply "deeds of Jesus." The stress is not on the miraculous nature of the deeds but on the person of the doer. In His deeds Jesus reveals His Person and character. He acts like the Messiah that He claimed to be (e.g., Is. 55). The miracles reveal Christ's will, motives, and mission. The deeds are significant because the promised Messiah is doing them and because they show us what kind of a Savior we have. This approach tells us our purpose in a sermon on this text. We want people to appreciate

what kind of Lord they have and to trust in Him to minister to their needs of body and soul.

3. The key word in this text is *esplagchnisthē*. His heart bled for the people. Our Lord is deeply moved by people's needs, and He exercises His Messianic office and authority on their behalf (see Heb. 4:15).

4. Our Savior is compassionate and powerful. This is demonstrated in His concern for our physical needs and weaknesses. However, His compassion is even greater for our miserable spiritual state and the doom of eternal damnation. For this He gave Himself as the ransom, and by faith in Him we are made spiritually well and strong to live in this life as His reborn disciples and to enjoy eternal life with Him.

Sermon Outline
APPRECIATING OUR MESSIAH

Do Christians appreciate Christ sufficiently? Do we fail to come to Him with great expectations? The apostles did not expect the miracle of the feeding. What Scripture recalls about our Messiah is a strong encouragement to draw near with confidence (Heb. 4:16). What does it tell us about Him?

I. Our Lord meets our needs with infinite compassion.
   A. He displays compassion for the earthly needs of people.
      1. He knows that many of our physical needs are brought about by our own forgetfulness and folly.
      2. He displays His divine compassion for the needs and hurts of people.
      3. His unique divine-human nature makes it possible for Him to identify with our needs and yet to do so with infinite compassion (Heb. 4:14–16).
      4. The same Jesus who fed the five thousand is still the God-man, but He now is seated at the right hand of God. Hence He is omnipresent, and His compassion is available to us now.
   B. He displays compassion for the spiritual needs of people.
      1. He is compassionate for the terror of our lost condition (Luke 19:10).
      2. He is compassionate for the suffering that our sinfulness brings to this world (weeping for Lazarus and for Jerusalem).
      3. He is compassionate for the missing joy in the

sinner's life and for the missing of eternal life (John 6:27).
II. Our Lord meets our needs with infinite power.
   A. He displayed His power in the face of human earthly needs.
      1. He fed the five thousand, healed the sick, cleansed the leper, raised the dead, etc.
      2. He commissioned His disciples to continue His ministry to meet the bodily needs of people.
   B. He displays the ultimate end of His Messiahship in meeting the spiritual needs of people.
      1. He is the Lamb of God, who takes away sin (John 1:29).
      2. He makes alive from the death of sin (Eph. 2:4–10).
      3. He gives eternal life (John 6:35–40).
      4. He gives a living hope in this life (1 Peter 1:3–9).

The Gospels show what a great Messiah we have. Bring all your needs to Him.

RICHARD J. SCHULTZ

Twelfth Sunday After Pentecost

EPISTLE   Romans 9:1–5

Sermon Notes/Introduction

The Old Testament Reading for this Sunday ties in especially well with the Epistle selection. Elijah is discouraged because he feels alone. God has not properly shown His power, he believes. In an encounter with the Lord, he observes God's power not in earthquake or fire but in the still, small voice and receives the command to continue his work of testifying. Paul has just finished his masterful exposition of the doctrine of justification by faith. Now he is confronted by the unbelief of his own relatives according to the flesh. The text begins a new section of the epistle, in which he deals with this problem, which was of great interest to both Jewish and Gentile Christians.

Verse 1: Two witnesses were needed under Jewish law to establish a point. Paul is calling as his witnesses his own statement and his conscience. Conscience speaks independently, not hesitating to disagree. Still conscience can err, but Paul speaks "in Christ"; he connects his conscience with the Holy Spirit, who enlightens and controls it through the Word.

Verse 2: Paul has the same anguish as Jesus, who wept over Jerusalem. The pain is not momentary but constant (*adialeiptos*).

Verse 3: Paul's pain is so great that he wishes himself "anathema" if this would effect the salvation of his brethren. Here he stands like Moses (Ex. 32:11–14, 31–32), but he goes beyond Moses. Moses' love for his people was so great that he did not want to be saved without them (Ex. 32:32); Paul wants to save his people at the cost of his soul.

"Anathema from Christ"—accursed, deprived of salvation because of separation from Christ.

Verse 4: These are Israelites, and therefore they have certain privileges. Paul does not name them Hebrews according to their language or Jews according to their nationality, but he calls them Israelites in honor of a faith that once prevailed (Gen. 32:24–28). He then goes on to list the privileges of the Israelites: adoption as sons in a special sense; the *kabod Yahweh*, the pillar of cloud and of fire, the Shekinah; the covenants, a plural referring to the repetition of these to the patriarchs; the giving of the Law on Sinai; the establishment of the cultus; and most important, the promises relating to the coming of the Messiah.

Verse 5: "The fathers," the patriarchs from whom the Israelites descended; the culmination is the Christ. He is from them according to the flesh, according to His human nature. This Christ is true God; Christ, an Israelite according to the flesh, is Lord of all.

Sermon Outline
SPURNED GIFTS

America has always been heralded as the land of opportunity. Rich in resources, a country of political freedom, it has provided men with the opportunity to escape oppression and to enjoy prosperity. But men have not always used the opportunities. The resources have been squandered; political freedom has been abused. God's gifts have, in effect, been spurned. So also has it been with God's spiritual gifts. In his Letter to the Romans, Paul calls our attention to this and to the sorrow it brought him.

    I. The privileges of the Israelites are eight, listed in four pairs. All of these God's chosen people spurned.
        A. Adoption (Ex. 4:22–23; Deut. 14:1; Hos. 11:1).
        B. Glory—the revealed manifestation of Yahweh (Ex.

24:16; 40:34; 1 Kings 8:10–11; 19:9–12 [Old Testament Reading]; Ezek. 1:28).
   C. The covenants (Gen. 12:1–3; 15:4–6; 17:4; 22:15–18; 26:4–5; 28:12–22).
   D. The giving of the Law (Ex. 20). Note that the giving of the Law was a privilege granted to the Israelites.
   E. The service of the sanctuary, the cultus (Heb. 9:1).
   F. The promises—Messianic blessings.
   G. The fathers—blessing in the seed of Abraham.
   H. Christ as the culmination (Rom. 1:3; 4:1). Note Paul's glorious doxology to Christ. God over all—Paul claims this for our Lord. He is blessed forever. He is not limited to time.
II. Paul's reaction is sorrow.
   A. It is a great sorrow. Unconverted man is indifferent to the misery of his fellowman; not so the Christian.
   B. It is a natural sorrow. Brothers and sisters according to the flesh are involved. Paul feels great sorrow and continual heaviness of heart for the misery of others.

We are all pained when we find those nearest and dearest to us rejecting the Lord's gifts. Many, perhaps most of us, have experienced the great sorrow of heart that Paul experienced. Paul did not give up on his kinsmen according to the flesh. Their unbelief only spurred him on to greater efforts on their behalf. So we too should make every effort to bring our unbelieving friends and relatives the Gospel.

JOHN W. KLOTZ

Twelfth Sunday After Pentecost

GOSPEL   Matthew 14:22–33 (RSV)

Sermon Notes/Introduction

"O man of little faith, why did you doubt?" How the words must have seared Peter's conscience, as they do ours. It is embarrassingly easy to identify with Peter.

Sermon Outline
WHAT JESUS THINKS OF LITTLE FAITH

I. It shouldn't exist.
   A. Jesus takes care of His disciples (Matt. 14:22–29).
      1. He sent them away; they would not be tempted to

join the crowd that wanted to make Him bread-king (v. 22; see John 6:15). It is similar with us; see 1 Cor. 10:13.
2. He came to be with them on the sea, though the danger was overpowering (Matt. 14:23 – 25; cf. 8:23 – 27). He is with us too (28:20).
3. He comforted them by identifying Himself (14:26 – 27).
4. He granted Peter's request with an enabling word (vv. 28 – 29).

B. But His disciples forget (v. 30).
1. Peter thought the wind and the waves were a bigger threat than Jesus was a help. We also face many forms of worldly forgetfulness.
   a. Teenagers half-jokingly say, "I hope Judgment Day doesn't come until after my date Friday."
   b. We forget the Lord in our day-to-day concerns, relying instead on ourselves, our friends, money, cleverness, etc.
   c. In the church there is a preoccupation with gimmicks. People then think it is only concerned with self-preservation.
2. We believe Jesus—but only part way. And that's worst of all. Peter was in no great danger until he got on the water and doubted.

II. Yet it doesn't stop Jesus.
A. He saves people of little faith (v. 31).
1. He is motivated by grace; there is no question who is caring for whom.
2. He substituted for all—even those of little faith.
   a. He lived with unflagging confidence in God (e.g., v. 23).
   b. He died facing the danger that results from little faith.
3. Believing is receiving. Even when Jesus works a miracle (v. 32), its meaning must be apprehended in faith (v. 33). But faith receives Him and His forgiveness regardless of how great or small it is (see John 1:12).

B. He is the Son of God (v. 33).
1. This is the great reality that exists prior to—or even apart from—faith. Even Jesus' enemies had to recognize it (cf. Matt. 4:3, 6; 8:29; 27:54).
2. He had come to save, not destroy (John 3:17;

12:47; cf. Is. 42:3). As the Son of God, He carried out the saving plan. His substitution worked *because* He was God (cf. 2 Cor. 5:19).
3. Those who have great faith are those who receive this great God in all His power and compassion (cf. Matt. 8:5–13; 15:21–28).
4. His Gospel Word tells us about Him and brings Him to us. It engenders faith, just as this event strengthened the disciples' faith.

The Lord is more than worthy of our trust. For a Christian to have faith in Him is like a child's loving his mother.

KEN SCHURB

Thirteenth Sunday After Pentecost

EPISTLE   Romans 11:13–15, 29–32 (RSV)

Sermon Notes/Introduction

Paul here deals with the failure of the Jews to accept the promised Messiah. Their failure has brought about a preaching of the Gospel to the Gentiles. But not all have spurned God's mercy; the remnant, of which Paul and the Jewish Christians at Rome are a part, has been saved, chosen by grace. Yet the Gentiles are not to boast; their salvation is as much a result of God's mercy as the salvation of the remnant. Their salvation and their preaching are to provoke the Jews to jealousy so that some may be added to the remnant and be saved.

The Old Testament Reading speaks of foreigners joining themselves to the Lord and the gathering of outcasts of Israel. The Gospel continues that theme in the story of the Syrophoenician woman.

Verses 13–14: For the first time in the Epistle, Paul addresses the Gentile Christians directly. Paul is an apostle to the Gentiles (Acts 9:15); yet here he does not glory in what he has accomplished among the Gentiles; rather, he looks beyond them to what he may accomplish among the Jews. The full glory of his Gentile ministry is to lie in its effect on the Jews. Jewish stubbornness has caused salvation to be brought as riches to the Gentiles (Rom. 11:11–12); the conversion of the Gentiles is to arouse Jewish jealousy, create a favorable climate, and bring about Jewish conversions; the latter are the real crown of Paul's ministry.

Verse 15: Note that Paul speaks of the casting away of the

Jews as a fact. He does not harbor the notion of the ultimate conversion of the entire Jewish nation. The "all Israel" of verse 26 is the total of the elect in Israel. The casting away of the hardened Israel brings its blessings to the Gentile world. The recovery of Jewish Christians, locked up in disobedience, is, like the recovery of the Gentile Christians, a restoration of life to a dead body. Both Jew and Gentile are dead in trespasses and sins (Eph. 2:1).

Verse 29: When God bestows His precious gifts (see the list discussed last Sunday, Rom. 9:4–5) and calls people, He never regrets the gift and the call.

Verses 30–31: The situation of Jew and Gentile is the same. The Gentiles were once disobedient; they obtained mercy because the Gospel was brought to them after the Jews showed themselves stubborn. The Jews, who have also become disobedient, are to be given mercy because of the mercy shown the Gentiles.

Verse 32: This verse ties it all together. Jew and Gentile are on the same level. All must be saved by the same means— God's mercy in Christ Jesus—for all have been locked up together in disobedience.

Sermon Outline
MERCY, ONLY MERCY

The success of Alcoholics Anonymous is based on the individual's recognition of his condition and his helplessness. Before he can be helped, he must recognize that he is an alcoholic. Then he must recognize that he needs help. So it is with the faith. We must recognize our sin and our helplessness in overcoming our condition.

I. Both Gentiles and Jews are disobedient.
   A. The Gentiles are disobedient as pagans.
   B. The Jews are disobedient to the Gospel promise.
   C. All—both Jew and Gentile—are locked up in disobedience.
II. God's mercy is offered to both Jew and Gentile.
   A. Neither deserved Christ's coming. Theirs was a hopeless condition. God's application of mercy brings life from the dead (v. 15).
   B. It was mercy, only mercy, to both.
III. God's mercy brings results.
   A. Those who receive it have gratitude.
   B. They also have zeal for those who do not know it.

1. God does not regret His special gifts and call (v. 29).
2. The disobedience of the Jews led to the extension of the Gospel to the Gentiles (v. 30).
3. Paul hopes his preaching to the Gentiles will lead some of his own people to salvation (vv. 13–14).
4. We must never regard unbelief as hopeless. There is such a thing as a hardening of the heart, the sin against the Holy Ghost. Yet Paul hoped that some of his kinsmen according to the flesh would still be saved.

Once a former alcoholic has recognized his need, has gotten help, and has overcome the habit, he seeks to help others. He wants them to enjoy the same freedom he now enjoys. So as Christians we seek to lead others to the same solution we have found in God's mercy.

JOHN W. KLOTZ

Thirteenth Sunday After Pentecost

GOSPEL   Matthew 15:21–28 (RSV)

Sermon Notes/Introduction

The encounter of Christ with the Syrophoenician woman initially creates in us a sense of puzzlement. "Am I hearing correctly?" we may well ask ourselves. "Is this the gentle Jesus I know?" Certainly, He heals the woman's child. That is to be expected from the Great Physician. What we would perhaps not expect is that He should have to be cajoled into doing so or that He should seemingly assert the superiority of one race of people over another.

But if we examine this incident more carefully, these questions are soon resolved. For as Jesus looked on the Syrophoenician woman, He did not see her as an interloper as did the disciples—an unwelcome intruder on His time and energy. Rather, He saw her as a woman of great personal faith, and His conversation with her was designed to test that faith. Instead of leaving us in doubt about the Lord's words and actions, the text can lead us to a better understanding of the nature of a persistent faith.

Sermon Outline
A PERSISTENT FAITH

I. Persistent faith gives Christ joy. "Without faith it is impossible to please" God (Heb. 11:6). This Scriptural truth is certainly an accurate one. However, the converse is also true: Every time we make the difficult venture of faith, we bring joy to God. We can just imagine the twinkle in the Lord's eyes as this encounter took place. "It is not fair," Jesus says, "to take the children's bread and throw it to the dogs" (Matt. 15:26). Although knowing that she, a heathen woman, is as unclean in the eyes of a Jew as one of the pariah dogs that prowled around ancient eastern cities, she does not contradict what Jesus is saying. "Yes, Lord," she replies, "yet even the dogs eat the crumbs that fall from their masters' table" (v. 27). Her response is quick. It exhibits a spirit—a faith—that no doubt gave Jesus joy. He had no time for those who just hoped for the best—those people, like many of us, who find it difficult to place complete and total confidence in God's good grace.

II. Persistent faith breaks barriers. Throughout the encounter described in the text, the woman's faith in the ability of Jesus to cure her daughter is the dominating factor. Indeed, her faith was subjected to an ordeal of endurance that was almost superhuman. There was the rude impatience of the disciples, who regarded her as little more than a nuisance (v. 23), and there was the seeming indifference of Jesus Himself. Still, her faith persisted, and that persistence paid off! Christ's power becomes ours as we believe that He can overcome any barrier, any obstacle, with His divine love. The Syrophoenician woman had such faith; she believed Christ's power was great enough to surmount the obstacles of race, distance, and disease. After Christ saw such faith in the woman, He said, "Great is your faith! Be it done for you as you desire" (v. 28).

III. Persistent faith is grounded in God's plenty. The persistent faith of the woman on behalf of her child exhibits a great confidence in the amplitude of Christ's resources as the Son of God. Mere crumbs are all she asks for, but she knows that behind this teacher with whom she is talking is God's plenty. The power of God can never be exhausted, for it has its foundation not in our good intentions or our own human resources but in Jesus Christ, whom the woman recognized as "Lord" (v. 22).

The words of Christ to the woman were not words of displeasure or arrogance, as it might appear initially. They brought to the surface a tenacious, persistent faith in the power of God. May we too offer to Christ the same utter loyalty, the same unquestioning obedience, the same persistent faith.

JOHN F. JOHNSON

Fourteenth Sunday After Pentecost

EPISTLE   Romans 11:33 – 36 (RSV)

Sermon Notes/Introduction

Paul, contemplating the mercy and love of God revealed in His dealings with Jews and Gentiles, adores the divine wisdom and knowledge that can never be fully known by human beings (Rom. 11:33). In v. 34 he quotes from Is. 40:13 to prove the unsearchableness of God's ways and to show that no one can be His confidant. In v. 35 he quotes from Job 41:11 to show that the initiative always belongs to God and that we have nothing that we did not receive. In v. 36 he emphasizes man's absolute dependence on God—"from Him" as the source, "through Him" as the power by whose energy the whole world is sustained and ruled, "to Him" as the goal for whose glory the world and all that is in it exists. Creation, redemption, providence, and all the phenomena connected with them are for the glory of God.

The central thought of the text is that God is supreme. The goal of the sermon is that the hearers will acknowledge God's supremacy. The problem is that we sometimes honor persons and things more than God. The means to the goal is God's ordering and controlling of the world to serve His love in Jesus Christ.

When we look at what human beings have accomplished, especially in medicine and computers, it is easy to give glory to man. The text shows that it is more appropriate to give the glory to God.

Sermon Outline
TO GOD BE THE GLORY

I. He is the source ("from Him," v. 36).
  A. He created the world and all that is in it (1 Cor. 8:6; 11:12).
    1. Researchers simply discover what was there all along.
    2. God's wisdom and knowledge are apparent in His

creation of the human eye and ear, for example.
  B. He initiated the world's redemption.
    1. The riches of His love moved Him to plan redemption as a gift (Rom. 11:35).
    2. His wisdom found a way to meet the demands of both His justice and His love. No one suggested to Him how to do this (v. 34).
II. He is the power ("through Him," v. 36).
  A. His energy sustains the world and the universe.
    1. He holds it all together (Col. 1:17; Heb. 2:10).
    2. He keeps us alive (Acts 17:28).
  B. He is the agent of salvation.
    1. In Christ He saw it through to the resurrection and the ascension.
    2. He brought us to Christ and keeps us with Him.
III. He is the goal ("to Him," Rom. 11:36).
  A. The world and the universe exist for God's praise.
    1. All created things praise Him (Ps. 19:1; 148:9–10).
    2. Our physical body joins in the praise (Ps. 139:14).
  B. We praise Him for who He is and for what He has done (our creation, redemption, and preservation).
  C. We praise Him with words and songs of adoration and with lives that honor Him.

It is exhilarating to focus on God rather than on ourselves. We become truly human when we give God the glory.

GERHARD AHO

Fourteenth Sunday After Pentecost

GOSPEL   Matthew 16:13 – 20 (RSV)

Sermon Notes/Introduction

Jesus had gone with His disciples to the district of Caesarea Philippi for a brief rest. The crowds kept pressing and now sought His words of wisdom and miracles of healing. Then He asked His inner circle of followers a searching question: "Who do you say that I am?" (v. 15). All of Christ's earthly ministry had been leading up to the query. All that was likely to follow would be determined by the view people took of His person. No doubt Jesus was profoundly aware that this was a pivotal question; it was, and in fact still is, the supreme question.

Sermon Outline
THE SUPREME QUESTION

I. This question is important because it is easy to give false answers or imperfect opinions.
  A. Christ prefaced the personal question with a more general one that had to do with the impression He had made on the people during His brief ministry (v. 13). This question brought forth many answers. The Sadducees said He was a lunatic. The Pharisees called Him a winebibber and glutton. The Scribes regarded Him as unlearned. On the other hand, some views of Jesus, though inadequate, were not entirely false. People had been impressed by His character, His personality. They had placed Him among the greatest sons of Israel. Some had been so impressed by His earnestness that they thought He might be John the Baptist come back from the dead or Elijah or Jeremiah (v. 14). But such opinions, however flattering, were not enough; they fell far short in describing Christ.
  B. People still offer good and favorable opinions about who Christ was. Many observations about the morality of the Lord's teaching or His concern for the well-being of mankind are complimentary. However, they express nothing about the true nature or mission of Jesus Christ. Our verdict on His person is inadequate if we merely elevate Him to the highest rank of men. Since this attitude is as prevalent today as it was when He first posed the question, we must face afresh the challenge of the Lord's query.
II. The question is also important in view of the rival claimants to men's loyalty.
  A. In his *Historical Geography of the Holy Land*, George Adam Smith draws attention to the importance of the locality where Jesus asked His question. One can imagine that the gleaming marble temple where Caesar was worshiped caught the attention of the disciples as they stood with Christ outside Caesarea Philippi. Near that temple was also a grotto devoted to the worship of the Greek god Pan. There they stood—two deities setting forth their rival claims. And over against them, challenging them both, stood the demands of Jesus, the "Son of the living God" (v. 16).
  B. The situation has not changed in 2,000 years. There

are those who still worship the idol of power, those who remain entranced by the pleasure of the world. If our faith presumes to make its historical claim about the person of Christ, all of the other rival claimants to the loyalty of men must be rejected.

III. Finally, the question of our Lord is important because our answer to it shapes our attitude toward Christ's cross and our own.

A. It is significant that in the Gospel of Matthew, from which the text comes, Jesus has nothing to say about His own sufferings and those of His followers until this crucial question has been faced and answered. But the moment Peter gives the right answer and affirms Christ's divinity, Jesus shifts the conversation to the suffering awaiting Him in Jerusalem (v. 21). The view one takes of the cross of Christ will depend on the view one takes of His person. If Jesus is only a great man, then His death has no more importance than that of any martyr who died for a noble cause. But if Jesus is God, then His cross becomes the vicarious suffering of God Himself, whose sacrifice avails for the sins of the world.

B. Suffering is also part of our calling as Christians. When the Gospel was first preached, Christians were persecuted; not to be ashamed of Christ meant torture and death. Witnessing to the faith may still lead to suffering and self-denial—our own personal cross. When we undergo such personal suffering and loss for Christ's sake, then the view we hold of His person must qualify our attitude toward such hardship. If He is truly divine and is with us and in us as only God can be, we shall not need to bear alone the burden of suffering and despair. He will always be at our side.

"Who do you say that I am?" This is still the supreme question. In every age it is the most important question with which men have to deal. How is it possible to reach the right answer regarding the deity of Christ? It is something revealed to us by the Holy Spirit through the Word. "Flesh and blood," Jesus says to Peter, "has not revealed this to you, but My Father who is in heaven" (v. 17). We must reach the answer in the same way.

JOHN F. JOHNSON

Fifteenth Sunday After Pentecost

EPISTLE   Romans 12:1 – 18 (KJV)

Sermon Notes/Introduction

The mercies (Rom. 12:1) are those God has shown in the redemption through Christ. Our body is the instrument by which we serve God. The "reasonable service" is the presenting rather than the sacrificing of the body; it is the act of offering, not the thing offered, that constitutes the service. It is reasonable service also because it is rational and not merely outward and mechanical. Christian renewal imparts not only the will and power to do God's will but also the intelligence to discern it (v. 2). The will of God here is what is good in a moral sense. The present tenses suggest ongoing renewal by the Holy Spirit. Although various degrees of self-estimation are proper, since God gives one person more and another less (v. 3), all are regulated by humility, for none of us has anything we have not received. Each of us has received a gift or gifts. Yet we are no more than members in the whole body (v. 4). We are mutually dependent on each other (v. 5). We are to exercise whatever gift we have as well as we can (vv. 6 – 8). Verse 9 stresses using the gifts on the basis of love, which never condones evil but clings to the good. Love is to be directed to the whole family of God (v. 10). It moves us to zealous performance of our duties as service to the Lord (v. 11).

The central thought of the text is that the mercy of God moves us to worship with our body, mind, and gifts. The goal of the sermon is that the hearers will worship God with their whole being. The problem is that fleshly rather than spiritual considerations often motivate and direct our worship. The means to the goal is the mercy of God in Christ, which impels and empowers our worship.

In the chapters preceding the text, Paul describes the mercies of God as they are demonstrated in the redemptive work of Christ. He reminds us that there is no condemnation for those who are in Christ (8:1), and that nothing in heaven, on earth, or beneath it can separate us from God's love in Christ (vv. 38 – 39). Such mercy calls for a response. However, Paul does not say, "I command you." Rather, he says, "I beseech you ... by the mercies of God" (12:1). To do what? To perform our "reasonable service."

Sermon Outline
OUR REASONABLE SERVICE

I. We present our bodies.
   A. It is a living sacrifice.
      1. It is not like slaughtered animals or perfunctory performances.
      2. We present them as instruments for rational, moral behavior (v. 1; 1 Peter 2:5; Rom. 6:13, 16, 19).
   B. It is acceptable to God.
      1. God's mercy motivates our behavior.
      2. God's mercy covers our shortcomings.
      3. God's mercy hallows our efforts.

Such presenting of our bodies is a reasonable service (1 Cor. 6:20). But this service involves the mind as well as the body.

II. We are renewed in our minds.
   A. The Holy Spirit enables us to discern God's will (Rom. 12:2).
      1. We become more sensitive to what is good.
      2. We become more watchful that the world does not squeeze us into its mold (Phillips).
   B. The Holy Spirit enables us to assess ourselves honestly.
      1. We neither denigrate ourselves nor think of ourselves more highly than we ought to think (v. 3).
      2. The awareness that all we have is from God makes us humble (vv. 3, 6).

So to be renewed in our minds is a reasonable service. Our bodies and minds are activated by mercy.

III. We use our gifts.
   A. We use whatever gifts we have as well as we can (vv. 7–8).
      1. Each of us has different gifts from God (v. 6).
      2. We are most ourselves when we use our gifts as fully as possible.
   B. We strive to use our gifts for the good of others (v. 5).
      1. We are dependent on each other.
      2. We each can contribute to the functioning of the whole body.

What a challenge to present our bodies as living sacrifices, to be renewed in mind, holiness, and humility and then with body and mind to use our gifts more fully! This is but our reasonable service in view of the magnificent mercies of God.

GERHARD AHO

Fifteenth Sunday After Pentecost

GOSPEL   Matthew 16:21 – 26 (RSV)

Sermon Notes/Introduction

Peter had just put into words the foundation fact on which the church of God is established: Jesus is "the Christ, the Son of the living God" (Matt. 16:16). The disciples had come to know the person of Christ, but they had an awful lot to learn about the work of the Christ. Just as God intended to create a servant people when He called Abraham's family to be His people, so He sent His Son to be the true Israel, the Suffering Servant and Redeemer of the world. For Jesus, the way to fulfilled purpose and glory was the way of the cross and the empty tomb. The way of cross-bearing and self-denial for those who would follow Him in faith was a difficult pill to swallow for Peter and the others—and still is for would-be disciples today! In fact, it is even difficult to preach about it unless we remain squarely under the cross and in the Spirit's light.

How great it is to know and relish Jesus, our "beautiful Savior," who by His cross has won for us forgiveness of sins and eternal life in heaven. But like the disciples in today's Gospel, we still have a lot to learn about cross life.

Sermon Outline
CROSS LIFE

I. Self-denial and burden-bearing are very contradictory to our normal goal for life.
   A. Peter's visions of sharing messianic glory and power collided with Jesus' announcement of His coming suffering and death.
      1. Peter and the other disciples were still blinded by the Jewish concept of the Messiah as an earthly king who would bring victory, glory, and wealth to his people.
      2. This explains why Peter so strongly resisted the Lord's prediction of suffering and the cross (v. 22).

B. In varying degrees the goals of people are oriented toward self and success.
 1. People live for wealth, health, happiness, and freedom to "do your own thing." (Illustrate with contemporary evidence in people's lives, advertising, etc.)
 2. Caught in the patterns of this world, many Christians have much trouble with self-denial (putting oneself out for others) and "crosses" (standing up for Christ).

Unfortunately, when we live for self-satisfaction only, at the end of life, that is all we have (cf. v. 26). God has something better for us.

II. Real life is ours when we deny self-fulfillment in order to follow God's claim on our lives.
 A. Christ's life was controlled by the divine "must" of the Father's will for Him, which climaxed on the cross (v. 21; John 4:34; Luke 22:42).
 B. In Christ God has filed His claim on our lives not only for the hereafter but for the here and now.
  1. By Baptism our sinful self died with Christ, and we were raised with Him to new life (Rom. 6:3–11; 2 Cor. 5:15).
  2. We now live with and for Christ.
   a. We must deny self ("deny" means "to turn someone off, to disown him").
   b. We must take up His cross, which was the sacrifice of servanthood (text; Rom. 12:1). "Cross" is not merely the pains of mortal humanity but the burden and cost of being Christlike in life.
   c. We must follow Christ in commitment to the will of the Father (Eph. 5:1–2; 1 Thess. 4:3). We are called to obedience after Christ's perfect example.

Peter missed the meaning and power of Christ's cross because he did not catch the promise of resurrection victory. In the power of our living Lord we can confidently live our cross life with and for Him.

EDWIN DUBBERKE

Sixteenth Sunday After Pentecost

EPISTLE   Romans 13:1–10 (RSV)

Sermon Notes/Introduction

In many places it is not wise to walk the streets alone at night. It is surely inadvisable to leave valuables in unlocked cars. And even when your house is locked, that is no assurance that your possessions will be secure. Laws of the land do protect property and people, but lawlessness has still not ceased to leave its ugly mark on society.

Sermon Outline
LAWLESSNESS—IT IS NOT THE CHRISTIAN WAY

I. Respect God-ordained government.

"There is no authority except from God" (Rom. 13:1). It is clear that Paul is speaking especially of government authority in this chapter (v. 3: *hoi archontes*). "Governing authorities" is, therefore, a legitimate rendering of *exousiais huperechousais* in the first part of verse 1. The lawlessness wrought by the entrance of sin into the world became apparent already when Cain murdered Abel, a time when the Creator Himself had to intervene to prevent utter chaos in human society. Understanding the rebellious nature of fallen mankind, God established the institution of government to maintain order in the world.

The purpose of God was loving and good, for evil is restrained as a result of government, and good can flourish—"he [i.e., government] is God's servant for your good" (v. 4). This "good" embraces, of course, the many factors that contribute to a productive and peaceable life. One ought to note especially, however, that the church has been able to carry on its tasks in the world because of ordered government. To be sure, there have been times when government has persecuted the church of God, but for the most part in human history, God-ordained government has contributed effectively to a societal order that promotes the advance of the Gospel. Even the ministry of a persecuted Paul benefited from the protection of Rome. Good government serves the cause of Christ.

Ordained by God, government invites the support of

God's people. They consider it their Christian duty to pay taxes and to honor and obey God's institution.

II. Obey God-empowered authority.

Because God has ordained government, it follows that government also has the right to demand obedience. Therefore, "let every person be subject to the governing authorities" (v. 1).

It is important to note that Paul was demanding this kind of allegiance to a government that was officially dedicated to idolatry and paganism. Corruption, too, was not uncommon within ancient Rome's efficiently managed empire. Paul does not urge obedience because of the moral quality of the government nor on the basis of its political design. Governments of all kinds, authoritarian and democratic, exist by God's appointment and invite the obedience of Christians. Only when government demands a violation of a commandment of God should this institution of God be disobeyed, for "we must obey God rather than men" (Acts 5:29).

To enable government to perform its tasks God has furthermore given it the power of the sword (Rom. 13:4). For that reason, government may engage in just wars to maintain itself or protect its people. It may choose not to exercise its prerogative, but it also has the right to exact capital punishment. God has thus empowered government so that it may function in its divinely appointed sphere.

III. Love your neighbor.

It should not be fear of punishment, however, that prompts the Christian to avoid lawlessness. The Christian is motivated to civil obedience by the love of Christ. Born guilty under God's perfect law and daily sinning against it, the Christian understands that he has been rescued by Christ from the condemnation of God's law. That law, which exposes sin, also guides the Christian in his relationships with other human beings. The Christian's desire to practice love is the motivation to respect and obey government. Government is ordained to order and protect human life and property. This involves our neighbor's welfare, and "love does no wrong to a neighbor" (v. 10).

Observe how love goes beyond even what government expects. Marriage is regulated to some extent by human laws, but the Christian understands God's more comprehensive protection of holy wedlock in the Sixth Commandment. Murder the government punishes, but the Christian seeks to remove hate from his life. Not just the overt act of stealing, but coveting is already the act of theft against which the new life in Christ wars (v. 9). There is little love for one's neighbor in lawlessness.

The Christian seeks to pursue the way of love. For that reason, he respects and obeys government, God's institution for the well-being of people.

WAYNE E. SCHMIDT

Sixteenth Sunday After Pentecost

GOSPEL   Matthew 18:15 – 20

Sermon Notes/Introduction

This text is commonly seen as the *sedes doctrinae* of church discipline. Two extremes are common in approaching it—seeing it as the "proper" procedure to remove undesirables from the church or defending a complete disregard of the Savior's instructions "because we don't have the right to judge people." We can only understand the text if we remember what the loving, seeking heart of our Savior is like. His all-consuming purpose was always to bring to the sinner the grace and forgiveness of God. The mechanics of church discipline are familiar, but the spirit of deep concern for weak, erring fellow believers should dominate in a sermon on these words of our Lord.

A vacationing family from the Midwest was visiting Niagara Falls. While on Goat Island above the falls, a younger son fell into the swift current. A teenage brother managed to grab him and cling to a rock. When it seemed the older boy's strength would not last until help arrived, the mother's cry, "Don't let go; he's your brother!" encouraged him enough to hold on so that both were saved. That mother's cry illustrates the Savior's concern for weak and endangered believers in the text and what He wants us to do about them.

Sermon Outline
DON'T LET GO—HE'S YOUR BROTHER

I. Whose responsibility is it to look out for stumbling Christians?
   A. Any believer who sees a brother or sister in spiritual danger is obligated by our Lord to reach out with help (Matt. 18:15; Gal. 6:1 – 2).

B. Not to help lift up a falling brother is to share his guilt (cf. Ezek. 3:18–21).
II. We must be fully aware of just who this "brother" is about whom we are to be concerned.
   A. Common faith in Christ links us together like mountain climbers who are tied together in one cause (1 John 3:14; also Communion).
   B. Each of us—not merely church officials—has responsibility for the weak and erring in the church, in the family, etc.
III. It is essential to consider what sins should concern us lest we become merely judgmental.
   A. Our concern is not just sins against our person but flagrant sins against God and His Word and sins that offend His people.
   B. While we all daily sin out of weakness, when a believer persists in sin against God's clear Word, his salvation is in jeopardy (Matt. 18:15).
   C. Since those closest to a person will first see the sin, they have the first responsibility to call the erring to repentance.
IV. The seriousness of this Christian duty is emphasized by what is at stake (vv. 15, 17).
   A. Since sin separates from God, the person's salvation is endangered.
   B. Continuing in open sin robs God of His glory and endangers other believers through a bad example.
   C. Because of all that is at stake, the strong measure of excommunication as a last step is essential.
V. It is the authority given by Christ Himself that promises effectiveness in this ministry to erring fellow believers (v. 18).
   A. God alone can forgive sins, but He works through His people to warn the straying and comfort the penitent.
   B. It is God's Word that really does both the judging and the comforting in Christ.

What a blessed work has been entrusted to us by our Lord. May He fill us with a unified concern to carry it out (vv. 19–20).

EDWIN DUBBERKE

Seventeenth Sunday After Pentecost

EPISTLE   Romans 14:7 – 9 (RSV)

Sermon Notes/Introduction

A popular singer of some years ago mournfully sang, "I owe my soul to the company store." Not infrequently do people in debt feel that they do not belong to themselves but to someone else. The local Friendly Finance Company expects the monthly house payment on time and Easy Pay Auto Loans wants its share, too. What those two don't get, the IRS surely will.

Although few enjoy being indebted to the point that they almost belong to someone else, the Christian knows of a most welcome and reassuring claim on his life. The apostle Paul expresses that claim in the words: "We are the Lord's" (Rom. 14:8).

Sermon Outline
WE ARE THE LORD'S

I. What does this mean for life?

"None of us lives to himself" (v. 7). The temptation looms large to expand on these words without a careful regard for the immediate context. Admittedly, Paul had spoken about sins unbecoming to the Christian life at the end of chapter 13. Chapter 14, however, deals with a different topic, namely, a specific worship practice among Christians. Some of the apostle's readers were apparently abstaining from certain kinds of foods in honor of the Lord, while others were enjoying those same foods and doing so in a spirit of thanksgiving to God. In both cases, however, there was a recognition that the Christian life is lived under God and that it includes acts of worship to honor and give thanks to Him. This is living not to oneself but to God.

The door stands wide open to speak about forms of worship in the church of the 20th century. No single form is prescribed. In fact, forms may be outwardly quite different from one another and may be used with profit, provided, of course, that the rubric of "what makes for peace and for mutual upbuilding" is still observed (v. 19).

The subject of eating and drinking is taken up in a different context by Paul in 1 Corinthians. There the apostle adds the admonition: "Whatever you do, do all (*panta*—all things) to the glory of God" (1 Cor. 10:31). In other words, the Christian is urged to view life's entire set of activities from the perspective of living to God rather than self.

II. What does this mean for death?

It is not only in this life, however, that we are the Lord's. The apostle Paul was always keenly aware of the end of his earthly sojourn. At the time of his impending death, he wrote to Timothy: "I am already on the point of being sacrificed; the time of my departure has come" (2 Tim. 4:6). Christians must daily face the reality of death, for "sin came into the world through one man and death through sin ... because all men sinned" (Rom. 5:12). In the stern hour of death, God's people can boast, "We are the Lord's." They have the confidence of Paul: "Henceforth there is laid up for me the crown of righteousness, which the Lord ... will award to me" (2 Tim. 4:8). Looking at death from the perspective that we are the Lord's, we can declare, "To me to live is Christ, and to die is gain" (Phil. 1:21).

Tou kuriou esmen (Rom. 14:8). The English construction, "We belong to the Lord," might convey the genitive with the copula more idiomatically than "We are the Lord's." To belong to the Lord means that God's people in Christ live life with thanksgiving and meet death with confident hope.

III. How did this come about?

It is well known, of course, that we did not become the Lord's without a price and without a divine victory. "For to this end Christ died and lived again" (v. 9). This last verse affords the opportunity to put the entire sermon within the framework of Christ's vicarious death and His glorious resurrection from the dead. Without that work of the Savior, no man could be the Lord's. Death conquered, however, and life won; Christ is now Lord of both the living and the dead. In fact, for those who are the Lord's, the word "death" is itself a happy contradiction, since those who believe in Him really never die.

Refer to the introduction again. To have one's soul belong to the company store is not an encouraging circumstance. To belong to the Lord, on the other hand, is unparalleled bliss.

WAYNE E. SCHMIDT

Seventeenth Sunday After Pentecost

GOSPEL   Matthew 18:21 – 35 (RSV)

Sermon Notes/Introduction

The central thought of the text is that we are to keep on forgiving others as God forgives us. The goal of the sermon is that we make forgiveness a way of life. The problem is our tendency to retaliate rather than to forgive. The means to the goal is God's generous, unstinted forgiveness of our sins for Christ's sake.

Not reconciliation but retaliation is the operating principle in the world. Jesus flatly contradicts the world's procedure and lays down a better principle.

Sermon Outline
MAKE FORGIVENESS YOUR AIM

I. Our forgiveness is empowered by God's forgiveness.
   A. The debt God forgave was great (Matt. 18:24).
      1. Our debt of sin includes not only our transgressions but what we should have done and failed to do, like not noticing that lonely person, not speaking an encouraging word, or not helping a neighbor in need.
      2. We cannot pay our debt (v. 26). Good intentions will not suffice. Our efforts won't expiate our guilt.
   B. God forgave at great cost.
      1. Our debt to God had to be paid. Jesus paid it, down to the last penny (1 Peter 2:24).
      2. God forgives us for Jesus' sake (Micah 7:18). When we experience God's forgiveness, that forgiveness can also be our aim.
II. Our forgiveness imitates God's forgiveness.
   A. We forgive from the heart (Matt. 18:35).
      1. This does not mean we are always able to forget the offense. The memory of it may still disturb us at times.
      2. It does mean that we do not allow the evil that was done to separate us from the other person.
   B. We set no limit on our forgiveness.
      1. The servant set a limit (v. 28).

2. Peter wanted to set a limit (v. 21).
   3. We too stand accused of setting a limit. Yet if we are to imitate God's forgiveness, the spirit of vengeance cannot be permitted to rise.
 C. We reflect the love of God.
   1. The unforgiving servant reflected hate, not love (vv. 28–30). Refusal to forgive causes distress among Christians and makes a mockery of God's forgiveness (vv. 31–33).
   2. We are to reflect God's love to the meanest and the worst. The worst that can be done to us is still only a pinprick compared to what we have done to God. By forgiving, we beget love rather than retaliation.

"Put on then, as God's chosen ones, holy and beloved, compassion ..." (Col. 3:12–13). Let us make forgiveness our aim.

GERHARD AHO

Eighteenth Sunday After Pentecost

EPISTLE　　　　　　　　Philippians 1:3–5, 19–27 (RSV)

Sermon Notes/Introduction

Consider for a moment Polish rabbi Hofetz Chaim. When an American tourist saw his simple room filled with books, a table, and a bench, he asked, "Where is your furniture?" "Where is yours?" replied the rabbi. "Mine?" retorted the puzzled American. "But I'm a visitor here. I'm only passing through." "So am I," said Hofetz Chaim.

St. Paul's attitude toward life was similar. In Phil. 3:20, for example, he speaks of a citizenship in heaven. But in the Epistle, Paul seems to be torn between the desire to depart to his home in heaven and the necessity of remaining. Why remain? Because of his partnership in the Gospel (1:5).

Sermon Outline
OUR PARTNERSHIP IN THE GOSPEL

I. We have a partnership of prayer.
 A. We pray for others as Paul prayed for the Philippians. Even while in the cell at Rome from which he was writing, he was thankful for them and their prayers. We, too, ought to pray for all those in God's family who share the Gospel with others.

B. We depend on the prayers of others. Paul believed he would be freed from prison through the Spirit and prayers on his behalf (v. 19). Paul always asked for prayers from others: "Pray for us" (1 Thess. 5:25; 2 Thess. 3:1–2). "You also must help us by prayer" (2 Cor. 1:11). He asked for prayers from the Romans (Rom. 15:30–32).

II. We have a partnership of growth.
   A. The goal is to live a life worthy of the Gospel. Paul uses the word *politeuesthe,* which means "to be a citizen" (Phil. 1:27). The word Paul normally used to refer to a person's conduct ("conversation" in the KJV) was *peripatein,* literally, "to walk about." Philippi was a Roman colony, where people lived and acted like Romans. Paul exhorts us: "Live as citizens of God's kingdom!"
   B. We grow in faith. Our progress and joy are in the faith (v. 25).
   C. We grow in love. Paul writes, "It is my prayer that your love may abound more and more" (v. 9). The life of love is a witness of deed, salt, and light (Matt. 5:14–16).

III. We have a partnership to spread the Gospel.
   A. We are witnesses for Jesus Christ. Note Jesus' last words (Acts 1:8). It was Paul's expectation that he would not be ashamed in this regard (Phil. 1:20). "Expectation" is an unusual word. It puts together *apo* ("away from"), *kara* ("the head"), and *dokein* ("to look"), making *apokaradokia,* meaning an eager, concentrated, intense look, which turns its gaze away from anything else but its one desire. (TEV: "my deep desire and hope.")
   B. We stand with all other Christians. In verse 27, Paul's concern was that people stand in one spirit and one mind, "striving side by side for the faith of the Gospel." We stand side by side in congregation, in denomination, and in the church universal.

What is your desire? Paul was "hard pressed" whether to depart or remain (v. 23). The Greek is *sunechomai,* which a traveler would use for a narrow road with a rock wall on each side so that he could go nowhere but straight ahead. The Greek for "depart," *analuein,* is the word for striking camp or pulling up anchor on a ship and setting sail. But Paul will "remain and continue with you all" (v. 25) for the partnership in the Gospel. Living out that partnership gives us joy (vv. 4, 18, 19, 25).

ERWIN J. KOLB

Eighteenth Sunday After Pentecost

GOSPEL Matthew 20:1–16

Sermon Notes/Introduction

It is natural to sympathize with the first workers. It seems only just that they should have received more than the last workers. But that is precisely the point Jesus is making. God operates differently from labor and management. God is so generous that we have difficulty accepting it. When Jesus first spoke this parable, the grumbling of the first workers was a reference to the grumbling of the scribes and Pharisees over the graciousness of Christ toward publicans and sinners. The Jewish leaders had not been wronged; they were jealous (had an evil eye) that others had been treated generously. These others (tax collectors and sinners), who were considered last, were nevertheless the first to receive God's gracious offer, while those considered first (Pharisees and scribes) were the last to receive it, if they received it at all (Matt. 20:16).

The point of the parable is that as the owner dealt very generously with all his workers, so God is generous beyond our understanding. The goal of the sermon is that we will be happy that God is so generous to all. The problem is that we sometimes live more under Law than under grace and do our share of pharisaic grumbling about others receiving more than we. The means to the goal is God's amazing and undeserved generosity to us all.

The wage question can be troublesome. Strikes and marathon negotiations are part of the economic picture in the world.

The wage question can be troublesome also in the spiritual realm. It troubled a rich young ruler who came to Jesus (19:16). Jesus offered him work and a fine wage (v. 21), but the young man went away dissatisfied. The question troubled Peter also (v. 27). We too are often concerned about what we will get for following Jesus.

Sermon Outline
THE WAGE QUESTION IN THE KINGDOM OF GOD

I. The wages are based on grace.

    A. God's pay scale contradicts our notion of rewards.
        1. The Jewish leaders grumbled about Christ's gracious offer to sinners (20:11–12).
        2. Even Peter thought he and the other disciples should receive more than those who had not left their homes and jobs (19:27).
        3. We too get jealous when God seems to be blessing others more than us.
    B. Yet God deals fairly with us.
        1. No injustice has been done, for we have received the agreed wage (20:13–14).
        2. God never promised to give us what we think we deserve for our efforts.
        3. Our grumbling reveals our loveless and unmerciful attitude and shows that we are under the Law instead of under grace more than we perhaps realize.
II. The wages are uniformly high.
    A. God is generous to all (v. 15).
        1. God is a real equal-opportunity employer.
        2. Whatever we give up we receive back a hundredfold, and finally we receive eternal life (19:29).
        3. Isn't it wonderful that even those of us who worked only one hour also receive a denarius?
    B. The work itself is already a reward.
        1. Just to be a Christian is a privilege—not a wearisome duty but a happy service, no matter how long God lets us serve.
        2. There is no richer, fuller life than that of a disciple of Christ.

The wage question in the kingdom of God need not trouble us, for in the kingdom there is no unemployment, and the wage level is uniformly high.

GERHARD AHO

Nineteenth Sunday After Pentecost

EPISTLE   Philippians 2:1–11 (RSV)

Sermon Notes/Introduction

After being separated for a number of years, two sisters came to live together again. After a while, one sister told the other, "I don't know what happened to you, but you're a great deal easier to live with than you used to be." The reason was given: "I have become a Christian." In today's text Paul is saying to the Philippians, "You are Christians. Learn to live together!" The appeal of Phil. 2:1–2 is for "full accord" in Christ, in love, and in the Holy Spirit; the final appeal is that all have the mind of Christ (v. 5). "Mind" here means disposition or attitude. (Beck: "Think just as Christ Jesus thought"; TEV: "the attitude.") That makes the difference in living together.

Sermon Outline
THE ATTITUDE MAKES THE DIFFERENCE

I. It is an attitude of humility.
   A. Let us sacrifice our selfish concerns. In verse 3, Paul is dealing with "selfishness or conceit." In contrast to this he posits Christ as the example. He was "in the form" of God. *Morphē* is an essence that cannot change. Jesus took the "form" of a servant. The *schēma* is the outward aspect of a person that is continually changing. For example, if *morphē* is the human person, his *schēma* would change from child to youth to adult. Jesus "emptied Himself" (v. 7); He did not "demand and cling to his rights" (Living Bible). What honor, prestige, respect, and rights do we demand?
   B. Let us become servants to others. Paul exhorts that we count others better than ourselves (v. 3). The essence of humility is exemplified in Christ's state of humiliation. See Luther's explanation to the Second Article or Matthew 8:20: "Foxes have holes ... but the Son of Man has nowhere to lay His head." For what positions, honors, or glory do we snatch? In family quarrels do we give in first? How far out of our way do we go to help others?

II. It is an attitude of obedience.
   A. Let us obey the will of God. Humility, sacrifice of self, and service to others are only possible in obedience. Jesus, as a sheep led to the slaughter, was obedient to death: "No one takes [My life] from Me, but I lay it down of My own accord" (John 10:18). Jesus was obedient *for us*. *Illustration:* While a boy and his father are driving down a road, a bee flies into the car. The boy goes into hysterics because he is allergic to bee stings. But the father catches the bee in his hand: "Don't be afraid; the stinger is in my hand." Jesus took

the sting of death in His body. We are free and forgiven, and we have eternal life. "For our sake He made Him to be sin" (2 Cor. 5:21).

B. Let us obey Jesus as our Lord. Yes, He died, but He also rose to seal the victory over sin and death. "God has highly exalted Him" (Phil. 2:9). His given name was Jesus, which means "Savior." But someday every knee will bow and confess that He is Lord. That was the first Christian creed: "Jesus is Lord." It is our confession today. *Kurios* means "master" or "owner"; it was used as a title of respect; it became the official title of the Roman emperor—in Latin *dominus*. This same title was attached to every heathen god and was the Greek word used for the Hebrew YHWH in the Septuagint. Paul is saying that Jesus is the master and owner of all life, King of kings, Lord of emperors, and Lord of all heathen gods. To say "Jesus is Lord" means to give Him the love, loyalty, and allegiance that we will give to no other person. It began in our baptism and continues to grow daily as we renew our baptism by contrition and repentance.

A trucker had a bumper sticker that read, "God is my partner." When a service station attendant tested him by giving an extra dollar in change, he said, "My partner won't let me keep it." That was his way of saying, "Jesus is *my* Lord."

ERWIN J. KOLB

Nineteenth Sunday After Pentecost

GOSPEL   Matthew 21:28 – 32 (RSV)

Sermon Notes/Introduction

This is the first in a series of three parabolic sayings in which Jesus reveals the basis of the Holy Week conflict between Himself and the religious leaders of the Jews. With gradual intensification He shows that a portion of the Jewish people (a) refused to give God obedience in deed and refused to heed the call to repent (Matt. 21:28 – 32), (b) mistreated God's emissaries and killed His Son (vv. 33 – 45), and (c) even turned down the free offer of the gift of righteousness by grace (22:1 – 14). The issue in this conflict is also shown by pointing out the continuity between the mission of John the Baptist and that of Jesus (compare Matt. 21:23 – 27 with vv. 31 – 32). *All* must enter the kingdom through a rite designed for sinners and proselytes—baptism unto repentance. Any who refuse John's path of righteousness reject Jesus also.

Matthew says (21:45): "When the chief priests and the Pharisees heard His parables, they perceived that He was speaking about them." What was He saying? "Therefore I tell you, the kingdom of God will be taken away from you and given to a nation producing the fruits of it" (v. 43). Here is the point for them and a warning for us.

Verse 28: "What do you think?" Like Nathan (2 Sam. 12:1), Jesus raises a hypothetical question whose answer will render a judgment against those who give it.

"Two sons." Some in the early church may have thought that these were the Jews and the Gentiles (see the discussion of the text-critical problem in v. 29). But the original reference would have been to two strata (*Schichten,* Schlatter) of the Jewish people.

"Son, go and work." The father uses a familiar address (*teknon* is equivalent to *huios*) and asks nothing but what would have been expected.

Verse 29: "And he answered, 'I will not.' " Comparison with the NEB translation or reference to a critical Greek text will show that a few manuscripts (including Vaticanus) have the *first* son say "Yes" and not go and the *second* son say "I will not" and then repent and go. (Most of these same manuscripts also then substitute "last" for "first" in the answer in v. 31.) But the order in the RSV should be retained; it has better external testimony, and it is easier to explain the origin of the Vaticanus reading as an alteration designed to make the "first" son equal the Jews and the "second" the Gentiles.

"I will not" is a rude refusal; the son uses no polite term of address to his father. This conduct corresponds to that of the "tax collectors and harlots," who show blatant disregard for God's will under the covenant.

"Afterward he repented." The first son had a change of will from within. This word for repent (*metameletheis*) is rare in the New Testament but not unusual in the Septuagint. This action corresponds to that of the sinners of Israel responding to the preaching of John the Baptist, repenting, and bringing forth (like Zacchaeus) the fruits of repentance.

Verse 30: Egō (preferred over the variant *hupagō*) corresponds to the Hebrew *'ani* (see Judges 13:11), but also in the Koine *egōge* represents a strong affirmation.

"Sir." This son was very polite, and yet he did not go. The

thought that deeds, not words, are required to fulfill the Father's will is applied to the Pharisees also in Matt. 23:3: "They preach, but do not practice."

Verse 31a: The consequences are drawn. The answer is a foregone conclusion. The application to the scribes and Pharisees is obvious (see v. 45).

Verses 31b – 32: Jesus drives home the point and parallels the situation to the responses to John the Baptist. Blatant sinners originally refused to obey, but they *repented* and so entered the kingdom of God. (Matthew usually uses "kingdom of heaven.") You (scribes and Pharisees) are also sinners in that you did not obey, but (unlike them) *you did not repent.* Both sons, all Israel, all mankind are sinners. The important difference (and the point of this passage) is that one son *repented,* and the genuineness of his repentance was shown in the results of his changed will; he went forth to obey his Father's will.

Sermon Outline
JESUS' MINISTRY CALLS SINNERS TO THE KINGDOM OF GOD THROUGH REPENTANCE

I. Lip service is inadequate, but how can we *do* the Father's will and not just *say* "I will"?
II. The way of righteousness is that Jesus calls us sinful sons to enter the kingdom through repentance. This involves sorrow over our sins; faith that God has forgiven our sins and declared us righteous because of the life, death, and resurrection of Jesus; and a God-given resolve to be righteous (by the power of the Holy Spirit) in our *everyday* life.
III. He who has entered the kingdom through repentance loves not just in word but in deed and in truth; his faith is not dead, without works, but alive and bearing fruit.

JONATHAN F. GROTHE

Twentieth Sunday After Pentecost

EPISTLE   Philippians 3:12 – 21

Sermon Notes/Introduction

Paul is pressing on to the final resurrection because Christ has laid hold of him (Phil. 3:12). In the preceding and following verses Paul makes clear that although he has broken with his past and is now living in Christ, he must still assume the lowly position of a learner. In the power of the resurrected Christ he is striving to live out Christ's victory over sin and death and to receive the final prize of heaven (v. 14). A sign of maturity is the humble conviction that we have not yet attained perfection. Paul adduces his own example of striving for the Philippians to follow. He warns against imitating professing Christians who have allowed their liberty to degenerate into license and who claim to be perfect while they are concerned only with their self-indulgence (v. 18). Christians are to crucify the flesh. Not to do so is to make oneself an enemy of the cross of Christ. In verse 10 Paul contrasts the prize to be won by those who bear the cross to the destruction that will be meted out to those who, while using the name Christian, mind earthly things. Those for whom the cross of Christ is central have a heavenly commonwealth, which inspires a heaven-oriented life. The perfection Christians strive for in daily crucifying their flesh will one day be manifested in a glorified body that will be in the likeness of Christ in glory and sinlessness (v. 21).

Sermon Outline
THE CHRISTIAN LIFE IS A PRESSING ON

Introduction: If there is nothing to strive for, no goal to achieve, life becomes drab and aimless. We all need something toward which to strive. In our text Paul describes the pressing on that characterizes our life as Christians.

I. We press on by crucifying the flesh.
   A. We are not yet perfect (sinless) (vv. 12 – 13).
      1. The sinful flesh asserts itself by enticing us to mind earthly things (v. 19).
      2. The sinful flesh, if habitually indulged, can eventually lead to our eternal destruction (v. 19).
   B. We can crucify the flesh because Christ has made us His own (v. 12).
      1. His resurrection power working in us energizes our new nature that says no to sin.
      2. His resurrection power is available to us in the Word of the Gospel, Baptism, and Holy Communion.

II. We press on by anticipating the prize.
   A. The prize of perfection awaits us.
      1. This perfection is heaven (v. 20).
      2. This perfection consists in our having a glorious body (v. 21).

B. We can overcome what causes us to lose sight of the prize.
1. The memory of past sins can cause us to lose sight of the prize. Yet we don't have to dwell on those sins because Christ's resurrection proves He atoned for all sin (v. 21).
2. The world around us can so allure us that we forget all about the prize. Yet we can become heavenly instead of earthly minded by pondering the ultimate purpose of Christ's death and resurrection—to subject all things to Himself and to bring us into His eternal kingdom.

Conclusion: Pressing on is what the Christian life is all about. It's a daily struggle against sin and a daily looking forward to the final victory.

GERHARD AHO

Twentieth Sunday After Pentecost

GOSPEL   Matthew 21:33 – 43

Sermon Notes/Introduction

This parable, recorded also in Mark 12:1 – 12 and Luke 20:9 – 19, describes the miserable treatment the Jewish leaders accorded the prophets and finally Christ. The chief priests and Pharisees realize that Christ was speaking of them as the wicked tenants of the vineyard (Matt. 21:45). These leaders also caught Jesus' reference to Is. 5:1 – 7 where Israel is described as God's vineyard. In response to Jesus' question (Matt. 21:40) they are forced to incriminate themselves. Then Jesus shifts the imagery by quoting from Psalm 118 and showing that the tenants were also stupid builders who, by rejecting the Stone (Christ), destroyed themselves.

The point of the parable is that while God has incredible patience, He will finally destroy those who obstinately refuse to bring Him the fruit He is entitled to. The goal of the sermon is that we bring to God the fruits of faith that He expects. The problem is that we who are tenants or renters too often act like owners. The means to the goal is that God is extraordinarily patient with us.

It's possible to rent an amazing variety of things. God too has a rental arrangement.

Sermon Outline
VINEYARD FOR RENT

I. The terms are specified.
   A. God puts the vineyard in excellent condition.
      1. He did so for Israel (Is. 5:1 – 7).
      2. He does so for us through the Good News of Christ, by which He gathers and preserves us as His people.
   B. God "rents out" the vineyard (the message of His love and forgiveness) by giving it to us and through it supplying us with faith, strength, and hope.
   C. God expects us to pay Him rent in kind.
      1. He wants the fruit of faith (Gal. 5:22 – 23).
      2. Because of the enabling power of the Holy Spirit, fruitbearing is not a chore but a spontaneous outpouring in response to God's benefits.
II. Difficulties are encountered.
   A. God had difficulties with His renters.
      1. They killed the prophets (Matt. 21:35 – 36).
      2. Finally they killed the Son Himself (vv. 38 – 39).
   B. God still has difficulties with us, His renters.
      1. We fail to love His mission to the world.
      2. We fail to love God's people.
      3. We fail to love God's messengers.
III. God takes action.
   A. God shows patience.
      1. He kept on sending servants (vv. 34, 36). What a contrast to what we probably would have done under similar circumstances!
      2. He went so far as to send His only Son (v. 37). Through Christ's death God atoned for the tenants' selfishness and ours. To what great lengths God went to show His love and patience!
      3. He is still giving us time to bring forth fruit. He keeps on loving and seeking our love.
   B. Yet God's patience has a limit.
      1. When the Jewish nation rejected Christ, God gave the vineyard (the Gospel message) to the Gentiles.
      2. If we reject Christ, the Gospel will be taken from us and given to others. Christ, the Cornerstone, will one day fall on us and destroy us.

God's sign is still out: Vineyard for rent. The terms are as generous as they can be. In His marvelous love God has surmounted all the difficulties we caused Him. How wicked we are if we spurn His love! What a privilege to be a tenant in God's vineyard and to bring Him His fruits!

GERHARD AHO

Twenty-First Sunday After Pentecost

EPISTLE   Philippians 4:10 – 13, 19 – 20 (RSV)

Sermon Notes/Introduction

1. Paul had a special, close relationship with the church at Philippi grounded in *koinonia* in the Gospel (Phil. 1:5). The closing verses of his letter again reflect the joy of that fellowship, and they lend some insight into the way Christians work together in love—and thereby share real rejoicing.

2. Apparently the Philippian church had supported Paul in some monetary way (4:10). Interestingly enough, the size and other timely details concerning the gift are not mentioned. In a sense, Paul may well agree, "It is not the gift, but the thought that counts." Yet he is also very mindful of the physical needs of the church, as his efforts toward the collection for the Jerusalem church indicate (Rom. 15:25 – 28; 1 Cor. 16:1 – 3).

3. In thanking the church at Philippi, Paul displays a good deal of Christian understanding and tact. For some reason the gift had been delayed; "now at length" the concern is revived (Phil. 4:10). This expression, used only here and at Rom. 1:10, indicates a process long under way that has finally reached completion. But Paul is quick to point out, with the imperfect tense in the next sentence, that the Philippians have certainly been concerned all along. He understands that the right moment, when everything fell into place, was a bit slow in coming. Certainly, one can find ready examples of the need for such patience and understanding when the well-intentioned plans and promises of even fellow Christians sometimes go awry.

4. Paul further softens the delay of the gift in Phil. 4:11. It was not that he did not need it or appreciate it. In no way is he less thankful. But he tactfully eases any embarrassment by reminding the Philippians that he has long since learned to be "content" and not to complain.

5. The real reason Paul is "content" reveals his focus on the "one thing needful." The Greek word translated "content" gives theological meaning to a Greek philosophical concept, as

Paul had also done in verse 8 (see last Sunday's Epistle). The Stoics used the word to describe the inward "self-sufficiency" they sought, but Paul is "self-sufficient" only because he is in Christ (3:8) and because he knows that "our competence is from God" (2 Cor. 3:5). Whether rich or poor (Phil. 4:12), in all things Paul can rejoice (cf. v. 4). He does not need to trust in himself or to evaluate his physical condition to determine success. Rather, he recognizes that any power or ability comes only from "Him who strengthens me" (v. 13).

6. Verses 14–18, omitted in the suggested reading, might well be included, especially verses 17–18, which describe the gift as a fruit of faith and a fragrant sacrifice (cf. Gen. 8:21; Lev. 1:9), a good example of what Article XXIV of the Apology to the Augsburg Confession calls a "eucharistic sacrifice" (*Dankopfer*). Again, the amount of the gift is not important. Paul rejoices simply in witnessing this act of faith and fellowship.

7. God alone fills needs (Phil. 4:19), which are determined not by a physical state (v. 11) but by what really matters: "His riches in glory in Christ Jesus." Christians find cause for joy in sharing that glory of Jesus Christ, the hope of eternal life; so Paul closes with a fitting doxology (v. 20).

Sermon Outline
REAL REJOICING: SHARING IN THE LORD

Last week we saw Paul emphasize the special and true joy we have in the Lord always and in everything. Certainly this affects our lives as we rejoice *together*. Real rejoicing means sharing—confessing together our faith in Jesus as Savior, supporting one another, working together, worshiping and praising God together.

I. Without Christ, we cannot share joy.
   A. Many try to live in a relationship of "joy" and "love" with their fellowman as though this were a panacea for a world of selfishness.
   B. "Charitable giving" is a major part of American life.
   C. But no horizontal relationships will ever produce real joy and love unless we first understand our vertical relationship with God.

II. Christian sharing means first sharing the cross.
   A. Paul emphasizes the secondary nature of the things of this world. They are less important. Paul can take them or leave them.
   B. One cannot be "content" or satisfied by the things of

this world. Pride, greed, and self-trust breed anxiety (cf. 4:6).
C. One is satisfied only when satisfaction is made for his sins. Contentment lies in the cross.
D. True riches are riches in glory in Jesus Christ, offered to us through the Gospel message of the forgiveness of sin and through the Sacraments.

III. Because of the cross, we share a fellowship in the Gospel (see 1:5).
A. Christian joy now finds contentment in Jesus Christ and in sharing Him.
B. Christian joy prompts physical, monetary support for one another in the work of the Lord where there is a need.
  1. This is done out of thanksgiving and rejoicing, as a fruit of faith and response to God's love in Christ.
  2. Such sharing presupposes understanding and concern, even when intentions may not be carried out smoothly.
C. Christians share in rejoicing by praising God together. This is real rejoicing—sharing the riches of the glory of God.

ANDREW H. BARTELT

Twenty-First Sunday After Pentecost

GOSPEL Matthew 22:1–14

Sermon Notes/Introduction

This parable, along with the parables of the two sons and the wicked tenants, should be understood against the background of the final events in Christ's ministry. Jesus is relating Israel's shameful treatment of the prophets God sent to call them to repentance. Christ's hearers were well aware that kings dispatched armies to destroy opponents and to set fire to their cities.

The emphasis in verses 9–10 is on the mercy God extends to all sinners. Yet each guest must have the proper clothes (vv. 11–14). The king himself provides the necessary garment. To refuse to wear it is to show contempt for the host. The person who insulted the king, refusing to sit at the banquet on the king's terms, represents the self-righteous person who rejects the righteousness God offers through Jesus Christ.

Anyone who thinks he does not need the garment of righteousness Jesus secured for him must suffer the consequences.

The point of the parable is that although everyone is welcome at God's wedding feast, one can be a guest there only on God's terms. The goal of the sermon is that the hearers will take seriously God's offer of grace. The problem is that we sometimes make God's gracious offer an excuse for sinning. The means to the goal is that God invites all sinners and provides them with the needed garment.

One of life's pleasures is to hear the announcement, "Dinner's ready." God has prepared a dinner—salvation, forgiveness of sins, and life eternal. That's quite a dinner! This dinner has been ready for a long time.

Sermon Outline
DINNER'S READY

I. God invites.
   A. He doesn't command people to come.
      1. He doesn't demand that we first make ourselves worthy.
      2. He won't force us to eat.
   B. Yet many refuse the invitation.
      1. They allow activities acceptable in themselves to become more important than God's invitation.
      2. We need to watch that we do not put off accepting God's invitation.
      3. The consequences of such procrastination can be drastic.

II. God invites all.
   A. He sends His messengers out again.
      1. He won't let rejection by some prevent the banquet from taking place.
      2. He wants the food to be eaten.
   B. God shows no partiality or prejudice. When the respectable people refuse, He invites the lowly and the despised.

III. God invites on His terms.
   A. He provides for each guest the needed wedding garment.
      1. Not only has He prepared salvation, but He also makes it possible for all to partake of salvation.
      2. The wedding garment is the righteousness Christ earned for us, which alone makes us acceptable to

God and qualifies us to be guests at God's wedding feast. We receive this garment by faith in Jesus.
3. Without Christ's righteousness we are doomed, for our righteousness condemns us.

B. While letting Christ's righteousness cover our sins, we must be on guard lest we continue to love and practice sin.
1. That would amount to playing games with the grace of God.
2. That would mean that we are no better off than the blatant unbeliever.

God Himself has prepared a wedding dinner. What joy to hear, "Dinner's ready"—to hear Him invite us and to receive from Him the beautiful garment of Christ's righteousness.

GERHARD AHO

Twenty-Second Sunday After Pentecost

EPISTLE   1 Thessalonians 1:1 – 5a

Sermon Notes/Introduction

1. The church at Thessalonica was founded by Paul on his second missionary journey (Acts 17:1 – 9). It was composed of converts from Judaism and from heathenism, including many devout Greeks and leading women of the community.

2. The birth of this church was marked by strife. Jealous Jews tried to label these new Christians as unpatriotic anarchists who upset the established order and advocated the replacement of Caesar with Jesus as king. In the midst of the strife, the fledgling Thessalonian Christians, out of loving concern for Paul (and for his co-worker, Silas), sent their pastoral leaders to Berea.

3. The pressures of persecution continued (1 Thess. 2:14 – 16; 3:3 – 4). In the absence of mature pastoral teaching and counsel, internal problems also arose. There was concern rooted in ignorance about the eternal destiny of believers who had died (4:13 – 18) and a parallel misunderstanding about the second coming of Christ (5:1 – 11), both of which combined to produce problems of idleness (4:11) and disorderliness (5:14 – 15). Some were tempted to return to heathen vices (4:1 – 8; 5:22). The bitterness of their situation seems to have prompted others to malign Paul and his ministry to them (2:1 – 12). Paul had gained an assessment of the condition in

Thessalonica by sending Timothy to visit and to bring back a report.

4. It was evident that the Thessalonian Christians had lost some of their realization of themselves as people of God, the church of God. Paul's first remedy for their need was to remind them that they had become God's people and church. In so doing, he also reminds us to look to our beginnings to gain a proper perspective on our present and on our future. By expressing thankful remembrance of the beginnings, Paul invites thankful remembrance as the conscious context for current believing and living.

Sermon Outline
REMEMBER YOUR BEGINNINGS WITH THANKSGIVING

(In all components of the outline, a running parallel should be maintained between the Thessalonians and the immediate hearers of the sermon.)

I. Remember your initiation as God's people and church.
   A. The Gospel came to you.
      1. It came in the larger sense of the Word of God, which by the Law convicts the hearer of his sin and by the Good News convinces the hearer of his Savior.
      2. It came both in word to inform and in the power of the Holy Spirit to give certain confidence.
   B. God's choice of you became evident to you.
      1. You took no initiative in hearing or believing the Gospel.
      2. The fact and the effect of your hearing the Gospel mark you as God's chosen ones from eternity (Rom. 8:28–30; Eph. 1:3–14; Formula of Concord, Epitome and Solid Declaration, XI).
II. Remember your continuation as God's people and church.
   A. Your faith has not been an idle or merely intellectual believing, but it has been fruitful in the works taught by Christ, the object of faith (1 Thess. 2:14; 4:1; 5:11).
   B. Your faith has not only led you to have a spiritual concern for others, but has also led you to perform labors of love for others (3:6, 12; 4:9–10).
   C. Your faith has not only been a blessing for the present life but has also given you steadfast hope in our Lord Jesus Christ for the future life (5:1, 9–10).

III. Remember your status as God's people and church.
   A. Give thanks for your conversion (1 Pet. 2:10; Eph. 2:19 – 22).
   B. Give thanks for the conformity of your life to Christ (Rom. 12:1 – 2).
   C. Give thanks for your being the church (the "called out") in God the Father and the Lord Jesus Christ (Rom. 8:15 – 17; Eph. 1:22 – 23; 4:15 – 16).

The present may be fraught with difficulties, as it was for the Thessalonians, and the future may be foreboding, as it seemed to them, at least in some respects. But remembering one's beginnings with thanksgiving keeps the powerfully effective Gospel uppermost in heart and mind so that the same means that worked such blessing in the past are there to work blessing in the present and for the future.

ROLAND A. HOPMANN

Twenty-Second Sunday After Pentecost

GOSPEL   Matthew 22:15 – 21 (RSV)

Sermon Notes/Introduction

This is the first in a series of three questions put to Jesus on Monday of Holy Week. The Pharisees (Matt. 22:15 – 22), the Sadducees (vv. 23 – 33), and a lawyer (vv. 34 – 40) each lay before Jesus a pitfall into which His Messiahship might plummet. Any of His expected or possible answers might open the door for charges against Him—insurrectionist, compromiser, innovator, someone loose in His attitude toward the Law. But in each case Jesus' answer transcends the sectarian views of the questioners; His enunciation of the truth exposes the limitations of each party's tenets. Jesus teaches them (and us) the true nature of His Messiahship (see also His counter-question, Matt. 22:41 – 46) and the reign of God.

Verse 15: "Pharisees." Jesus' conflict with Judaism was often a clash with this sect, which was oriented toward a twofold system of law (written and oral). The Pharisees enjoyed great influence over the people. They desired to avoid war with Rome, but their hope for the salvation of Israel included the removal of the foreign oppressor.

"Entangle Him." This is no polite or bona fide inquiry. As His enemies, they plot to expose and discredit Jesus, so that they may be justified in doing away with Him.

Verse 16: "Herodians." The ruler's party compromised and cooperated with the Romans. The Pharisees were ordinarily opposed to their policy, but the reason for which they invited them to this occasion is obvious: Jesus might brand Himself an insurrectionist.

"You are true." The flattery is designed to force Jesus to make a self-indicting answer or be discredited as a fearless prophet and teacher of truth.

Verse 17: "Tell us, then, what you think." One of Jesus' favorite devices (see Matt. 21:28) is turned against Him.

"Is it lawful?" Supposedly, *God's* will and Law are the subject of the inquiry. But the pointed question invites no discussion; it seeks a yes-or-no answer. Either answer will discredit Jesus, and that is the question's goal. The Pharisees probably expected that He would answer no and fall into a conflict with Rome. A Messiah who could recognize the political sovereignty of Caesar was unthinkable for all Jews. His opposition to Rome would naturally be expressed in His attitude toward paying the tribute tax. (The Zealots, in fact, said that to pay the tribute tax was to give up the yoke of the reign of God.)

Verse 18: "Hypocrites." Jesus recognizes their intent. By their association with their usual opponents, the Herodians, the Pharisees show their hypocrisy.

Verses 19 – 20: "Show Me the money." This demand also makes the Pharisees reveal the hypocrisy of their question, and at the same time it prepares for the principle enunciated in the next verse. For the Jews, the image and inscription of Caesar (*divus Augustus*) on a coin was technically a violation of the commandment against graven images of other gods. These coins were offensive to the Pharisees, and yet they themselves had compromised enough to allow them to be handled in the payment of the tax. By making them bring such a coin to Him, Jesus pointed out the Pharisees' own compromise on the very issue with which they were trying to entrap Him.

Verse 21: "Render therefore to Caesar." The coin is Caesar's possession. It is not with such things that man honors God. Religious zeal that expresses itself in a demand to refuse to pay taxes has a low estimation of what true piety is. The Zealots and the Pharisees had too worldly a view of the reign of God.

"The things that are God's." What is it that bears the stamp of God's image? It is the human soul itself, made in God's image and redeemed by Christ's life, death, and resurrection! Let Caesar have his wretched coins. Give God what is His— your very selves, a living sacrifice (see Rom. 12:1). With these words Jesus freed His followers from moving to oppose Rome, while still maintaining His claim to be the Messianic bringer of the reign of God.

Sermon Outline
OF COINS AND SOULS

Jesus' Messiahship establishes the reign of God in a way that does not rival the kingdoms of this world but rather makes a radical demand for man's ultimate allegiance and worship. Jesus' atoning work, applied by the Holy Spirit, enables us to meet this radical demand.

I. The significance of the Pharisees' question is in their Messianic expectations and practical compromises.
II. The significance of Jesus' answer is the distinction between what pertains to earthly citizenship and the honor and worship men owe to God.
III. Jesus' answer avoided the trap.
   A. He defused the Pharisees' question and exposed their hypocrisy.
   B. He established the two-kingdom teaching for the church throughout history.
   C. He gave Christians today clear direction for living as good citizens with their religious priorities straight.

JONATHAN F. GROTHE

Twenty-Third Sunday After Pentecost

EPISTLE   1 Thessalonians 1:5b – 10

Sermon Notes/Introduction

Paul marked the church of the Thessalonians as an "example" (1 Thess. 1:7)—literally, a type. The word "type" not only is transliterated from Greek into English but carries essentially the same cluster of meanings in English as in Greek (cf. Greek and English lexicons).

Ask people, "What type are you?" Some hear it neutrally as a request for a self-evaluation, some negatively as a threat to oversimplify their valuable complexities and diversities, and some positively as an invitation to identify their best and most useful qualifications. To the Thessalonians, Paul gave the answer without asking the question and did so in a way that led them to recognize their goodness and its usefulness. For us, in the spirit of appreciation established by the paragraph's first sentence (vv. 2–3), this text should rouse realization of our useful goodness and prompt us to be thankful for being God's type.

Sermon Outline
BE THANKFUL FOR BEING GOD'S TYPE

I. God makes people His type.
   A. God made Paul His type, a figure formed by Him, in a spectacular conversion (Acts 9:5), for which the groundwork had been laid in Paul's rich knowledge of the Old Testament (22:3) and of the tradition concerning Jesus Christ (8:1).
   B. God made the Thessalonians His figure, His type, in an impressive conversion by the power of the Spirit in Paul's preaching of the Word (1 Thess. 1:6; Acts 17:2–4) so that they turned from idols to the living and genuine God and to His Son, Jesus, the Deliverer, (1 Thess. 1:9–10).
   C. God has made us His impressions or types in a miraculous conversion, whether observable or not, by the power of His Spirit in the Word as received in Baptism (Titus 3:3–7; Rom. 6:3–4) or through reading and hearing that led us to Baptism (Acts 8:26–39), so that we have been turned from hopeless sinfulness and death to righteousness and life in Christ (Eph. 2:1–9). To God be our thanks.

II. God leads people to live as His types.
   A. Paul shamelessly referred to his own life among the Thessalonians (1 Thess. 1:5) as God's own exhibition of having shaped him (Phil. 2:13; Heb. 13:20–21; Eph. 2:10) and made him an imitator of God (1 Thess. 1:6) in such things as courage (2:2), trustworthiness (vv. 3–6), kindness (v. 7), and selflessness (v. 9). His unwilling continued sinfulness confirmed rather than denied his being the figure and pattern of God (Rom. 7:21–25; 1 Tim. 1:15).
   B. Paul prompted the Thessalonians unabashedly to see themselves as God-made figures and patterns in their imitation of the Lord, their endurance of affliction (1 Thess. 1:6), their speaking the Word (v. 8), their service to God (v. 9), and their waiting for Jesus' triumphant return (v. 10). The weakness of their continued sinfulness (4:3–6, 11–12; 5:14–15) did not destroy God's impression on them (4:1).

C. These Scriptures prompt us to see the ways in which God causes His imprint on us to show, even in His turning us to Himself for the forgiveness of the sin that still clings to us. To God be our thanks.

III. God blesses His types in each other.
  A. Paul, God's chosen instrument to carry the Gospel to the Gentiles (Acts 9:15), was a blessing and source of strength not only to those whom he served directly so that they became imitators of him (e.g., the Thessalonians, 1 Thess. 1:6) but also to those believers who had only heard of him (Rom. 1:8 – 15).
  B. The Thessalonians were a blessing and encouragement not only to each other (1 Thess. 5:11) but also to the believers in Macedonia, Achaia, and beyond (1:7 – 8).
  C. God uses His impression on us as a spiritually edifying influence on those with whom we live face to face and on many more of whom we may never be aware in this life. To God be our thanks.

God made us His types, maintains us as His types, and uses us as His types or patterns to be imitated in order to bless each other and many believers beyond our acquaintance with strengthening and encouragement. For what our Lord does to us and through us we can give thanks every day.

ROLAND A. HOPMANN

Twenty-Third Sunday After Pentecost

GOSPEL   Matthew 22:34 – 40

Sermon Notes/Introduction

Verse 34: Jesus has just silenced the Sadducees on the question of resurrection, no doubt a source of satisfaction to the rival Pharisees (Acts 23:8). Now they gather together (*epi to auto*) to question Him directly and not through intermediaries as in Matt. 22:16.

Verse 35: The *nomikos,* an expert in the Mosaic law, tests (*peirazōn*) Jesus. The Markan account (12:28 – 34) reflects that this encounter is not hostile, unlike many of the other encounters between Jesus and the Pharisees (Matt. 9:3; 15:12; 16:21; 20:18; 21:15 – 16; 22:15).

Verse 36: The lawyer's question shows that the commandments have varying degrees of importance. *Poia:* "What kind of commandment" rather than "which individual commandment." The rabbis had some 613 commandments, 248 positive and 365 negative. Such a large number necessitated the classification reflected in *poia*.

Verse 37: Jesus offers no rebuke at all to the lawyer (see 22:18, 29) but answers his question. The first commandment, like the second (v. 39), is a commandment of selfless and purposeful love, *agapē*.

Love for God is to fill the entire person's heart (the center of the personality), soul (life itself), and mind (intellect). Deut. 6:5 reads "heart, ... soul, and ... might"; Mark 12:30 has "heart, ... soul, ... mind, and ... strength." The totality of one's existence is meant. Note the repetition of *holē*. God can demand man's total love because He has totally loved man, to the extent of entering into a covenant with man and giving up His own Son. His total love offers the fine opportunity to present the Gospel in this text and to avoid descending to legalism.

Verse 38: This commandment is *megalē kai prōtē*, "great and first," because it is the foundation of all actions detailed in the other commandments.

Verse 39: The second commandment (Lev. 19:18), treating duties toward our fellowman, is like the first because of the requirement of love. Love for neighbor is modeled on God's love for all (Matt. 5:43 – 45) and on self-identification with the neighbor (Matt. 7:12; 19:19). Mark 12:32 – 34 indicates the lawyer's satisfaction with Jesus' answer.

Verse 40: Not legal requirements of Scripture but the entire Law *and* Gospel hang on these two commandments. Indeed, only the Christian motivated by the Gospel of Christ is able to fulfill these commands (Heb. 11:6).

Sermon Outline
ALL OR NOTHIN'

In the musical *Oklahoma!* Wil tells Ado Annie to love him "all or nothin'. It's all or nothin' with me." This is a good description not only of God's love for us but also of His expectations of us in our relationship with Him and with one another.

I. God's total love for you.
   A. It is seen throughout Bible history.
      1. It is promised in Israel and the covenant.
      2. It is fulfilled in the life of Christ.

    B. It is active in your life.
        1. It is applied to you in Baptism.
        2. It is proclaimed to you through the Word.
        3. It is shared with you in Holy Communion.
II. God yearns for all your love—for Himself.
    A. The first commandment is the greatest commandment.
    B. We often fail to keep it.
    C. God's love forgives and strengthens us for better future fulfillment.
III. God yearns for all your love—for others.
    A. The second great commandment depends on the first.
    B. We also fail to keep this commandment.
    C. God and Christ are the source and models for improvement.

DALE A. MEYER

Twenty-Fourth Sunday After Pentecost

EPISTLE 1 Thessalonians 4:13 – 18 (RSV)

Sermon Notes/Introduction

When a loved one dies, it is bad enough. But when one is perplexed about the possibility that death may rule out any participation in the joy of the second coming of Christ, that perplexity adds much more grief to the sorrow ordinarily experienced.

This is the situation addressed by St. Paul in the Epistle for today. The new Christians in Thessalonica apparently had come to fear that death might negate involvement in the great day of the Lord Jesus' parousia. Timothy had brought this news to Paul. Hence, the inspired author wrote tender, comforting words to his beloved friends in Macedonia, which retain their cogency and power to this very day.

Sermon Outline
GOD'S PROMISE MAKES A DIFFERENCE

I. The absence of the promise brings ignorance, misunderstanding, and heartache.
    A. "We would not have you ignorant, brethren" (1 Thess. 1:13a). This is inevitably the result when, for some reason, the Word of God is not faithfully taught or is resisted or rejected. Ignorance, superstition, misunderstanding, and a host of other tragic cir-

cumstances may be found everywhere when the Word is not taken seriously. One of the primary functions of the Word is to dispel ignorance.

B. "That you may not grieve as others do who have no hope" (v. 13). Ignorance of the Word leads to heartache and grief. The Christians of Thessalonica were needlessly grieved over the loss of loved ones because they feared that those who died prior to Christ's return would have no part in that great event. They saw the evidence of the dire result of man's sin in the face of death (Law) but were not able to appreciate the healing effects of the Gospel.

II. The acceptance of the promise brings knowledge and comfort.

A. Christ's death and resurrection assure the resurrection of those who die in Him (v. 14). St. Paul's use of the Greek *ei* does not imply doubt; on the contrary, it is a virtual assertion that they do indeed believe that Christ died and rose again. This confidence has the further ramification that those who die in faith will be brought together by God with Christ at His coming.

B. The Word of the Lord gives some details of the parousia (vv. 15–17).

1. "The Lord Himself will descend from heaven" (v. 16). As He descends, there will be a cry of command, an archangel's call, and the sound of the trumpet of God. The emphasis is on the Lord Jesus Himself. He is the One who died, who was buried, who rose again, who ascended into heaven, and who has promised to return in like manner (see Acts 1:11; 1 Thess. 1:10). He is the focus of attention and the object of adoration.

2. "The dead in Christ will rise first" (1 Thess. 1:16). This assurance St. Paul received as a special revelation from the Lord (v. 15). Those who are alive at the parousia will not precede those who died; rather, the dead in Him will rise first, then those who are alive will rise to meet the Lord in the air. Therefore, the loved ones who have fallen asleep have a special place in the parousia (v. 17).

3. "So we shall always be with the Lord" (v. 17). It is interesting to note that there is no reference to a thousand-year reign of Christ at this juncture. The focus is on the believers, those who died and those

who remained, being united together with the Lord Jesus Christ, their only hope and only salvation.

C. The Word of the Lord gives comfort to the believers (v. 18). That authoritative Word not only is able to comfort the individual, but it is to be shared among the community of saints. "Comfort one another with these words."

When the "bottom line" reads "death," man needs more than speculations to reassure him. At that hour man needs a word from God. It matters not whether that "death" is the "falling asleep" of a loved one or the moment of his own death. Thanks be to God, that Word has been spoken. In Jesus Christ, who died for our sins and rose again for our justification, we have forgiveness of sins and assurance of life eternal. All this is mediated through the Word and the sacraments.

RUDOLPH H. HARM

Twenty-Fourth Sunday After Pentecost

GOSPEL   Matthew 23:37 – 39 (KJV)

Sermon Notes/Introduction

1. Like many other pericopes for Sundays late in the Pentecost season, the Series A readings for the Twenty-Fourth Sunday After Pentecost are concerned with the End Time, God's judgment, and our preparation for it. Our text captures both the somber notes of the Old Testament Reading (compare Matt. 23:38 with Amos 5:18 – 24) and the brighter notes of the Epistle (compare Matt. 23:39 with 1 Thess. 4:13 – 14), which describes the blessed resurrection of those who have availed themselves of the protection of God—the ultimate Pentecost gathering!

2. In relation to its immediate context, the Gospel comprises an oasis in a desert of Law. Immediately preceding our text is a lengthy "woe" section, in which the scribes and Pharisees are denounced for various evils, and after our text is a lengthy description of the chaotic conditions that will prevail before Judgment Day. While Matt. 23:38 is a continuation of the mood of both precontext and postcontext, verse 37 shows the compelling love of God toward those just denounced, and verse 39 holds out a ray of hope.

3. "Jerusalem, Jerusalem" (v. 37) is an apostrophe, a digression in which the speaker turns aside to address an absent

or imaginary addressee. The repetition calls attention to the intensity of the feeling that prompts the remark and to the importance of the substance of the remark. (Think of "Absalom, Absalom"; "Martha, Martha"; "Saul, Saul.")

4. "Jerusalem" is also metonymy; that is, the city stands for the people of the city—in fact, for the people of the entire nation.

5. Since "Jerusalem" means literally "city of peace," the name, in view of the people's evil deeds and their dire consequences, is ironic in this context.

6. The present participles "killing" and "stoning" (v. 37) are significant in that they imply that the dastardly deeds described are still being committed. They are not merely past misdeeds, but they persist to the present.

7. The metaphor of the hen gathering her chickens under her wings, besides being a concrete and specific description of that God described in more general and abstract terms in Ezek. 33:11 as having "no pleasure in the death of the wicked" and in 1 Tim. 2:4 as wishing to "have all men to be saved," echoes the frequent Old Testament metaphor of God as an eagle, whose wings bear us up (Ex. 19:4) or cover us with feathers (Ps. 91:4) and under which we take refuge (Ps. 57:1). When we bear in mind that the Greek word for hen may also refer to any kind of bird, the parallelism in imagery between the Old and New Testaments is all the more remarkable. Aware of this parallelism, the preacher and his audience, when confronting our text, may have a delightful "Aha!" experience, suddenly recognizing in the coupling of the eagle-hen images a powerful tribute to the unity of the two Testaments, as well as a reassurance that Jesus is indeed "the same yesterday, and today, and forever" (Heb. 13:8).

8. If only our Lord's addressees would respond to His plea to be gathered together under His protection as chickens are gathered together under the wings of a hen, they could avoid both the "Roman eagle" that later destroyed their city in A.D. 70 as well as that divine eagle of judgment described in Matt. 24:28 as hovering over the carcass.

9. Note in 23:37 the sharp contrast between the "would" of Jesus and the "would not" of His addressees ("how often *would* I have gathered thy children together" versus "and ye *would not*").

10. "House" (v. 38) is regarded by many commentators as the temple at Jerusalem. Note how subtly God's absence is communicated in the fact that the temple is called "*your* house"

(not "*God's* house"). Since the temple was the heart and center of Jewish worship and life, God's absence from it signifies His absence from His addressees if they persist in their godless conduct.

11. "Desolate" (v. 38) means bereft of God; thus it is a symbol of that ultimate and permanent absence of God that is more commonly called hell.

12. Note the contrast between verse 38 and verse 39. If the former threatens the absence of God, the latter promises His presence (a superb Law-Gospel combination). Not all is hopeless; at some future time (after Jesus' resurrection? at Pentecost? at the Second Coming? perhaps better left unspecified?) some of Jesus' addressees will welcome the Lord Jesus in words similar to those used by the Palm Sunday multitude (see also Ps. 118:26). In so blessing the Lord, they, of course, will themselves be blessed.

Sermon Outline
GOD'S "WOULD" VERSUS OUR "WOULD NOT"

I. Our "would not" (sin).
   A. The evidence.
      1. Then.
      2. Now.
   B. The Outcome: "Your house is left unto you desolate."
II. God's "would" (grace).
   A. The evidence.
      1. It is stated generally and abstractly in Ezek. 33:13 and 1 Tim. 2:4.
      2. It is stated specifically and concretely in verse 37 of the text.
      3. It is demonstrated dramatically on the cross.
   B. The outcome.
      1. We repent and welcome the Lord; we say (in effect): "Blessed is He that cometh in the name of the Lord."
      2. Jesus says to us: "Come, ye blessed of My Father, inherit the kingdom prepared for you from the foundation of the world" (Matt. 25:34).

FRANCIS C. ROSSOW

Twenty-Fifth Sunday After Pentecost

EPISTLE   1 Thessalonians 5:1 – 11 (RSV)

Sermon Notes/Introduction

In view of the fact that the question of the second advent of Christ plays such an important part in both letters to the Thessalonians, it appears that this subject constituted one of the major thrusts of St. Paul's initial teaching and preaching activity in that city. The text before us today teaches that the properly instructed Christian has a distinct attitude and life-style in prospect of the realities connected with the "day of the Lord." This constitutes the major emphasis of our message.

Sermon Outline
THE CHRISTIAN AND THE DAY OF THE LORD

I. What does the Christian know of the day of the Lord?
  A. The day comes suddenly "like a thief in the night" (1 Thess. 5:2). The people of the world will be misled by "peace and security" (v. 3), but the Christian will not be surprised (v. 4), for he is a son of the day and of light (v. 5).
  B. The day brings "sudden destruction" (v. 3). Just as the pangs of childbirth come suddenly and are impossible to avoid, so the day of the Lord brings inescapable destruction on the unsuspecting and unprepared person of the world. Of this the Christian is aware, and by grace he is properly prepared to meet it. God's wrath against sin is clearly discerned. Only the child of God, who finds safety in the wounds of Jesus Christ, can face that day without fear.
II. What is the Christian's destiny in light of the day of the Lord?
  A. The Christian is not destined to wrath (v. 9). Wrath is the just penalty for all who, like Adam, have "sinned and fall short of the glory of God" (Rom. 3:23). Paul obviously is including all mankind. By birth and by choice all are numbered among those deserving the name "sinner." God would be completely justified in assigning all people to destruction because of their private and public rebellion against Him. Apart from

the grace of God, everyone is without hope and without God.
- B. The Christian is destined to salvation through Christ (1 Thess. 5:9). Though the Christian deserves to die just as any other person, Christ died on the cross for the sake of all mankind. Because of His sacrificial death and resurrection, all who trust in Jesus receive through their faith the forgiveness of sins and the assurance that they will be able to stand in the day of the Lord. God, working through His Word and sacraments, creates faith in the Christian's heart, making it possible for him to escape the wrath to come.

III. How does the Christian behave in view of the day of the Lord?
- A. The Christian should "keep awake and be sober" (v. 6). As he anticipates the sudden advent of Christ, the Christian ought to remain alert and in control of all his senses. (Note that the present tense of the subjunctives in the original indicates continued action.)
- B. The Christian is to be on the defense against evil forces (v. 8). Since the best defense is a good offense, God urges each Christian to put on faith and love as his breastplate and the hope of salvation as his protecting helmet. The Christian knows, indeed, that it is only the power of God's Spirit working through the means of grace that empowers him to "put on" these good gifts. Therefore, he realizes his need to live in utter dependence on resources that are not his own but come from the Spirit of God.
- C. In life or in death the Christian lives with Christ (v. 10; cf. Rom. 14:8). The Christian's whole existence is centered in Jesus Christ. He can say with the apostle Paul, "It is my eager expectation and hope that ... now as always Christ will be honored in my body, whether by life or by death. For to me to live is Christ, and to die is gain" (Phil. 1:20–21). The Christian's prayer and worship express the reality of this conviction. A Christ-centered life has its own present and future reward.
- D. Christians ought to "encourage one another and build one another up" (1 Thess. 5:11). The Christian life is not lived in isolation; it is lived in community. In that communion of the saints, the Christian should share the good things of God with his brothers and sisters in

faith. God's grace is not inactive in the individual but shows continued expression of His love through Jesus Christ in the life of the Christian (cf. Smalcald Articles, III, IV).

RUDOLPH H. HARM

Twenty-Fifth Sunday After Pentecost

GOSPEL   Matthew 25:14 – 30 (KJV)

Sermon Notes/Introduction

Citizens of the kingdom of God are responsible for the use of the gifts and abilities God has given them. They are to be actively engaged in speaking and doing those things that their abilities best fit them to say and do. There will be time to use our abilities, but the day of reckoning will come. Therefore the matter is urgent. As Christ's servants we are to use our talents profitably by helping others, improving ourselves, and honoring Christ. This parable illustrates Paul's words in 1 Cor. 6:20, "Glorify God in your body, and in your spirit, which are God's."

A talent in New Testament times was a large unit of money. Because of Jesus' use of the word in the text, talent has acquired the meaning of gift, aptitude, or ability. The question raised by the text is whether our talents are being used.

Sermon Outline
ARE YOUR TALENTS AT WORK?

I. God gives each of us talents.
   A. He gives to each of us according to our ability.
      1. Our talents are personal and diverse.
      2. Talents may be musical, intellectual, or organizational.
   B. Our talents are a trust from God.
      1. We have been privileged to receive them.
      2. Surely we would not wish to disappoint Him who has given us what we had no right to demand.
II. God provides each of us with opportunities to use our talents.
   A. Faithful use of our opportunities is never in vain (1 Cor. 15:58).
      1. Benefits are multiplied.

        2. An equal sense of responsibility will sometimes produce different results.
    B. We are faithless when we do not grasp our opportunities.
        1. When we do nothing, we dishonor the Lord.
        2. Doing nothing is just as bad as wasting our opportunities in riotous living.
III. God requires an accounting.
    A. There will be commendation for some.
        1. We who are clothed in the goodness of Christ are commended for any gain through the use of our talents.
        2. The Lord's "well done" is a gracious assurance of heavenly joy.
    B. There will be condemnation for others.
        1. The condemnation is just, for no servant is burdened with more than he can handle.
        2. The condemnation is warranted, for unprofitable servants look on the Lord as a "hard man" and not as the gracious Master that He is.

Are our talents at work? What a privilege to let them work for a Lord who has entrusted them to us and who graciously commends our responsible use of them!

GERHARD AHO

Third-Last Sunday in the Church Year

EPISTLE 1 Thessalonians 2:8 – 13 (KJV)

Sermon Notes/Introduction

1. The readings in some of the other pericopal systems for the last Sundays in the Trinity season deal with eschatology—the end of time, the second coming of Christ, the judgment, and the resurrection of the dead. The ancient Christians looked forward to the second coming with great longing. During the Middle Ages, a time very otherworldly in some ways, some subtle changes were introduced on the topic of the second coming. Christians began to feel dread and terror rather than earnest longing. In the Medieval Mass, the day of the second coming was referred to as the day of wrath. The hymn "Day of Wrath, O Day of Mourning" reflects this clearly.

2. Modern man is much more blasé, devoid of yearning as well as of dread and terror. This may or may not be the reason

that the ILCW series pericopes for the last Sundays after Pentecost depart substantially from the theme of eschatology.

3. The standard Gospel, Matt. 24:15–28, speaks of the coming of the Son of Man and of the terrors and delusions that will precede. In the standard Epistle, 1 Thess. 4:13–18, St. Paul speaks very clearly of the comfort of the resurrection associated with the second coming of Christ. The pericopes in the three-year series are much more personal. They depart considerably from the main theme, thus missing most of the emphasis on the second coming of Christ. Even if we pass up the eschatology emphasis of other pericopes—a sad loss, to be sure—it may be salutary, possibly provocative, for both pastor and people to make a comparison with St. Paul. Probably not many of us may truthfully say to a contemporary congregation what St. Paul wrote to the Christians in Thessalonica about the sacrifice he made in ministering to them. But at least Paul may serve as a model: "Not as though I had already attained, either were already perfect; but I follow after" (Phil. 3:12).

4. This text in a way is paired with that for next Sunday. 1 Thess. 2:8–13 highlights the apostolic concern for the congregation. In 3:7–13 Paul stresses the mutual concern among pastor and people, with the response of the congregation occupying an important part of the content.

Sermon Outline
THE MODEL OF SELF-SACRIFICING APOSTOLIC MINISTRY

Highlight the second coming of Christ, the resurrection, and the judgment. In the light of this certainty, the ministry of the Word takes on a new urgency.

I. The Roots of This Self-Sacrificing Ministry.
   A. They are found in the love of God for sinful men.
      1. The love of God is expressed in the Gospel. The broader dimensions of the Law-Gospel theme must be described here. Paul stresses that he imparted the Gospel (2:8–9), the Word of God (v. 13).
      2. God had a special love for the apostle. It had pleased Him to entrust St. Paul with the Gospel (v. 4). This must be the basis of a self-sacrificing ministry even today.
   B. They are found in the apostle's love for his people.
      1. The apostle had a kindly feeling for people, so that he might in no way be a financial burden (v. 9).

2. The apostle had a love for his people. He was quite gentle with them (v. 7); he was concerned with them as a father is for his children (v. 11).
II. The Results of This Self-Sacrificing Ministry.
   A. They are seen in the apostolic witness.
      1. The apostle was willing to impart his own life to them (v. 8). St. Paul boldly stresses his "labor and travail," which he willingly endured for the sake of an unencumbered ministry in Thessalonica (v. 9). St. Paul also stresses his holy, just, and unblamable conduct. Action must follow attitude, but the proper attitude for a self-sacrificing ministry must be based on God's love and must be sincere and unfeigned in the heart of God's servant.
      2. The apostle exhorted, comforted, and charged each one of the members to walk worthy of God.
   B. They are seen in the response of the congregation.
      1. The people received the apostolic witness as the Word of God (v. 13).
      2. The people received the efficacious Word, which worked effectually in those who believed (v. 13).

God's love expressed in the Gospel and His special ministry entrusted to Paul served as the roots of Paul's self-sacrifice on behalf of the Thessalonians. As men entrusted with the same Gospel and a similar ministry, we can do no better than to try, with God's help, to imitate Paul's apostolic pattern.

ROY A. SUELFLOW

Third-Last Sunday in the Church Year

GOSPEL   Matthew 23:1–12

Sermon Notes/Introduction

According to Matt. 23:2–3 the scribes and Pharisees were worthy of respect because they had inherited the authority of Moses. Insofar as their teaching was derived from the Scriptures and not from their own interpretations, that teaching was to be heeded. It was their practice that was to be shunned, for they bound or tied together like sheaves (*desmeuousin*, v. 4) heavy burdens of rules but made not the least effort to follow their own rules. Here Christ is denouncing not the Law itself but the false inferences and deductions that put a yoke on the neck of disciples.

A second pharisaic evil Jesus warns against is ostentation in religion. Insofar as they did comply with their rules, they did so only to get the honor of men. Phylacteries were little boxes attached to the forehead and the left arm near the heart containing pieces of parchment with injunctions written on them to keep in memory God's laws and dealings. The more zealous teachers enlarged the phylacteries to focus attention on their religious and careful observance of the Law. The tassels fastened to the corners of the garments were supposed to remind the wearers of God's commandments. The Pharisees also coveted the place of honor at banquets and in the synagogues and loved to be respectfully greeted in public places (vv. 6–7). In verse 8 Christ does not forbid respect for teachers but condemns eagerness for titles and the desire for abject discipleship from followers. A good teacher will influence his followers to look to God and not to himself (v. 9). In verse 10 Christ censures the kind of spirit that manifested itself in the Corinthian church (1 Cor. 1:11–13), where one said that he belonged to Paul and another said he belonged to Apollos. Paul and Apollos were servants of Christ, who alone is the supreme teacher because He is the Messiah, the Savior. True greatness lies in servanthood (Matt. 23:11). Such servants God Himself exalts (v. 12).

The central thought of the text is that religious forms must not degenerate into mere formality. The goal is that the hearers will use the forms of religion to serve God and not themselves. The problem is that we often use the forms of religion to exalt ourselves. The means to the goal is that Christ, who humbled Himself all the way to the cross, will Himself exalt His humble followers.

Christians, both clergy and lay people, are often criticized for not practicing what they preach. Disagreement between word and deed can cause offense and weaken the church's witness. The leaders of the church in Christ's day were notorious for saying one thing and doing another.

Sermon Outline
WE ARE TO PRACTICE WHAT WE PREACH

I. Let's not substitute forms for true religion.
  A. We do that by emphasizing externals.
    1. We may observe certain Christian customs for no other reason than to fulfill what we regard as a divine requirement.
    2. We may use God's Word mechanically so that it

loses its meaning and we quench the Holy Spirit (vv. 2–3).
- B. We do it by loading people with obligations that we do not take seriously ourselves (v. 4).
- C. We do it by greedily grasping for titles and recognition and by using any means to get them (vv. 5–7). The result of not practicing what we preach is self-righteousness, unbelief, and perdition (the "woes" Jesus pronounced on the scribes and Pharisees, vv. 13–36).

II. Let's use the forms of religion to exalt God rather than ourselves.
- A. Jesus is not opposed to our calling someone our father in the faith as long as in doing so we give highest honor to the Father who is in heaven (v. 9).
    1. Our fathers in the faith have led us to know that we are children of the heavenly Father by faith in the Christ (v. 10), who died for us and reconciled us to God.
    2. Our fathers in the faith encouraged us to live in the grace of the heavenly Father.
- B. Nor does Jesus forbid the use of titles of respect and the giving of recognition for work well done.
    1. These formalities can be a means of honoring God, who provides leaders and blesses their work.
    2. Jesus wants us to quench the desire for self-glory that makes us eager for respect and recognition.
    3. He wants us to serve not ourselves but others.
- C. Whatever we do for others, even for the least of Christ's disciples, we do for Him, and we shall not lose our reward (Matt. 10:42).
    1. The Christ who has exalted us by making us sit with Him in heavenly places (Eph. 2:6) regards highly the smallest good we do for others.
    2. When we follow the forms of religion—worshiping, praying, giving money, observing God's laws so that we can serve others—we are thereby serving God. And God exalts those who serve Him. What an encouragement to practice what we preach!

GERHARD AHO

Second-Last Sunday in the Church Year

EPISTLE   1 Thessalonians 3:7 – 13 (KJV)

Sermon Notes/Introduction

This text is paired with that for the preceding Sunday. Also in this text the apostle is fairly personal, expressing his inner thoughts and feelings about the congregation in Thessalonica.

Paul had been very anxious for the Thessalonian Christians because they had endured all manner of afflictions (1 Thess. 3:3). Of these the apostle had warned them when he had been there in person (v. 4). Paul sent Timothy to Thessalonica to strengthen and encourage the Christians. Timothy brought back the news that the Christians were standing firm and were most anxious to see the apostle again and to receive his ministrations. This text is part of the response of Paul to the good news that Timothy brought.

Sermon Outline
THE THREE C'S OF CONGREGATIONAL CONCERN

I. Comfort. "We were comforted over you in all our affliction and distress by your faith" (v. 7). "Over you" and "by your faith" show the emphasis.
   A. The firm faith of the congregation is a source of comfort and encouragement to the apostle.
   B. The perseverance of the congregation in firm faith is indicative of life to the apostle.

II. Celebration.
   A. There is celebration for sinners found by God (v. 9). The apostle can hardly find adequate words to express his thanksgiving to God for the converts in Thessalonica.
   B. There is celebration in Christian fellowship (vv. 10 – 11). The apostle yearns for renewal of fellowship with his fellow Christians, "night and day praying exceedingly."

III. Confirmation.
   A. He desires confirmation in the faith for this life (vv. 10, 12). The apostle was keenly aware of the need to continue to grow in understanding and faith and wanted to perfect what was lacking in their faith. It was

obvious that in Thessalonica some did not fully understand the second coming of Christ or the Christian attitude in view of the parousia.
B. He desires confirmation in the faith for the appearing of Jesus for judgment. In the last verse of this pericope, St. Paul touches on the central theme of the second coming of Christ, which the standard pericope for this Sunday stresses. Pastors today need to stress for themselves as well as for their congregations that where the emphasis on confirmation in the faith in view of the second coming is lacking, there is insufficient congregational concern.

ROY A. SUELFLOW

Second-Last Sunday in the Church Year

GOSPEL   Matthew 24:1 – 14

Sermon Notes/Introduction

The disciples, disturbed by Jesus' words about the destruction of Jerusalem (Matt. 23:38), call His attention to the seeming solidity of the magnificent temple complex (24:1). Jesus speaks even more pointedly (v. 2), uttering a prophecy that was literally fulfilled when Titus ordered the total demolition of the temple, the walls, and the city. The disciples' question in verse 3 was prompted by their assumption that the temple's destruction was connected with Christ's final coming and the end of the world. They wanted to know whether this would come to pass in their lifetime or in the distant future. Jesus does not satisfy their curiosity but warns them of the dangers they will have to guard against before the end, the consummation of the age. In the succeeding verses (vv. 4 – 42), Christ foretells events that for the most part will precede both the destruction of Jerusalem and His final coming. The popular messianic hope of that day was political independence, and there were political Christs who advocated war against Rome. Other kinds of false Christs have continued to deceive. Jesus warns the disciples and us to stay aloof from any such movement (vv. 4 – 5). The prediction concerning wars, famines, and earthquakes applied to the period both before and after the destruction of Jerusalem. While these things were taking place, the disciples would be propagating the faith in many areas of the world. That activity and the resulting persecution will be duplicated in the lives of Christ's followers in future generations (v. 9). Many Christians, fearful of losing their lives, would inform against friends (v. 10). As if this were not bad enough, from within the Christian fold false teachers would arise—Judaizers, Gnostics, and their present day counterparts—deceiving many with their pernicious doctrines (v. 11). All these troubles will contribute to a spirit of worldliness and selfishness that will weaken the love of Christians for one another. What is needed is patient perseverance in the faith (v. 13). The primary task of the church is to get the Gospel message out to all nations (v. 14). Christ does not promise wholesale conversions, only that there will be extensive evangelization before the final day.

The central thought of the text is that Christ prepares us to cope with the crises preceding the end. The goal of the sermon is that the hearers will endure to the end by persevering in the faith. The problem is that we allow crises to weaken and destroy our faith. The means to the goal is that through the Gospel we make known that Christ Himself works to preserve our faith.

There will be an end to earth's poverty and riches, joys and sorrows, plans and enterprises. The last hymn will be sung, the last sermon preached. The earth we know, the life we experience, the existence we share with all human beings will end.

Sermon Outline
THEN THE END WILL COME

I. Jesus gives the signs of the end.
   A. Many will be deceived (vv. 4–5, 11).
      1. Some will purport to be Christs.
      2. There will be false religious movements.
   B. Nations will be distressed (vv. 6–7).
      1. There will be wars and rumors of war.
      2. There will be earthquakes, famines, and recessions.
   C. Christians will be persecuted (vv. 9–11).
      1. The world's antagonism will be sharp.
      2. The result will be that the love of many Christians will grow cold.
   D. The Gospel will be preached.
      1. The Bible will be translated into more and more languages.
      2. Salvation will be offered to more and more people.

II. We must endure to the end.
   A. We endure by remaining in the truth.

1. We are established in the truth through diligent use of God's Word.
   2. We thereby guard ourselves against false teachings.
   B. We endure by continuing in the faith.
      1. We cling to Christ as our Savior.
      2. We find in Christ strength to overcome callousness and despair.
   C. We endure by exercising our faith in kingdom work.
      1. We are to spread the Good News of salvation and also help others spread it.
      2. This proclamation hastens the end so that the period of suffering is shortened and fewer fall away.

The end will come. But to be forewarned is to be forearmed. We who are in a faith relationship to Jesus Christ can endure to the end.

GERHARD AHO

Sunday of the Fulfillment: Last Sunday in the Church Year

EPISTLE   1 Corinthians 15:20 – 28 (KJV)

Sermon Notes/Introduction

1. The bodily resurrection of Christ, so vigorously asserted in 1 Cor. 15:20, was not the point at issue between Paul and his Corinthian readers. That event the latter readily agreed to. What they doubted, however, was the possibility of *our* bodily resurrection. Christ rose, true, they thought, but that doesn't mean we will rise. To assert it is a non sequitur. Paul then endeavors to show them the logical outcome of their position: Denying our resurrection—the thing they were doing—would compel them ultimately to deny Christ's resurrection—something they wouldn't think of doing (cf. v. 13). Thus the unique situation in our text indirectly corroborates the fact of Christ's resurrection. None of Paul's readers thought of denying that phenomenon. They knew better. Christ's resurrection was an established fact. It was a given, a common ground of agreement on which they and Paul could begin to explore what they didn't agree on—our resurrection. Paul's cry, "But now is Christ risen from the dead" (v. 20), is not a gauntlet he throws down to his doubting readers; it is rather a stirring reminder of what they all agree to be true.

2. Christ is "risen." Paul, of course, means exactly what he says. He doesn't mean that the memory of Jesus lives; he means that *Jesus* lives. It isn't just His spirit that still exists; the Man Himself exists, the same one who was actually sentenced and executed. It isn't simply His teaching that survives; the Teacher survives, in spite of the fact that men killed Him and buried Him.

3. As elsewhere in the Bible, death in verse 20 is described as a "sleep." This is not a euphemism, not an unrealistic way of viewing death. Our sinful flesh tempts us to quip that if death is a sleep, it certainly is a very sound sleep, and surely the sleeping quarters leave much to be desired. But we have no right to dismiss the analogy suggested, and all the more so because it isn't presented as an analogy. If death resembles anything, it resembles a sleep. It's more like that than like anything else in our experience. So what follows? Where there is sleep, there is awakening. God's pleasant alarm goes off on Judgment Day, and we arise from our grave as we arise from our bed.

4. There is "Gospel extra" in verse 24 in the words "God, even the Father." In a passage dealing primarily with the awesome power and dazzling glory of the First Person of the Trinity, we are told that He is also the "Father," both Jesus' Father and ours, a thrilling reminder that, for all His might and splendor, He is a God of infinite mercy, of tender care, and of stirring compassion.

5. Verses 27–28 are not intended to invite speculation about rank or hierarchy within the Trinity but are rather meant to portray graphically the give and take of love and respect, of trust and obedience, between Father and Son. The Father puts all things under Jesus' feet (v. 27). The Son, in turn, delivers the kingdom to the Father (v. 24) and then subjects Himself to Him (v. 28) so that God may be "all in all." "God is love" is not an abstraction. It has teeth in it. For love goes on within the Trinity itself!

Sermon Outline
CHRIST'S VICTORY AND OURS

The same note of triumph that marked the end of Jesus' life on the cross characterizes the end of all things described in our text. "It is finished!" was a cry of victory, not of defeat. Similarly, in our text, "Then cometh the end" (v. 24) is a proclamation of triumph, not a message of doom. What we celebrate today at the end of another church year is Christ's victory and ours.

I. We triumph over death (vv. 20–23).
   A. Adam is the origin of our problem.
      1. Adam sinned.
      2. Death was the penalty for his sin.
      3. We inherit Adam's sin (Rom. 5:12).
      4. Therefore, we inherit Adam's penalty, death (1 Cor. 15:21–22).
   B. Christ is the solution to our problem.
      1. Christ became our sin (2 Cor. 5:21).
      2. Christ became our penalty for sin (Gal. 3:13).
      3. Christ rose from death (1 Cor. 15:20).
      4. His resurrection is "the firstfruits," the guarantee of our resurrection (vv. 20, 23).
II. Christ is King over all (vv. 24–28).
   A. Our victory over death is really Christ's victory. We are the beneficiaries, but His is the power and the glory (v. 26).
   B. His victory over death is only one of many triumphs.
      1. Death is "the last enemy that shall be destroyed" (v. 26).
      2. But Christ "hath put all enemies under His feet" (v. 25). He has "put down all rule and all authority and power" (v. 24).
   C. Having won the battle that God, His Father, entrusted to Him (v. 27), Jesus, the Son, now delivers the kingdom to God (v. 24) and in voluntary obedience subjects Himself to His Father that "God may be all in all" (v. 28).

The end of the Lord's Prayer captures the stirring message of our text about the end of all things: "For Thine is the kingdom and the power and the glory forever and ever. Amen."

FRANCIS C. ROSSOW

Sunday of the Fulfillment: Last Sunday in the Church Year

GOSPEL   Matthew 25:1–13 (RSV)

Sermon Notes/Introduction

The concluding verse of the text shows that the context of the parable is Christ's teaching about His final return. The parable makes clear that those who are not prepared for His return will be excluded forever from His kingdom. When Christ comes it will be too late to get ready. Those who are unprepared are contrasted to those who are prepared. The ending of the parable echoes Jesus' teaching in Matt. 7:21–23. Since the wise as well as the foolish girls fell asleep while they were waiting, watchfulness does not appear to be the point of this parable but rather preparedness.

The goal of the sermon is that the hearers will wisely prepare for Christ's coming. The problem is that we foolishly tend to neglect preparing. The means to the goal is that Christ the Bridegroom Himself enables us to make the proper preparation and will receive us into His eternal kingdom.

It is important to be prepared for life's exigencies—tests in school, market fluctuations in business, changes in middle life and old age. It is more important still to be prepared for the final event in human history.

Sermon Outline
BE PREPARED FOR THE LORD'S COMING

I. We are foolish if we do not prepare.
   A. We are not prepared if we rely on Christian associations.
      1. Mere membership in the church is not preparation.
      2. Neither is having the designation "Christian" or "Lutheran."
   B. We are not prepared if we rely on someone else's faith.
      1. We cannot rely on the faith of our parents.
      2. We cannot rely on the faith of an illustrious Christian ancestor.
   C. To be inadequately prepared is foolish because when Christ comes it will be too late to make proper preparation.
      1. Our fate will then be irrevocably fixed (v. 10).
      2. We will be left in darkness behind the closed door

II. We are wise if we prepare.
   A. We must have an ample supply of oil.
      1. This is a way of saying that only through Christ are we adequately prepared because by faith we receive the forgiveness of sins that Christ earned for us.
      2. Wise preparation is possible because of God's gift of faith to us.

B. We must trim our lamps.
   1. This is a way of saying that our faith must be nurtured by regular use of Word and Sacrament.
   2. As our faith is being nurtured, we can go about our ordinary activities in the relaxed confidence (v. 5, "all slumbered and slept") that we are prepared to meet Christ whenever He comes.
C. To be prepared is wise because we have attended to what is most important—our relationship to God through Jesus Christ.
   1. Christ will know us as His own.
   2. We will enter the heavenly marriage feast with Him.

The Bridegroom is coming. Are we prepared to meet Him? It is possible to make preparations and yet not be prepared.

> The Bridegroom soon will call us, "Come to the wedding feast."
> May slumber not befall us nor watchfulness decrease,
> But may our lamps be burning with oil enough and more,
> That, with our Lord returning, we find an open door.

GERHARD AHO

SCRIPTURE INDEX

Studies marked CTQ originally appeared in *Concordia Theological Quarterly;* those marked CJ originally appeared in *Concordia Journal.*

Matthew 1:18 – 25, Gerhard Aho (CTQ), 24
Matthew 2:13 – 15, 19 – 23, Alfred Fremder (CJ), 32
Matthew 3:1 – 12, Stephen J. Carter (CTQ), 16
Matthew 3:13 – 17, Andrew H. Bartelt (CJ), 40
Matthew 4:1 – 11, Francis C. Rossow (CJ), 75
Matthew 4:12 – 23, Warren Messmann (CTQ), 47
Matthew 5:1 – 12, Quentin F. Wesselschmidt (CJ), 51
Matthew 5:13 – 20, Quentin F. Wesselschmidt (CJ), 55
Matthew 5:27 – 37, Roger J. Humann (CTQ), 59
Matthew 5:38 – 48, Roger J. Humann (CTQ), 63
Matthew 6:24 – 34, Roger J. Humann (CTQ), 67
Matthew 7:21 – 29, Terence R. Groth (CJ), 147
Matthew 9:9 – 13, Daniel H. Pokorny (CJ), 151
Matthew 9:35 – 10:8, Steven C. Briel (CTQ), 156
Matthew 10:24 – 33, Terence R. Groth (CJ), 161
Matthew 10:34 – 42, G. Waldemar Degner (CTQ), 165
Matthew 11:2 – 11, Andrew H. Bartelt (CJ), 19
Matthew 11:25 – 30, Arthur F. Graudin (CJ), 168
Matthew 13:1 – 9 (18 – 23), Mark R. Oien (CTQ), 172
Matthew 13:24 – 30, L. Dean Hempelmann (CJ), 175
Matthew 13:44 – 52, George R. Kraus (CTQ), 179
Matthew 14:13 – 21, Richard J. Schultz (CJ), 182
Matthew 14:22 – 33, Ken Schurb (CTQ), 186
Matthew 15:21 – 28, John F. Johnson (CJ), 190
Matthew 16:13 – 20, John F. Johnson (CJ), 193
Matthew 16:21 – 26, Edwin H. Dubberke (CTQ), 198
Matthew 17:1 – 9, Louis A. Brighton (CJ), 71
Matthew 18:15 – 20, Edwin H. Dubberke (CTQ), 202
Matthew 18:21 – 35, Gerhard Aho (CTQ), 206
Matthew 20:1 – 16, Gerhard Aho (CTQ), 209
Matthew 20:17 – 28, Louis A. Brighton (CJ), 88
Matthew 21:28 – 32, Jonathan F. Grothe (CJ), 212
Matthew 21:33 – 43, Gerhard Aho (CTQ), 216
Matthew 22:1 – 14, Gerhard Aho (CTQ), 220
Matthew 22:15 – 21, Jonathan F. Grothe (CJ), 224
Matthew 22:34 – 40, Dale A. Meyer (CJ), 228
Matthew 23:1 – 12, Gerhard Aho (CTQ), 240
Matthew 23:37 – 39, Francis C. Rossow (CJ), 232
Matthew 24:1 – 14, Gerhard Aho (CTQ), 244
Matthew 24:37 – 44, Stephen J. Carter (CTQ), 12
Matthew 25:1 – 13, Gerhard Aho (CTQ), 248
Matthew 25:14 – 30, Gerhard Aho (CTQ), 237
Matthew 26:6 – 13, Gerhard Aho (CTQ), 96
Matthew 28:16 – 20, Richard Klann (CJ), 143
Luke 2:8 – 20, Gerhard Aho (CTQ), 28

Luke 24:13–35, Henry J. Eggold (CTQ), 116
Luke 24:44–53, Richard G. Kapfer (CTQ), 130
John 1:1–18, Alfred Fremder (CJ), 37
John 1:29–41, Harold H. Zietlow (CTQ), 44
John 4:5–26, Gerhard Aho (CTQ), 79
John 9:26–41, Gerhard Aho (CTQ), 83
John 10:1–10, Henry J. Eggold (CTQ), 119
John 11:47–53, Francis C. Rossow (CJ), 91
John 13:1–17, Gerhard Aho (CTQ), 100
John 14:1–12, Henry J. Eggold (CTQ), 122
John 14:15–21, Richard G. Kapfer (CTQ), 126
John 16:5–11, David E. Seybold (CTQ), 138
John 17:1–11, Andrew H. Bartelt (CJ), 134
John 19:30b, Gerhard Aho (CTQ), 105
John 20:1–9, Henry J. Eggold (CTQ), 109
John 20:19–31, William J. Schmelder (CJ), 112
Acts 2:1–21, David E. Seybold (CTQ), 136
Acts 10:34–38, Robert G. Hoerber (CJ), 39
Romans 1:1–7, Richard Klann (CJ), 21
Romans 3:21–28, John F. Johnson (CJ), 145
Romans 4:1–5, 13–17, Quentin F. Wesselschmidt (CJ), 77
Romans 4:18–25, Mark R. Oien (CTQ), 149
Romans 5:6–11, Mark R. Oien (CTQ), 153
Romans 5:12–15, Francis C. Rossow (CJ), 158
Romans 5:12–19, William J. Schmelder (CJ), 73
Romans 6:2b–11, Gerhard Aho (CTQ), 163
Romans 7:15–25a, George S. Robbert (CJ), 166
Romans 8:1–10, Louis A. Brighton (CJ), 86
Romans 8:11–19, Henry J. Eggold (CTQ), 89
Romans 8:18–23, Harold H. Zietlow (CTQ), 170
Romans 8:26–27, Erich H. Kiehl (CJ), 173
Romans 8:28–30, George S. Robbert (CJ), 177
Romans 8:35–39, Wayne A. Pohl (CTQ), 181
Romans 9:1–5, John W. Klotz (CJ), 184
Romans 11:13–15, 29–32, John W. Klotz (CJ), 188
Romans 11:33–36, Gerhard Aho (CTQ), 192
Romans 12:1–18, Gerhard Aho (CTQ), 196
Romans 13:1–10, Wayne E. Schmidt (CJ), 200
Romans 13:11–14, Henry J. Eggold (CTQ), 11
Romans 14:7–9, Wayne E. Schmidt (CJ), 204
Romans 15:4–13, Martin H. Scharlemann (CJ), 14
1 Corinthians 1:1–9, Francis C. Rossow (CJ), 42
1 Corinthians 1:10–17, Andrew H. Bartelt (CJ), 46
1 Corinthians 1:26–31, Andrew H. Bartelt (CJ), 49
1 Corinthians 2:1–5, David L. Bahn (CTQ), 53
1 Corinthians 2:6–13, David L. Bahn (CTQ), 57
1 Corinthians 3:10–11, 16–23, Harold H. Zietlow (CTQ), 62
1 Corinthians 4:1–13, Gerhard Aho (CTQ), 65
1 Corinthians 11:23–26, Gerhard Aho (CTQ), 98
1 Corinthians 15:20–28, Francis C. Rossow (CJ), 246
2 Corinthians 13:11–14, Francis C. Rossow (CJ), 140
Galatians 4:4–7, Francis C. Rossow (CJ), 30
Ephesians 1:3–6, 15–18, Ronald Irsch (CTQ), 35
Ephesians 1:16–23, Bruce J. Lieske (CTQ), 128
Ephesians 5:8–14, Quentin F. Wesselschmidt (CJ), 81
Philippians 1:3–5, 19–27, Erwin J. Kolb (CJ), 207
Philippians 2:1–11, Erwin J. Kolb (CJ), 210

Philippians 2:5–11, Henry J. Eggold (CTQ), 94
Philippians 3:12–21, Gerhard Aho (CTQ), 214
Philippians 4:10–13, 19–20, Andrew H. Bartelt (CJ), 218
Colossians 3:1–4, Gerhard Aho (CTQ), 106
1 Thessalonians 1:1–5a, Roland A. Hopmann (CJ), 222
1 Thessalonians 1:5b–10, Roland J. Hopmann (CJ), 226
1 Thessalonians 2:8–13, Roy A. Suelflow (CJ), 238
1 Thessalonians 3:7–13, Roy A. Suelflow (CJ), 243
1 Thessalonians 4:13–18, Rudolph H. Harm (CJ), 230
1 Thessalonians 5:1–11, Rudolph H. Harm (CJ), 235
Titus 2:11–14, Francis C. Rossow (CJ), 26
Hebrews 4:14–5:10, Gerhard Aho (CTQ), 102
James 5:7–10, Edwin H. Dubberke (CTQ), 17
1 Peter 1:3–9, Lowell F. Thomas (CTQ), 110
1 Peter 1:17–21, Richard J. Schultz (CJ), 114
1 Peter 2:4–10, Jerrold A. Eickmann (CJ), 120
1 Peter 2:19–25, Richard J. Schultz (CJ), 117
1 Peter 3:15–18, Jerrold A. Eickmann (CJ), 124
1 Peter 4:13–19, David E. Seybold (CTQ), 132
2 Peter 1:16–21, William J. Schmelder (CJ), 69